The Intellectual Crisis in American Public Administration

Third Edition

The Intellectual Crisis in American Public Administration

Third Edition

Vincent Ostrom

With a Foreword by Barbara Allen

The University of Alabama Press
Tuscaloosa

Third Edition
Copyright © 2008 by
The University of Alabama Press
Tuscaloosa, Alabama 35487
All rights reserved
Manufactured in the United States of America

First Edition Copyright © 1973
Revised Edition Copyright © 1974
Second Edition Copyright © 1989
Third Edition Copyright © 2008 by
The University of Alabama Press

∞
The paper on which this book is printed meets the minimum requirements of American National Standard for Information Sciences—Permanence of Paper for Printed Library Materials, ANSI Z39.48-1984.

Library of Congress Cataloging-in-Publication Data

Ostrom, Vincent, 1919–
  The intellectual crisis in American public administration / Vincent Ostrom ; with a foreword by Barbara Allen. — 3rd ed.
      p. cm.
  Includes bibliographical references and index.
  ISBN-13: 978-0-8173-5462-6 (pbk. : alk. paper)
  ISBN-10: 0-8173-5462-X
  1. Political science—United States—History. 2. Public administration—United States—History. I. Title.
  JA84.U5O88 2007
  351.73—dc22
                                                  2007007304

For my Mother,
Alma Knudson Ostrom,
who taught me my first
lessons in democratic theory.

There is a paradox . . . in the long
series of discussions over the theory of
bureaucracy. During the last fifty years,
many first-rate social scientists have thought
of bureaucracy as one of the key questions of
modern sociology and modern political science.
Yet the discussion about bureaucracy is still,
to a large extent, the domain of myths and
pathos of ideology.
On the one hand, most authors consider
the bureaucratic organization to be the
embodiment of rationality in the modern world,
and, as such to be intrinsically superior to
all other forms of human organization. On the
other hand, many authors—often the same
ones—consider it a sort of Leviathan,
preparing the enslavement of the human race.
This paradoxical view of bureaucracy in
Western thought has paralyzed positive
thinking . . . and has favored the making of
catastrophic prognostications.

Michel Crozier, *The Bureaucratic Phenomenon*

Contents

Foreword

One may well ask if the word "crisis" really applies to the decades of institutional failure that signal humanity's chronic return to bureaucratic administration. In the years since its first publication, *The Intellectual Crisis in American Public Administration* continues to offer a fresh perspective to discourses on governance, policy analysis, and public administration. When *The Intellectual Crisis in American Public Administration* first appeared in 1973, the immediate response told of an opening fissure in political science and public administration. The five essays comprising the first edition had initially been presented at The University of Alabama in lectures signaling a new scholarly and practical focus on the public choices of self-governing polities. "Democratic administration," as Vincent Ostrom labeled the general idea of a highly engaged, entrepreneurial citizenry, challenged "bureaucratic administration"—and corresponding attitudes toward expertise, command, and control.

Although the idea of a command economy had never enjoyed a strong following in American political thought, the same cannot be said of an increasing reliance on technical experts, hierarchical organizational plans, and training for top-down management of a growing federal bureaucracy that took root alongside the vibrant associational activity of Progressive Era reformers. The belief in administrative centralization and comprehensive planning would ultimately be articulated on many fronts in mid-twentieth-century battles against the uncertainties of life. From the Cold War to the War on Poverty, an "imperial presidency" prospered; from a multi-decade environmental crisis to a host of chronic problems once understood as issues best addressed locally, consolidation movements sought central regulation of school curricula, street lighting and repair, law enforcement, and environmental quality through "uni-gov" reforms. Among scholars and practitioners who seemed suddenly aware that "everything" is connected, highly centralized responses to myriad problems seemed efficient, effective—and absolutely right.

Without denying that Americans (and others) had engaged in environmentally destructive ways of life, failed to eliminate poverty and illiteracy, and now stood at the brink of catastrophe, Vincent Ostrom questioned the basic propositions of administrative centralization and the indictments of federalism voiced by many in public administration. In work that challenged advocates of consolidation, Ostrom, Charles Tiebout, and Robert Warren advanced new understandings of *public* economies as vital complements to *market* economies (Ostrom, Tiebout, and Warren 1961, reprinted in McGinnis 1999b: 31–51). Their theoretical contribution, which focused on metropolitan service delivery, is today considered among the most influential works introducing "public choice" scholarship into the disciplines of political science and public administration. Appearing first in the *American Political Science Review (APSR)*, their analysis rebutted a central premise of bureaucratic administration: that mature, effective organizations must have a single locus of administrative control. According to this characterization, "overlapping jurisdictions" were a symptom of administrative failure. In contrast, Ostrom, Tiebout, and Warren offered insights about the benefits of "polycentricity" in their analysis of the effective, efficient delivery of public goods in metropolitan Los Angeles. Their analysis of public economies also raised normative concerns about various civic virtues, including the role of citizen participation in a democratic community. In their work, the quality of institutional arrangements governing public choices would be evaluated along several dimensions, including local self-determination, participation, and representation, as well as opportunities for limiting externalities, rent-seeking, and other opportunistic behaviors, and offering citizens possibilities for dispute resolution as well as choices among competitive alternatives. "Overlap" could be a sign of health and functionality; the condition of a polycentric system must be evaluated by the strength of relationships among constituent parts, not by the strength or degree of power concentrated at some imagined center of control.

From this pioneering work, Vinçent Ostrom turned to the topics found in the Alabama lectures, suggesting that the patterns found in mid-twentieth-century demands for administrative centralization had much deeper roots—in the fascination with European bureaucratic forms of administration and the mistaken conception of American federalism held by such prominent political actors as Woodrow Wilson. In 1973, Ostrom offered an alternative paradigm, transcending his early work on *collective* choice by examining systematically the *constitutional* choices that provided the foundation for such public activity.

The introduction of economic theory into the study of politics in the mid-twentieth century had largely focused on the disjunctions between individual and collective choices. In 1950, Kenneth Arrow ([1951] 1963) revealed the Impossibility Theorem, showing that faced with three or more options in a given situation of choice, we have no method of determining a single collective preference as an aggregate of individual preferences that meets a set of reasonable conditions corresponding to a democratic ideal of collective choice. Using simplifying assumptions that to some extent set Arrow's theorem aside, Anthony Downs (1957) proposed that, in the aggregate, all policy issues reduced to a unitary left-right dimension of preference; if this is so, such generalization would allow candidates for office to maximize their chances of election by staking out a policy position at the median of a normal distribution of voters arrayed along this ideological dimension of choice. This "median voter" thesis stood in some degree of tension with two other conjectures about the political economy of voting. The effort of voting may be expected to exceed the impact a single vote could have on the outcome, resulting in a rational choice not to participate. For similar reasons, voters, as rational actors, may have little incentive to educate themselves about candidates for office. The dismal prognosis emerging from an economic theory of democracy was soon generalized by Mancur Olson (1965) as the intractable problem of collective action faced whenever public goods or common-pool resources were to be produced or sustainably consumed.

For some scholars, the application of economic theory to political phenomena was simply anathema. However, if such ideas merited any consideration, they indicated a need for governors to care for the "irrational" voter and leviathan-like solutions to save "rational fools" who would otherwise face a terrible fate in the "tragedy of the commons." Vincent Ostrom envisioned other possibilities.

Experiences as a consultant on natural resources policy and law as the territories of Alaska and Hawaii drafted constitutions in their bids for statehood, as well as work on the Water Commission of the State of Oregon, convinced Ostrom to return to earlier theorists of constitutional choice, James Madison and Alexander Hamilton, in this quest for a paradigm shift—away from Wilsonian bureaucratic administration. The exposition of institutional development articulated in *The Federalist*, coupled with the institutional analysis of Alexis de Tocqueville, brought Ostrom to a whole new line of inquiry, resulting in *The Political Theory of a Compound Republic*, published by the Public Choice Society in 1971. Encouraged as well by insights from James Buchanan and Gordon Tullock's *Calculus of Consent* (1962), Ostrom insisted that we step back to consider the constitutional choices that frame collective-action situations. Both the Alabama lectures and the detailed analysis of American federalism in *The Compound Republic* marked a turning point in public choice theory as well as in public administration.

In distinguishing constitutional choice from other ordinary collective decisions, Buchanan and Tullock had underscored the importance of conceptual unanimity—the exceedingly high level of agreement necessary for a collective choice that would establish the rules for all subsequent decision making. As they explained, the political economy of constitutional choice suggested that individuals might agree in advance to a particular set of rules, even knowing that the rule could occasionally work to one's detriment, if the overall benefits of constituting the group *according to such rules* are expected to exceed the costs. To know if a given decision rule for collective choice is worth the risk implied in accepting the rule of unanimity necessitated by constitutional choice, various decision rules must be compared analytically (Buchanan and Tullock, 1962). In *The Intellectual Crisis in American Public Administration*, Ostrom undertook this task.

Rather than simply countering "bureaucracy" or hierarchy with "markets" and conflating organizational forms with the degree of voluntarism implied by a given structure (e.g., bureaucratic coercion against free markets), Ostrom asked readers to consider a broader level of design, comparing the constitution of monocentric and polycentric frameworks in which a particular organization may function. Although he accepted the approach of political economy, methodological individualism, and an analysis of the diverse types of "goods" or events that would be the subject of administration, Ostrom also challenged some of the conclusions reached by Buchanan, Tullock, and other members of the Public Choice Society (of which he was also a founding member). He suggested that whether a given organizational form "worked" (as a shorthand for various evaluative criteria including claims of efficiency, efficacy, effectiveness, and equity) had to do with the nature of the good to be administered *and* with the broader framework of constitutional choice in which a good—and the *understanding of goods or events*—was embedded. Public goods and common-pool resources could become subjects of a collective-action dilemma, but whether "tragedy" ensued depended on the constitutional framework surrounding collective choice and the corresponding shared understandings of goods and events that ultimately inspired individual and collective action. Self-organization and self-governance were possibilities; if scholars and practitioners hoped to make such civic virtues likely, they should look to the levels of constitutional and epistemic choice.

Ostrom also took another step beyond Buchanan and Tullock, emphasizing what was implicit in their work: that those who consent—that is, citizens themselves—must have a theory of constitutional choice if they are to take part in a democracy. "Self-governance" could emerge in a variety of organizational forms. Ostrom explained and advocated "concurrent administration in a federal system," but bureaucracy as an *organizational* strategy was not precluded. He noted that analysts should not assume that the "bureaucratic free enterprise" of individuals who create their own missions and goals to enhance their private welfare is inevitably corrupt, suggesting instead that the proper constitutional constraints may turn such "goal displacement" toward beneficial forms of "public entrepreneurship." The primary message of the original five lectures was obvious: Administrative structures could be neither effectively organized nor analyzed, nor could policy outcomes be meaningfully projected, unless scholars, practitioners, and *other citizens* considered the constitution of order in which administration and policymaking takes place. In the battles against public choice theory and institutional analysis waged during the last quarter of the twentieth century, this message was scarcely audible.

In 1977, *The Intellectual Crisis in American Public Administration* became the vehicle for a caustic rebuke of public choice theories published in the *APSR* by Robert Golembiewski (1977a). When the review article, "A Critique of 'Democratic Administration' and Its Supporting Ideation," arrived unannounced in the journal's plain brown wrapper on Ostrom's desk, it commenced lengthy discussions among a network of scholars associated with the Indiana University Workshop in Political Theory and Policy Analysis co-founded by Vincent and Elinor Ostrom. "Workshop analytics" had indeed developed along pathways complementary to many aspects of public choice analysis. Yet, important differences emerged from the Workshop emphasis on constitutional and epistemic choice that would ultimately yield the Institutional Analysis and Development (IAD) framework discussed in chapter 7 of the present volume.

The Golembiewski critique offered an important occasion for elucidating these differences and highlighting the central puzzle of *The Intellectual Crisis in American Public Administration*: Why have scholars and practitioners of American public administration ignored the political theory of a compound republic and the constitutional level of analysis, opting instead for the pale version of Max Weber's insights about monocentric order found in Woodrow Wilson's conception of "Congressional government?" Ostrom's response (1977) remains one of the most lucid short accounts of public choice theory as it applies to public administration as well as the developing institutional analysis that would soon characterize the Workshop approach.

When the opportunity to produce a second edition of *The Intellectual Crisis in American Public Administration* came in 1989, the

Golembiewski-Ostrom debate figured significantly in clarifying notes added to the original five chapters, especially chapter 3, "The Work of the Contemporary Political Economists." Ostrom responded to methodological misunderstandings and Golembiewski's assertion that the theses of democratic administration lacked empirical support. Workshop scholars—guided initially by Elinor Ostrom, Roger Parks, and Gordon Whitaker—had engaged in several empirical studies of metropolitan service delivery that confirmed many of the conjectures made by Ostrom, Tiebout, and Warren. These findings were added to the 1989 edition. Ostrom also clarified several methodological issues in his response to Golembiewski, underscoring, for example, distinctions between methodological individualism and philosophical (possessive) individualism. The former, Ostrom's *APSR* and 1989 works explained, concerned an analytical presupposition that human beings are the authors of choice. While we may move among levels of analyses, taking associations created by individuals as a unit of analysis for some purposes, failing to disaggregate motives in an organization—not to mention thinking in terms of holistic construction—can blind us to the diverse incentives and motives that produce an "organizational choice." More significantly still, we will find it difficult to undertake an analysis of constitutional choices that lay the foundation for individual conceptions of value, motive, and incentive if we cannot think in terms of individual actors. No denial of culture, broad structures of history, or claims of universality need to be implied in the choice of methodological individualism over holism, as much of Ostrom's later emphasis on time and space specificity in constitutional analysis would explain in even greater detail (V. Ostrom, 1991; 1997).

Following Ostrom's response, Golembiewski enjoyed the last word in a rejoinder arguing, "central action *often* has been required—in economic development, in matters of racial justice, segregation, civil rights, organized crime, and so on through a long list" (Golembiewski 1997b: 1531, original italics). Golembiewski made light of Ostrom's concerns about the popularity of monocentric approaches; Ostrom had characterized this orientation as a belief that "national authorities have full competence to make constitutional decisions about the general structure of

local government" and that "national authorities are to control
the allocation of power in society." To Ostrom's disquiet about
such thinking, Golembiewski answered with the rejoinder's final
rhetorical jab: "Good grief." Chapters 6 and 7 of the 1989 edition
covering the Watergate and Iran-Contra constitutional crises challenge that sanguine reply.

In the immediate aftermath of the Watergate Crisis, as Americans congratulated themselves for having a system that ultimately had "worked," Vincent Ostrom asked how the "imperial presidency" responsible for these crises had come into being, *despite
the original intent of federal institutional designs.* What mental orientation and underlying logic could account for the public and
professional acceptance of administrative centralization? Increasingly, these chapters suggest, an epistemology of the State and
ideal of unitary sovereignty have had a dilatory influence on constitutional choices in the twentieth century. These are among the
most provocative insights of Ostrom's work—and potentially the
most helpful as we face the continuing constitutional crises of the
twenty-first century.

Scholars in public administration and policy analysis have begun to incorporate the ideas of political economy more systematically into their texts, using transaction cost analysis (Horn, 1995),
concepts of institutional design and choice (Chubb and Moe, 1990;
Moe, 1990; Knott and Miller, 1987), and, in some cases drawing on
the same Austrian economists and early theorists of *political choice*
as Ostrom did nearly five decades ago (Stone, 1988). Yet the central problem of constitutional analysis remains to be taken up as
more than a tool for public management.

In the present edition of *The Intellectual Crisis in American Public
Administration,* Vincent Ostrom again tackles what today seems a
more chronic than crisis-inspired constitutional malady. In chapter 6, an expanded discussion of contemporary efforts to revive
an imperial presidency reiterates the alternative design of a compound republic based on limited, distributed, and shared constitutional authority. The political capacity of citizens who ultimately must enforce limits on officials if federal designs are to prevail,
take center stage with perhaps greater urgency. In an updated and
expanded chapter 7, the ideas of public entrepreneurship and civ-

ic enlightenment made possible by the vibrant associational life of a polycentric constitutional structure signal an alternative to political spectatorship. Civic enlightenment becomes possible when citizens tackle shared problems directly and when administrators think beyond the microcosm of management to compare alternative forms of service production and provision. We must consider the constitution of orders that motivate such engagement in diverse communities. Political capacity is part of the answer; in some cases, only by being assigned the direct responsibility for the consequences of their choices will individuals enlighten themselves, moving beyond illusion, slogan—and ignorance, which, as several early critics of command economies and administrations held, will otherwise "persist in the face of masses of information however complete and correct" (Schumpeter, [1942] 1950: 262; Simon, 1957; 1959; 1965a). As Tocqueville argued and as Vincent Ostrom underscores, direct experience with self-organization can teach the art and science of association necessary for democratic self-government, enabling citizens to know enough to instruct and judge their representatives as well as act on their own initiative. Citizens must also develop an analytics of constitutional choice. As the following chapters show, it will not do to transfer administrative forms from one context to another without carefully considering the diverse exigencies of life as they vary in time and space. More than ever, the expanded argument suggests, the conception of State omnipotence stands as an obstacle to the open public realm—*res publica*—that alone provides the space for experimentation and civic enlightenment.

I was very happy that Vincent asked me to coauthor chapters 6 and 7. I share his enthusiasm for Madison and Hamilton as well as Tocqueville, and believe it is essential that we think seriously about the ideas of polycentricity and the compound republic that these early analysts and practitioners of democratic administration bequeathed to us.

Barbara Allen
Minneapolis, Minnesota

Preface to the Third Edition

Many years of teaching and research have contributed to this effort to reconsider the intellectual foundations for both the study and practice of public administration. My graduate education in public administration was in the traditional mainstream. Leonard White's *Introduction* was *the* basic text in my first introduction to the subject.

While on the faculty at the University of Wyoming, I became interested in the development of public organizations associated with water-supply and land-use problems in the arid regions of the American West. I gave serious thought to writing a dissertation on politics and grass as a study of institutional and policy developments associated with public land management. When I decided to return to Los Angeles to begin the dissertation, I shifted my focus to the fashioning of water policies and institutions in the development of Los Angeles and the Southern California metropolitan region.

The traditional theory of administration was not very helpful in understanding the different forms of public organization that were created to provide water supplies and manage public lands in the arid West. The works of John W. Powell, Elwood Mead, William Hammond Hall, Frederick Jackson Turner, Walter Prescott Webb, and Samuel Wiel were more helpful.

At the University of Oregon, I became associate director of the Cooperation Program in Educational Administration for the Pacific Northwest region. The CPEA was funded by the W. K. Kellogg Foundation to improve graduate education in educational administration. Officials in the Kellogg Foundation, on the basis of experience in the field of medicine, drew the analogy that improvements in training educational administrators would depend upon better intellectual foundations in the social sciences in the same way that professional education in medicine had been based upon intellectual foundations in the biological sciences. My task was to work with colleagues in the social sciences to develop those intellectual foundations. This became an occasion for exploring a very wide range of literature related to public administration in anthropology, economics, psychology, and sociology, as well as in education and political science.

This was the period when the debate engendered by Herbert A. Simon's challenge was at its peak. In my efforts to come to terms with the issues that were then being discussed and debated, I found John Dewey, Mary Parker Follett, Chester I. Barnard, Homer Barnett, Harold Lasswell, Kurt Lewin, and Elton Mayo to be most useful in reformulating my thinking. Public administration became a form of problem solving writ large. Somehow problem solving, learning, epistemology, decision making, and organization were all threads in a common fabric.

Work with problems of educational administration fueled my skepticism regarding the traditional principles of public administration. The contention that independent school districts should be eliminated and integrated into a single general unit of local government was becoming less and less persuasive. Independent officials could collaborate as colleagues within a community without being subordinated to a single chief executive. Furthermore, the largest school systems were clearly not the "best." Somehow, a multiplicity of independent jurisdictions had not generated chaos. The American system of education had many surprisingly consistent patterns of organization in the absence of any overarching hierarchy of authority. No master-general of American education could look at his watch and know what lesson students in each school would be studying at any one moment.

Yet students, teachers, or school administrators could transfer from Maine to California and be required to make relatively small adjustments in pursuing their course of work in a new situation. Similarities in graduate education, rivalry for personnel through competitive placement offices, accrediting associations, and professional associations of teachers, administrators, and school board members were a few of the institutions through which consensus evolved from discussion of problems and possibilities. New ideas that offered the possibility of greater return for the effort were worth trying.

My work with the Kellogg project was interrupted by a year at the Center for Advanced Study in the Behavioral Sciences. This was an occasion for rethinking the intellectual foundations of political science and public administration. Problems raised by Dewey and Lasswell led me off into analytical, historical, and comparative jurisprudence. Patterns of social organization are constituted by reference to decision rules. Somehow we needed to work with structures of legal relationships if we were to understand the architecture of organization. K. N. Llewellyn and E. A. Hoebel's *Cheyenne Way* (1941), W. N. Hohfeld's *Fundamental Legal Conceptions* (1964), and John R. Commons's *Legal Foundations of Capitalism* (1968) contributed important intellectual tools in this effort.

Residence at the center also provided an opportunity to become acquainted with the work of W. Ross Ashby. Ashby's *Design for a Brain* (1960) is essentially a theory of adaptive behavior, which enables one to comprehend problem solving, learning, epistemology, decision making, and organization as parts of a common fabric. Ashby's theory of adaptive behavior is today a basic foundation for my own work in political or organization theory.

The year at the center and a Faculty Research Fellowship from the Social Science Research Council provided the occasion whereby I began to recognize the importance of economic theory for the study of public administration. I had become interested in bargaining as a decision process occurring among organizations in the public sector. Charles Lindblom's work on bargaining was a helpful beginning. The interest expanded to major proportions after I joined the faculty at UCLA and began a period of collaboration with Charles M. Tiebout, a political economist concerned with the provision of public goods and services by local governmental agencies. Ostrom, Tiebout, and Warren, "The Organization of Government in Metropolitan Areas: A Theoretical Inquiry" (1961), was a product of that effort. Further studies by Robert

Warren, Robert Bish, Elinor Ostrom, Louis Weschler, and many others have since extended that analysis.

Further work in the political economy tradition was supported by Resources for the Future, Inc., for a study of the California water industry. My efforts to deal with patterns of organization in the California water industry are presented in a study for the National Water Commission, *Institutional Arrangements for Water Resource Development* (1971).

Without the opportunities afforded by support from the W. K. Kellogg Foundation, the Center for Advanced Study in the Behavioral Sciences, the Social Science Research Council, the National Water Commission, and Resources for the Future, Inc., I doubt that I would have been able to work my way through to an alternative approach to the study of public administration.

These essays are only a beginning that points in new directions while drawing on a much older approach. The relationship of the new to the old is indicated by my book *The Political Theory of a Compound Republic* (1987 [a third edition is forthcoming in 2007]), in which I attempted to reconstruct the political theory inherent in *The Federalist* papers on the assumption that Alexander Hamilton and James Madison were political economists doing a policy analysis regarding a problem of governmental organization in 1787. This analysis applied to the terms and conditions of government— the constitutional level of analysis—not to what the "government" should do.

The format of a lecture series afforded by the Alabama lectures in public administration provided a most stimulating environment for exploring the intellectual crisis in American public administration. I am grateful to Professors Robert B. Highsaw and Coleman B. Ransone, Jr., for the opportunity to write these essays and present them in lecture form. I am especially appreciative of the students and faculty at The University of Alabama who carried on a lively discussion of the issues raised. It was a memorable experience for me.

Since these lectures were first published in 1973, James Buchanan suggested that I should pursue the relationship between the intellectual crisis and the major constitutional crisis that arose in the Watergate affair. This was the occasion for adding a post-script entitled "Watergate and the Constitutional Crisis of the 1970s." That postscript now forms the first part of chapter 6 in this edition.

The 1970s were marked by joint efforts with Elinor Ostrom to organize the Workshop in Political Theory and Policy Analysis and to pursue theoretically informed empirical research. Elinor and her colleagues pressed on with a series of studies beginning with conjectures advanced in Ostrom, Tiebout, and Warren as these related to the delivery of public services, especially police services. Major advances were made in addressing problems associated with the multiorganizational level of analysis. I began a further effort to rethink the foundations of political theory prodded by issues raised by students and colleagues.

In the mid-1970s, we began discussions with European scholars at the International Institute of Management in Berlin about the multiorganizational level of analysis. In 1980, we were invited by Franz-Xaver Kaufmann to join discussions in forming a multinational, multidisciplinary research group concerned with "guidance, control, and performance evaluation in the public sector" at the Center for Interdisciplinary Research, Bielefeld University, Germany. One result of that work is represented by Franz-Xaver Kaufmann, Giandomenico Majone, and Vincent Ostrom, eds., *Guidance, Control, and Evaluation in the Public Sector* (1986).

Two major themes ran through much of the work of the Bielefeld research group. First, what constitutes the public sector is not a matter of simple definition but is itself a contestable matter that must necessarily be contestable in modern societies. Second, the major challenge confronting modern societies is increasing complexity; and this implies that the social sciences and related professional fields such as law and public administration need to develop both conceptions and methods for addressing problems of complex organization in modern societies. In Kaufmann's words, we face the challenge of working with "multibureaucracies" rather than "megabureaucracies" (Kaufmann, Majone, and Ostrom, 1986: 790).

The most fundamental challenge presented by work with the Bielefeld research group arose from the German tradition of scholarship in *Ordnungstheorie* (theory of order). This tradition began with a challenge laid down by Walter Eucken in his *Foundations of*

Economics (1951). Eucken indicated that economics, and by implication the social sciences, were confronted with a great antinomy.
Human societies depend upon achieving extraordinarily complex
chains of transactions in relating the activities of people to one
another. Graham Wallas (1921) had been concerned with the same
problem in his reference to the "Great Society."

Patterns of interdependencies in modern societies become extraordinarily complex and reach out to global proportions. Yet
economists, other social scientists, and social professionals in
their efforts to explain social reality rely upon extraordinarily
simplified concepts that increasingly distance themselves from
social reality. Eucken argued that we as social scientists face the
problem of developing analytical tools to penetrate social reality
rather than distancing ourselves from it. Eucken did not resolve
the challenge he presented; it remains a challenge for all of us who
are concerned with the study of human societies. Eucken's challenge, like the conceptualization of what is public, will probably
always confront scholars in the social sciences, humanities, and
social professions.

The basic presupposition inherent in scholarship in the theory-
of-order tradition is that human beings, to some significant degree, create their own social reality. Order in human societies is
constituted by concepts and beliefs that human beings share and
hold in common with one another. Customs, laws, or rules more
generally, are used to order relationships with one another and
with the events of the world in which we live. Seen from this perspective, human beings are the "artificers" who create their own
social reality as Thomas Hobbes expressed much the same idea in
his introduction to *Leviathan* (V. Ostrom, 1980). There is no reason
to assume as Hobbes did that there is only one way to fashion
human societies and create social realities. Yet we have reason to
believe that fundamental constraints exist and not everything is
possible.

Furthermore, it becomes apparent upon reflection that we cannot assume that human beings can *know* the truth. No one can
"see" the whole picture and accurately portray and understand
social reality. We must rely upon some intellectual apparatus that
helps us to inquire about social reality. As we attempt to change

that reality, we engage in practical experiments to reconstruct it. A science of administration informed by a theory of bureaucracy, a political science informed by a theory of the state, and an economics informed by a theory of the market do not exhaust the possibilities. There comes a point at which exclusive reliance upon such intellectual constructs becomes an obstacle to further inquiry.

Anyone who has devoted him or herself seriously to the study of seventeenth- and eighteenth-century political thinkers will become aware that much of their efforts applied to a constitutional level of analysis. Their concern was with thinking through issues that pertained to the terms and conditions of government. Much of what has become known as policy analysis is, instead, concerned *not* with the terms and conditions of government but with what "the government" should do. A choice of policy is, however, not necessarily controlling in what happens. Policies enacted by "the government" are no more than words on paper. Thus we always have "implementation" problems. What happens in the world of action is something else. Policies might conceivably be based on erroneous conceptions, which, when acted upon, yield different consequences than were intended. Human social experience is plagued by circumstances that can be both counterintentional and counterintuitive. We need to test our conjectures and our practical experiments by what happens in the world of experience.

From such reflections it becomes apparent that one way to cope with increasing complexity is to have recourse to multiple levels, facets, and foci of analysis. At a most primitive level, it becomes possible to distinguish constitutional levels of analysis from collective choice and operational levels of analysis. Each becomes operable in any effort to address a problem that involves communities of people. Recourse to concepts of state and bureaucracy is only one way to address problems at a constitutional level of analysis. Choices can also be made about patterns of governance with reference to other configurations of institutional arrangements. When pursuing such issues, a "policy analyst" is working at the constitutional level of analysis.

It should also be apparent that a focus on organizations is different than multiorganizational arrangements. A focus on relationships within firms is different than a focus on interfirm relationships in markets. One needs to take account of interorganizational arrangements as well as organizational arrangements to achieve a level of analysis that is appropriate to a multiorganizational level of analysis. The working of processes at the interorganizational level yields emergent properties that cannot be understood by recourse to "the government" or "the organization" as the basic unit of analysis. Theories of the state and bureaucracy place analysis in an intraorganizational context because a unitary state is presumed to be an all-encompassing organization. A theory of federalism would necessarily imply multiorganizational arrangements unless the term "federal" has lost all meaning to those who place primary reliance upon a theory of state and bureaucracy. In that case, "federalism" can be *made* to work only by superimposing a unitary command structure as James Sundquist (1969) has suggested and as President Richard Nixon tried to realize in his effort to fashion a new "federalism" subject to control from the Executive Offices of the President.

A challenge we face in the social sciences and in the study of public administration is to recognize that our intellectual efforts require recourse to multiple levels, facets, and foci of analysis. This has also been a basic challenge in the other sciences. Charles Darwin's work on the theory of evolution was primarily concerned with offering an account for the extraordinary variety of life forms. Darwin's conjectures were only the beginning of a series of investigations regarding the laws of heredity, genetics, and the effort to unravel the molecular structure of genes. No single level of explanation is adequate. Life is a multifaceted, complex "reality." We cannot expect social reality to be any less complex because, to a significant degree, human beings create their own social realities. We can, however, use our own cognitive facilities as human beings to communicate with and learn from one another so that we might better understand the nature and constitution of order in human societies.

In view of these intellectual developments, I decided to revise *The Intellectual Crisis in American Public Administration* for the second edition in 1989. I did not feel that the first five chapters, originally presented as lectures at The University of Alabama, were in need of substantial revision. Becoming aware that human beings can draw upon different conceptions and systems of ideas to fashion different social realities is a fundamental first step to becoming a master artisan in public administration and in the study of human societies. This purpose is reasonably well served by the first five chapters.

Chapter 6 begins with reference to Watergate and the constitutional crisis of the 1970s and then considers the continuing constitutional crises of the 1980s. Unless we return to the constitutional level of analysis to address these problems, we can neither expect Americans to cope successfully with domestic problems nor exercise the appropriate leadership for coping with alternative patterns of organization among the peoples of the contemporary world. If my analysis is correct, students of public administration will need to become increasingly sensitive to the constitutional level of analysis. It is not good enough to address policy issues by analyzing alternatives about what "the government" should do. Instead, much more attention will need to be given to exploring alternative options that apply to the terms and conditions of governance in the context of public entrepreneurship pursued under many different circumstances in a democratic society. Professor Barbara Allen of Carleton College, who did serious work on public entrepreneurship, has joined me in drafting chapters 6 and 7 of this third edition.

In the concluding chapter, "Intellectual Crises and Beyond," we argue that an awareness of an "intellectual crises" is only a first step in the pursuit of further inquiry. The future of public administration depends upon fashioning communities of scholars who can go far beyond the conjectures that we can advance. If we do not get hung up in trying to repudiate one another, we have the possibility of coming to a reasonable level of awareness of what human beings can and cannot do in fashioning their social realities. Each of us in our lifetimes can take but a few steps in such an endeavor. We must appreciate that what we might achieve depends on what we learn from others; and we can contribute to others only when we build on intellectual foundations that take account of the diversity of human experience.

Finally, we must acknowledge the challenge, stimulation, and assistance that have come from those associated with the Workshop in Political Theory and Policy Analysis at Indiana University. One who has a strong interest in political theory and its practical applications is continually challenged there by colleagues who share similar interests. Our program for advanced study in comparative institutional analysis and development has brought colleagues from Western Europe, Eastern Europe, Africa, Asia, and Latin America, who have challenged our ethnocentric presuppositions and helped us reach a better understanding of the nature and constitution of order in human societies. We cannot acknowledge their individual contributions: there are too many. But those who have shared that experience will know to whom we refer. We can only attempt to convey some of this shared community of understanding to others who read this volume.

The professional staff at the Workshop has done the demanding work of arranging and preparing this manuscript for publication; I am most appreciative of the opportunity to work with such diligent and helpful professional colleagues. I am especially indebted to Elinor Ostrom, who is both a strong critic and a helpful colleague, to Patty Lezotte, who is the invaluable link in translating my work into forms that become accessible to others, and to David Price for help on all fronts. Thanks also to Donald Lutz, Filippo Sabetti, and Jacqueline Bauer who provided helpful edits on revised chapters 6 and 7 and Brian Steed, who revised the index. A generous grant from the Earhart Foundation supported the completion of this enlarged and expanded third edition.

The Intellectual Crisis in American Public Administration

Third Edition

1

The Crisis of Confidence

As we enter the third century of American nationhood, we are losing confidence that the twenty-first century in the Christian era will be an American century (Hacker, 1970). Instead, we have been seized by a maelstrom of crises. Some have even begun to wonder whether there will be a twenty-first century in the Christian era and whether the United States of America will survive as a nation.

Whatever fate or destiny the future may hold for human civilization, that future will be a product of human choice. Technical capabilities now exist for human beings to choose a fate marking the end of modern civilization as we know it. Today, the choice to destroy much of mankind can be made by a mere handful of men. If that choice is ever made, we can be reasonably confident that Americans acting in "the line of duty" will have participated in that fateful decision. Such a decision can, indeed, be taken with considerable "speed and dispatch" and with relatively small expenditures of "time and effort" in decision making.

The range of possibilities at the command of human choice today far exceeds those available to prior generations. But a wealth of possibilities always interposes proportionately higher decision costs. The more benign the future of this civilization, the more time and effort will be required in fashioning decision structures appropriate to human creativity and the less we can afford to rely upon preemptive strategies involving speed and dispatch. The course of destruction is simple; the course of constructive action is much more complex and difficult.

1

If the practice of public administration is based on a knowledge of the organizational terms and conditions that are necessary to advance human welfare, then those of us who teach public administration should be able to indicate what those terms and conditions are. In short, we should be able to specify the consequences that will follow from different organizational conditions. To assert that consequences follow from conditions is to say that effects have their causes. Knowledge depends upon the specification of relationships between conditions and consequences, between causes and effects. We should be able to indicate the conditions and consequences that derive from the choice of alternative organizational arrangements if theories of organization have scientific warrantability.

We must, however, distinguish between a determinate causal ordering and a quasi-causal ordering. In a determinate causal ordering a cause impinges diectly upon and determines an effect. A quasi-causal ordering depends upon the intervention of human actors who are capable of thinking, considering alternatives, choosing, and then acting. The one is determined; the other is constituted. In such circumstances we are required to take account of how individuals view themselves, conceptualize their situation, and choose strategies in light of the opportunities available to them. Analysis in the social sciences requires recourse to strategic thinking in quasi-causal orders. The rule-ordered relationships that are constitutive of human organization function as soft constraints that are themselves subject to choice.

If we have a body of knowledge that enables us to estimate the probable consequences evoked by different organizational arrangements, we should then be able to pursue two forms of analysis. One form uses theory to draw inferences about consequences to be anticipated. These inferences can be used as hypotheses to guide empirical research and test the predictive value of theory. We can have some confidence in a theory that has predictive value for indicating consequences that can be expected to flow from specifiable structural conditions.

A second form of analysis derives from the first. When relationships between conditions and consequences can be specified and when any particular set of consequences is judged to be detrimental to human welfare, we should then be able to specify the conditions that lead to that set of consequences. Consequences of organizational arrangements that are detrimental to human welfare can be viewed as social pathologies. If the conditions leading to those pathologies can be specified, then the basis exists for diagnosing the organizational conditions of social pathologies. If conditions can be altered so as to evoke a different set of consequences, then different forms of remedial action can be considered. By altering the appropriate conditions, one set of consequences judged to be pathological might be avoided and another set of consequences judged to be more benign might be realized.

The relationships that I have just specified indicate the connection between theory and practice in the use of any body of knowledge. The practice of any **profession** depends upon the knowledge its members **profess**. The worth of professional practice depends upon the difference that professional advice will make in the opportunities made available to those who rely upon that advice. If I seek professional advice and that advice either reduces the misery I would otherwise have suffered or improves the advantage I might realize, then such advice is of value to me. If, on the other hand, professional advice leaves me worse off, I would have to conclude that such advice is harmful.

Organizational arrangements can be thought of as nothing more or less than decision-making arrangements. Decision-making arrangements establish the terms and conditions for making choices. Consequently, we would expect that the practice of public administration will increase in importance as the domain of choice is extended to include an increasing range of opportunities. I doubt that there are many today who anticipate a decline in the relative importance of the practice of public administration as long as opportunities exist for continued advancement in human welfare.

We are, however, confronted with a substantial question of whether the bodies of knowledge used by those who practice public administration will lead toward an improvement in or an erosion of human welfare. If, perchance, the consequence of acting upon knowledge used in the practice of public administration were a decline in human welfare, we would have to conclude that such knowledge contributes to social pathologies. Conventional wisdom in public administration indicates, for example, that efficiency will be enhanced by eliminating overlapping jurisdictions and fragmentation of authority. What, for example, would be the consequence of eliminating 80 percent of the units of local government in the United States (Committee for Economic Development, 1966)? Would the consequence of such action substantially enhance or diminish human welfare? We could hardly expect such action to be **without** consequences.

Dare we contemplate the possibility that the contemporary malaise in American society may have been derived, in part, from the teachings of public administration? The consolidation or merger of units of local government has, in some cases, attained substantial success. Have those successes been congruent with the consequences we expected? Is New York City a model of what we would like to achieve? Or is it a gargantuan system that has become virtually ungovernable? If our teachings have contributed to the contemporary malaise, we might further contemplate the possibility that continued reliance upon those teachings, as the basis for prescribing remedies to contemporary social pathologies, can lead to further deterioration in human welfare.

If such a circumstance prevails, we are confronted with a growing dilemma. On one hand, the practice of public administration will increase in relative significance. But as it grows in importance, those affected by public administration would be confronted with a progressively deteriorating situation. Actions taken to remedy conditions would exacerbate problems. In such a circumstance, we might expect to find that those educated in public administration were no more successful in its practice than those who were not educated to do so. They might be even less successful than others not so educated.

Perhaps this is an occasion on which we should entertain an outlandish hypothesis: that our teachings include much bad medicine. I have reached this conclusion after considerable agonizing about the problem. I once hoped that I could be proved wrong. I have since abandoned that hope; and I have attempted to work my way through to alternative resolutions. I am now persuaded that the major task in the next generation will be to lay new foundations for the study of public administration. If these foundations are well laid, we should see a new political science join a new economics and a new sociology in establishing the basis for a major new advance upon the frontiers of public administration.

The Persistent Crisis in the Study of Public Administration

When I was first introduced to the study of public administration on the eve of World War II, the confidence reflected in the theory and practice of public administration impressed me. The theory of administration presumed that technical solutions were available to solve public problems. Once decisions specifying policy objectives were reached, we assumed that the translation of these objectives into social realities was a technical problem within the competence of professional administrative expertise. The social problems associated with the Great Depression were transformed into new programs by enlightened political leadership and the technical proficiency of those who staffed the public service. Students in the late 1930s displayed as much enthusiasm for the public service as many of their counterparts in the 1970s had for the movement.

Perhaps the high point of that era was reflected in the publication of the *Report with Special Studies* of the U.S. President's Committee on Administrative Management (1937) and the companion volume edited by Luther Gulick and Lyndall Urwick as *Papers on the Science of Administration* (1937). The *Papers* stated the theoretical foundations for the science of administration. The *Report* proposed a bold new reorganization plan based on that science of administration to rationalize the host of New Deal agencies into a coherent administrative structure.

The war years provoked a challenge from which the study of public administration has never recovered. Wartime control measures were plagued by persistent failures.[1] Public administration sometimes appeared to involve greater measures of unprincipled expediency than of principled action. The principles of administrative organization were honored more in their breach than by their observance. The gap between theory and practice became increasingly difficult to bridge.

The wartime experiences with civil and military administration were more congruent with the work of Elton Mayo and his colleagues (Mayo, 1933) in the Western Electric experiment than with the work of Gulick and Urwick. The human relations aspect of organization appeared to have a greater effect on productivity than did formal tables of organization. The gulf between theory and practice was, indeed, formalized by distinguishing between a theory of formal organization and a theory of informal organization.

Perhaps the most devastating blow came in the carefully reasoned analysis sustained by Herbert Simon in his study *Administrative Behavior*. Simon explicitly rejected the principles of public administration as little more than proverbs (Simon, 1946; 1965a: 20–44). Simon concluded upon analysis that the traditional principles of public administration, like proverbs, could be arrayed into logically contradictory sets. One or another principle could always be invoked to justify contradictory positions.

The central thrust of Simon's challenge has never been effectively faulted. Considerable debate was engendered by his fact-value distinction. His call for an administrative science was widely supported. His organization theory was different but not unfamiliar.

Many of us who lived through the era following Simon's challenge found ourselves in basic agreement with a number of his contentions. At other points we sustained serious reservations. For example, many of us have been concerned with Simon's use of the fact-value distinction to dichotomize policy and administration (Simon, 1965a: 52–59). In addition, some have had a sense that Simon did not go far enough, that his theoretical thrust implied much more than he developed.

Leonard White, in the third edition of his *Introduction to the*

Study of Public Administration (1948), for example, reviewed Simon's contention that the rule implied by unity of command was logically incompatible with the rule implied by specialization in technical competencies. White, however, was able to demonstrate that "Simon eventually grants priority to the rule of unity of command but reformulates the proposition in these words: 'In case two authoritative commands conflict, there should be a single determinate person whom the subordinate is expected to obey; and the sanctions of authority should be applied against the subordinate only to enforce his obedience to that one person' " (38). Somehow, the thrust of Simon's theoretical criticisms should have generated a far less conventional conclusion. Perhaps this observation applies to all of us: that the extent of our theoretical doubts should lead to far less conventional inquiries than we are willing to pursue.

By a curious coincidence, the translated works of Max Weber were published in America at the same time that Herbert Simon's *Administrative Behavior* first made its appearance (Gerth and Mills, 1946). Weber's *Economy and Society* (1978) was a powerful effort to fashion a general sociological theory based on what he presumed to be a value-free approach to the study of social phenomena. In formulating his general sociology, Weber established certain ideal types to define social structures that functioned as elements in the organization of societies. Weber conceived a hierarchically ordered system of public administration, which he identified as "bureaucracy," to be one of the necessary organizational requisites for a modern society. Bureaucracy provided a rational basis for social organization. Weber's theory of bureaucracy became an important influence on work both in the sociology of large-scale organizations and in public administration during the post–World War II era.

Weber's commitment to a value-free social science was congruent with Simon's fact-value position. His concept of bureaucracy was offered as an ideal type to be used as a measure analogous to a well-calibrated yardstick. Weber's conception of bureaucracy would, thus, serve as a model which scholars could use in arraying imperfect cases of human organization. Weber's theory of bureaucracy was fully congruent with the traditional theory of public administration in both form and method.

In this circumstance, the postwar challenge to the traditional approach to public administration was accompanied by a new intellectual thrust that tended to reinforce traditional commitments of American scholarship in public administration. Woodrow Wilson and his contemporaries, such as Frank J. Goodnow, drew their inspiration for the study of public administration from French and German scholarship concerned with highly centralized bureaucratic structures. Weber, whose lifework was largely contemporary with Wilson's, provided a powerful restatement of that theory of administrative organization. The very theory that was being challenged by Simon was at the same time being reinforced and sustained by Weber, one of the twentieth century's most powerful social theorists. A theory challenged in one context reappeared in the cloak of different words and phrases to realize a new era of splendor.

The ambiguities of the shifting theoretical scene were accompanied by shifting styles of work in scholarly research. Early research in public administration had been management-oriented. Typically, such research included reference to organization, planning, budgeting, personnel, and selected aspects of program operation. The empirical thrust was diagnostic in character. Conclusions were usually accompanied by policy recommendations congruent with the prevailing theory of public administration.

The wartime experiences of many of the students of public administration led to a new style of research reflected in case studies designed to provide a narrative about the "realities" of administrative decision making (Stein, 1952). Case studies dramatized issues and pointed to the pervasiveness of conflict within the administrative setting. They were used extensively as teaching materials to give students a sense of reality about administration. In the absence of a reformulation of administrative theory, these accounts of reality become increasingly incongruent with theory.

Still another research tradition was stimulated by students of administration who came to adopt the behavioral approach and its commitment to building theory by generating and testing hypotheses. Theory, the behavioralists hoped, might gradually evolve from the accumulation of tested hypotheses. The work of the behavioral scientists made important contributions to the challenge to traditional theory. Emphasis on goal displacement and bureaucratic dysfunctions appeared in much of the behavioral research and reinforced the prevailing doubts about bureaucratic rationality (Merton et al., 1952; Blau, 1956; March and Simon, 1958; Crozier, 1964). The strategy of the bureaucratic personality who followed the rule of thumb "when in doubt, don't," stood in sharp contrast to the presumptions of efficiency, speed, and dispatch which Weber had attributed to bureaucratic organization (Merton et al., 1952: 378). The new research strategies that developed in light of the wartime and postwar challenge to the theory of public administration merely served to deepen and reinforce the challenge.

By late 1967, Dwight Waldo was able to characterize the crisis of confidence in public administration as a crisis of identity: "*Both the nature and boundaries of the subject matter and the methods of studying and teaching this subject matter became problematical. Now, two decades after the critical attacks, the crisis of identity has not been resolved satisfactorily. Most of the important theoretical problems of public administration relate to this continuing crisis, to ways in which it can be resolved and to the implications and results of possible resolutions*" (Waldo, 1968: 5; Waldo's emphasis).

Waldo is pessimistic about the resolution of this identity crisis—this failure to know what we are (subject matter) or how we should proceed (methods). Indeed, he concludes that there is no solution to the problem at the level at which it was originally posed. The crisis, he contends, cannot be resolved by choice between the alternatives presented in the traditional theory and in Simon's challenge. Both have proved wanting: neither is viable. The search for a solution must occur outside the frame of reference provided by either the traditional theory of public administration or Simon's theory of organization.

Waldo's proposal for a short-term solution pending a longer-term resolution of the identity crisis is as follows: *"What I propose is that we try to act as a profession without actually being one and perhaps even without the hope or intention of becoming one in any strict sense"* (Waldo, 1968: 10; Waldo's emphasis). Waldo then goes on to observe, "Frankly, it took some courage to say that, as it is patently open to ridicule." Waldo's advice is indeed open to ridicule. It is the advice of a friend who at a time of overwhelming tragedy counsels that one should concentrate on keeping a stiff upper lip.

If the methods of studying, teaching, and practicing the subject matter of public administration have become problematical, then that profession **cannot** have much confidence in what it professes. The practice of a profession rests upon the validity of the knowledge it professes.[2] When the confidence of a profession in the essential validity of its knowledge has been shattered, that profession should be extraordinarily modest about the professional advice it renders while keeping up its appearances.

Waldo's proposal has a fatal flaw if practitioners in the profession of public administration render professional advice when they do not know the grounds upon which their advice is predicated. In an era of political turmoil, when everyone is being challenged to demonstrate the relevance of his or her knowledge to the solution of pressing social problems, it is difficult, if not impossible, I fear, to profess modesty and doubt.

The nature of the flaw is emphasized by an announcement that the American Society for Public Administration (ASPA) had established a Task Force on Society Goals. The announcement was somewhat ambiguous as to whether the term "society" in "Society Goals" referred to ASPA, the United States of America, or even more broadly to human society in general. Let me read a few sentences from the announcement to indicate the problem: "Today's crisis exceeds all historical crises in public administration. . . . Public executives, taken as a group, have not yet awakened to the fact that they are in charge. They are responsible for the operation of our society; they cannot wait around for someone to tell them what to do. If they don't know, we're lost."[3] From such a statement one might observe that exuberance for action need not be limited because people know not what they do. Times are critical. We rush to meet crises with calls for urgency and fears of impending disaster.

In these circumstances the first order of priority in the study of public administration is to come to grips with the crisis of confidence—the identity crisis—that has clouded work in the field for the last generation. I am persuaded that we can begin to take important steps toward clarifying conceptual problems that are the source of this crisis of identity.

The Crisis as a Paradigm Problem

A first step in proceeding toward an understanding of our problem is to diagnose our crisis of identity as a recurrent problem in the history of scientific inquiry. Thomas S. Kuhn in his study *The Structure of Scientific Revolutions* (1964) provides us with a useful perspective. Kuhn, as a historian of science, distinguishes between the practice of normal science and of the extraordinary science associated with scientific revolutions.

The essential characteristic of normal science is general agreement upon a basic theoretical paradigm or framework in which a community of scholars shares common theoretical assumptions and a common language defining essential terms and relationships. The "agreement" upon an underlying paradigm is usually implicit. Each scholar takes it for granted in the organization and conduct of his or her work. Methods of work, conceptions of what is problematical, and criteria for what is to be included or excluded from the field of inquiry follow from a theoretical paradigm. The basic concepts and assumptions in a theory establish the defining sets and determine what is to be included and what is to be excluded from a scholar's frame of analysis. They tell the scholar what to "take hold of" in the conduct of an inquiry.

The basic concepts establish the essential elements of analysis; and relational postulates and axioms specify the essential computational rules. These computational rules enable members of an intellectual community to pursue a structure of inferential reasoning in which the work of one can be added to the work of others. Frontiers of knowledge can be extended with reference to the understanding shared by all members of the community.

When general agreement on a paradigm prevails, scholars work within the confines of that framework pursuing inquiry into a range of problems inferred or suggested by the paradigm. As long as work proceeds with a reasonably good fit between expectations and occurrences, scholarship is advanced in a step-by-step fashion. Normal science proceeds in a cumulative way in which bits and pieces are added to the frontier of knowledge by those who work within a prevailing community of scholarship.

Kuhn contends, however, that probing into new problems, inherent in the method of normal science, can evoke anomalous consequences which deviate radically from expectations. Such anomalies cannot be satisfactorily explained within the traditional framework. As those anomalies persist, the theoretical paradigm will itself come into question. When that happens, a crisis occurs for the community of scholars. The common understanding that provided the bond of community is beclouded with doubt. Scientific work shifts from the application of the prevailing paradigm to new problems and turns back to questioning the sufficiency of the theoretical framework itself.

During a period of paradigmatic crisis, a proliferation of competing articulations of the prevailing paradigm will occur. As the common bond of understanding is relaxed by contentions over the prevailing paradigm, members of a scholarly community will be more random in their choice of research strategies. Methodological experimentation will also be accompanied by debates over basic philosophical and epistemological issues. The doubts, methodological experiments, and philosophical debates lead to explicit expressions of discontent and unhappiness. When these characteristics prevail, a community of scholars is experiencing an intellectual crisis. The theoretical framework that provided the common bond of understanding has itself become problematical.

The process of normal science ends in crisis. The stage for scientific revolutions occurs within this background of crisis. When the proliferation of alternative versions of the traditional theory has failed to resolve the prevailing crisis, a radically different formulation is needed. But the more radical the reformulation, the less will be the common basis for making a choice between a traditional paradigm, its numerous variations, and a new, more revolutionary paradigm.

A new paradigm implies that a different form of basic ABC's is required for thinking about a subject matter. New concepts, different terms, and different postulates will give rise to a different pattern in inferential reasoning among the community of scholars and professional practitioners associated with that field of study. Scholarship that qualified and modified the old ABC's will be insufficient because the basic structure of thought was unsatisfactory. A new ABC's needs to be considered as a possible substitute for the old.

Sophisticated scholars in the old tradition will view efforts to reconstruct the logic inherent in the old ABC's as resurrecting a "dead horse." Those old ideas have been critically scrutinized over and over again. But it is the old ABC's that need replacing. A new qualification or a new extension in their use will not resolve the intellectual crisis.

The setting for fundamental change occurs when none of the alternative versions of the traditional theory has succeeded in resolving the issues created by the anomalies generated in the course of prior work. The process of scientific revolution can begin only after an alternative paradigm has been articulated to a point at which it is perceived to be an alternative. The alternative may not be appropriately stated in its early forms. Thus the process of scientific revolution may be prolonged. The Copernican revolution in astronomy, for example, covered a period of more than a century.

The articulation of an alternative paradigm is, however, a necessary condition before a scientific revolution can occur. Scientific revolutions require a choice among alternative paradigms. If Kuhn's theory of scientific revolutions is valid, we can anticipate a resolution of the intellectual crisis in public administration only if an alternative paradigm is available. If a new paradigm is to succeed, it must offer a formulation that is able to resolve some of the persisting anomalies and to provide an explanation that takes account of more extended intellectual horizons. A new paradigm, thus, might also be expected to open new frontiers of research. The new formulation may allow for the conception of relationships such that problems previously excluded from inquiry are now perceived to have an ordered relevance to the previously defined field of inquiry. In addition, a new paradigm may permit a greater precision in explanation and in measurement. These considerations involve potential gains that might be realized from the development of a new paradigm.

These potential gains need, however, to be viewed in light of potential losses. A change in paradigm is likely to require the abandonment of previously held beliefs, specialized language, and methodological tools and skills acquired in the practice associated with those beliefs. Retooling is a costly process. As long as prevailing tools appear to work in solving problems, we would expect scholars to take advantage of those opportunities which remain available to them. We would not expect scholars to abandon lightly their prior investment in skills and tools without anticipating a payoff that would justify the added expenditure of time and effort to acquire a new way for approaching one's field of study and developing new methods of work.

The more fundamental the revolution, the fewer the commensurabilities that will exist between the old and the new. The degree of incommensurability which we might expect to find can be estimated by reference to the constitutive effect of a paradigm. If there is a shift in basic organizing concepts, we would want to know whether the new will take account of the old and simultaneously at least some of the prior anomalies. If there is a change in the basic unit of analysis, scholars may be required to "take hold of" their subject in quite a different way. The basic assumptions may imply different boundary conditions for estimating the essential relevance or irrelevance of the larger universe of events. The relational postulates and axioms may imply a different structure of reasoning about the subject. Finally, the horizon viewed from a new perspective may include many unfamiliar features as well as some familiar landmarks, which now appear in a new context. It is even faintly possible that the beauties of a yesteryear may be revealed as ugly illusions; and some of those obscure figures in the background may shine with a new brilliance.

The Paradigm Problem in Public Administration

In the course of these lectures, I shall advance the thesis that the sense of crisis that has pervaded the field of public administration over the last generation has been evoked by the insufficiency of the paradigm inherent in the traditional theory of public administration. Simon's challenge will be viewed as a challenge to the traditional theory of public administration based on a number of anomalies inherent in that tradition. The study of public administration during the postwar period has all the characteristics that Kuhn associates with a paradigmatic crisis.

Kuhn's own work was concerned with the physical sciences of astronomy, physics, and chemistry. Yet the study of public administration during this period of crisis has been characterized by the proliferation of numerous versions of the prevailing theory, by the willingness of scholars to engage in methodological experimentation, by the expression of explicit discontent, by recourse to philosophical speculation, and by debate over fundamental epistemological issues. These are Kuhn's symptoms of crisis.

I agree with Waldo's conclusion that the resolution of the crisis cannot be attained by a choice between the traditional theory of administration and Simon's theory of organization. Simon's theory was essentially cast within the same mold as the traditional theory of administration. It was an alternative articulation of the old theoretical paradigm. Neither is a viable alternative.

Simon's effort to reconstruct organization theory made a number of critical breaks with tradition. His reconstruction gave a new emphasis to the psychology of decision making and to considerations bearing upon a model of organization man. His formulation of the criterion of efficiency proposed the application of a cost calculus that would allow for an independent test of efficiency other than presuming the efficiency of bureaucratic structures. Before his publication of *Administrative Behavior*, Simon did pioneering work on measuring the output of public service agencies (Ridley and Simon, 1938; Simon et al., 1941). He conceived a solution to the problem of identifying and measuring the output of public agencies as necessary to a rational theory of public administration (Simon, 1965a: 189). His subsequent work, however, has been preoccupied with a different range of problems (Simon, 1965b; 1969).

The principal efforts to conceptualize and define social production functions have instead been pursued by political economists in work on externalities, common properties, and the theory of public goods. Based on a theory of public goods, these political economists are developing a theory of collective action, which assumes that the principles of organization required for the efficient conduct of **public** enterprises will be different from the principles of organization for private enterprises. Competition among private enterprises in a market structure will tend to regulate activities among firms without regard for the structural characteristics of any particular firm. In the absence of a product market in which a consumer is not free to choose among alternatives, public enterprises must provide complex political decision-making arrangements for translating individual preferences into collective choices regarding the provision of public goods and services. The constitution of public enterprises will thus create significant differences in the way consumers' preferences are translated into the provision of public goods and services.[4] These differences emphasize what would be traditionally identified as the **political** aspects of public administration.

The theory of **public goods** is the central organizing concept used by these political economists in conceptualizing the problem of collective action and of public administration. By contrast, the theory of **bureaucracy** is the central concept in the traditional theory of public administration. When the central problem in public administration is viewed as the provision of public goods and services, alternative forms of organization may be available for the performance of those functions apart from an extension and perfection of bureaucratic structures. Bureaucratic structures are necessary but not sufficient for a productive and responsive public service economy. Particular public goods and services may be jointly provided by the coordinated actions of a multiplicity of enterprises transcending the limits of particular governmental jurisdictions. Some of these multiorganizational arrangements may take on characteristics analogous to industries composed of many different governmental agencies. Can we best understand the structure, conduct, and performance of the American system of higher education, for example, by reference to a bureaucratic chain of command accountable to a central chief executive or by reference to a relatively open but constrained rivalry among a diversity of collective enterprises?

In these lectures I shall be primarily concerned with revealing the underlying logic inherent in each theoretical paradigm. Logic is an important tool which enables us to draw plausible inferences from an expected choice of strategy in postulated conditions. When postulated conditions approximate the conditions of the empirical world, we can test inferences derived from theory by whether those inferences enable us to anticipate or predict the consequences that flow from action in specified conditions.

A danger always exists that theories may proliferate to such an extent that reasoning through logical inferences is abandoned and replaced by a process of naming different theories and writing narratives about theory. The study of theory then can become little more than interesting stories about the lives, loves, and miscellaneous thoughts of political philosophers or the quaintness of different sets of ideas. We spend a great deal of time **talking about** theory and surprisingly little effort in the **use** of political theory. Scholars should know how to **use** theory and to **do** theory, not just **talk** about theory.

The next two lectures will be devoted to a clarification of each of the alternative approaches. In the second lecture of this series, I shall examine the traditional theory of public administration, using Woodrow Wilson's work to state the basic argument. I shall then review Max Weber's theory of bureaucracy as an independent formulation similar to the classical theory, turning in particular to Luther Gulick's "Notes on the Theory of Organization" (Gulick and Urwick, 1937). Surprisingly, Gulick's analysis destroys the integrity of the traditional theory, although he patched over the wreckage with an incantation of appropriate words and phrases as though he were reaffirming the faith. The task of explicitly challenging the faith was reserved for Simon. The alternative paradigm inherent in the work of the contemporary political economists will be examined in the third lecture.

These two approaches can provide alternative constructs for viewing the experiential world of public administration. An intellectual construct is like a pair of spectacles. We see and order events in the world by looking through our spectacles and by using intellectual constructs to form pictures in our mind's "eye"—an intellectual vision. We are apt to neglect a critical examination of the spectacles or the constructs themselves. As Stephen Toulmin has observed, "We shall understand the merits of our ideas, instead of taking them for granted, only if we are prepared to look at these alternatives on their own terms" (Toulmin, 1961: 102).

In the fourth lecture, on democratic administration, I shall use the spectacles of the political economists to reflect upon the paradigmatic choice made by Wilson when he rejected the "literary theories" and "paper pictures" used by Alexander Hamilton and James Madison in *The Federalist*. The theoretical paradigm of the contemporary political economists enables us to find a theory of administration in Hamilton's essays on taxation and defense which is more general than his theory of the national executive contained in *Federalist* 70 and 72. Alexis de Tocqueville drew upon a comparable political theory when he compared the patterns of democratic administration in America with the patterns of bureaucratic administration in France. Tocqueville's theory and empirical findings are congruent with the work of the contemporary political economists.

Finally, in what in earlier editions was the concluding lecture, I focus on the implications that these two different theoretical approaches have for the study and practice of public administration. If different ways for conceptualizing administrative arrangements are available, then different concepts may serve as a basis for the design of different organizational arrangements.

New designs may, in turn, provide new remedies for some of our contemporary problems in public affairs. Perhaps we can begin to contemplate how these new remedies might affect the future. If we believe that the new remedies will be an improvement over the old, we may be confronted with a task of reformulating the study and practice of public administration. Perhaps there are alternatives to some of our contemporary crises.

In Chapter 6, I explore the continuing constitutional crisis in American government, which derives from the acceptance of the Wilsonian thesis that the more power is unified, the more responsible it becomes. In doing so, I focus on the Watergate affair as a crisis in constitutional government, which flows from the strengthening of the presidency as a consequence of reform efforts advanced by the President's Committee on Administrative Management (and other similar efforts), and the subsequent Administrative Reorganization Acts. The Watergate affair has been replaced by the Iran-Contra affair. Constitutional crises continue. The problem is not confined to executive instrumentalities. The conduct of legislative and judicial processes is also in disarray.

Finally, in Chapter 7, I return to the intellectual challenge that presents us with one intellectual crisis heaped upon others. To sort these out it is necessary to extend the frontiers of inquiry, recognize different levels of analysis, and move to deeper issues pertaining to the nature and constitution of order in human societies and view American experience in that context. I press onward to challenge ways of thinking about the constitutive nature of order in human societies. When administrators act, they constitute as well as manage. But what is being constituted—Leviathans or self-governing communities of relationships in compound republics (V. Ostrom, 1987)?

2

The Intellectual Mainstream in American Public Administration

Wilson's Point of Departure

The beginning of modern inquiry in American public administration is often identified with Woodrow Wilson's essay "The Study of Administration" published in 1887. Frank J. Goodnow's *Politics and Administration* (1900) is another important statement of the classical theory of administration which is highly congruent with Wilson's formulation. In this discussion I shall rely upon Wilson's essay and his book *Congressional Government* (1956; originally published in 1885) for an analysis of the theoretical foundations of American scholarship in public administration.

I do not wish to imply that the theory was original with Wilson and that others consciously followed in his footsteps.[1] Rather, I assume that Wilson used an approach which he found helpful in his work and that this approach was shared by other scholars who undertook graduate study in the newly organized departments of political science during the late nineteenth century. Many scholars in succeeding generations have, in turn, gone back to Wilson's work and found affirmation and inspiration for their own work (e.g., Caldwell, 1965; Dimock, 1937; Millett, 1959; Wengert, 1942; White, 1948).

Wilson's Theoretical Presumptions

Wilson's choice of where to "take hold" of his subject is best formulated in *Congressional Government* (1956). The essential concern of a political scientist, according to Wilson, is to reveal "the real depositories and the essential machinery of power." Wilson's conception of "reality" in politics rests on the presumption that "there is always a centre of power" within any system of government (my emphasis). The task of the scholar is to identify (1) "where in this system is that centre?" (2) "in whose hands is [this] self-sufficient authority lodged?" and (3) "through what agencies does that authority speak and act?"(Wilson, 1956: 30). Once the center for the exercise of sovereign prerogative is identified, the structure of authority can be unraveled and the symmetry of social life in that political order can be understood.

Scholars must be prepared to penetrate the facade of political forms and focus upon the essential realities of power. The "literary theory" of the American Constitution, according to Wilson, was based on "a balance of powers and a nice adjustment of interactive checks," which deny the presumption of a single controlling force in American politics. This was the facade, the "literary theory," or the "paper picture" of the American political system (Wilson, 1956: 31).

But what are the realities in the practical conduct of government? Wilson's central thesis in *Congressional Government* is a response to that question: "The predominant and controlling force, the centre and the source of all motive and all regulative power, is Congress." He then goes on to observe: "All niceties of constitutional restriction and even many broad principles of constitutional limitations have been overridden, and a thoroughly organized system of congressional control was set up which gives a **very rude negative** to some theories of balance and some schemes for distributed power, but which suits well with convenience and does violence to none of the principles of self-government contained in the Constitution" (Wilson, 1956: 31; my emphasis). Throughout his analysis in *Congressional Government*, Wilson recognized that the forms inherent in the "literary theory" of the American constitutional system did have substantial significance for political practice. The checks and balances created impediments to a smooth and harmonious relationship among the various decision structures within the

American system of government. To drive his point home, Wilson observed that "**those checks and balances have proved mischievous just to the extent to which they have succeeded in establishing themselves as realities**" (Wilson, 1956: 187; my emphasis).

The central axiom in Wilson's political theory is the proposition that "the more power is divided the more irresponsible it becomes"[2] (Wilson, 1956: 77). Wilson's model for political organization was the British parliamentary system. "The natural, the inevitable tendency of every system of self-government like our own and the British," Wilson observes, "is to exalt the representative body, the people's parliament, to a position of **absolute supremacy**" (Wilson, 1956: 203; my emphasis). The forces of reality were leading the Americans to adjust sovereignty accordingly. "The plain tendency" that Wilson saw "is toward a centralization of all the greater powers of government in the hands of federal authorities, and toward the practical confirmation of these **prerogatives of supreme over-lordship** which Congress has been gradually arrogating to itself. The central government is constantly becoming stronger and more active, and Congress is establishing itself as the **one sovereign authority** in that government" (Wilson, 1956: 205; my emphasis).

Once the principle is accepted that the representatives of the people are the proper ultimate authority in all matters of government, the originating and controlling force in the politics of a nation resides in its legislative body. It determines what shall be done; and the executive "is plainly bound in duty to render **unquestioning** obedience to Congress" (Wilson, 1956: 181; my emphasis). Those who fix the policies that the administration is to serve should be strictly accountable to the choice of the majority. Beyond that, the condition of self-government requires that "a sharp line of distinction" be made "between those offices which are political and those which are *non*-political" (Wilson's emphasis). "The strictest rules of business discipline, of merit tenure and earned promotion, must rule every office whose incumbent has not to do with choosing between policies" (Wilson, 1956: 190).

Wilson's Theory of Administration

Wilson's theory of administration is based on this "sharp line of distinction" between "politics" and "administration." He defines politics as the enactment of public law, as the formulation of public policy (Wilson, 1887: 198, 212). Public administration is defined as the detailed and systematic execution of public law (Wilson, 1887: 212). Governments may differ in the political principles underlying their constitutions; but principles of good administration are much the same in any system of government. That there is "but one rule of good administration for all governments alike" is the basic thesis in Wilson's theory of administration (Wilson, 1887: 202).[3]

The science of administration, according to Wilson, was most fully developed by French and German scholars at the turn of the century (Wilson, 1887: 202). The practice of administration was most highly perfected in Prussia under Frederick the Great and Frederick William III and in France under Napoleon (Wilson, 1887: 204–205). Monarchies and democracies may differ with respect to the political structures of their constitutions, but their administrative systems operate on the same technical principles (Wilson, 1887: 218): "When we study the administrative systems of France and Germany, knowing that we are not in search of *political* principles, we need not care a peppercorn for the constitutional and political reasons which Frenchmen and Germans give for their practices when explaining them to us. . . . If I see a monarchist dyed in the wool, I can learn his business methods without changing one of my republican spots" (Wilson, 1887: 220; Wilson's emphasis).

Wilson's thesis that there is "but one rule of good administration for all governments alike" carries two correlative implications. First, a theory or science of public administration is applicable to all political regimes; and second, a theory of administration is a general theory as distinct from the limited theories inherent in the ideological preoccupations of political theorists. Administration is an invariant relationship in all systems of government; thus a science of administration has universal applicability to all political systems. Wilson could conceive of a theory of democratic government but **not** a theory of **democratic administration**.

Wilson also sustains the conclusion that modernity in human civilization is associated with the perfection of a system of "good" administration (Wilson, 1887: 204).[4] A system of "good" administration will be hierarchically ordered in a system of graded ranks subject to political direction by heads of departments at the center of government. The ranks of administration will be filled by a corps of technically trained civil servants "prepared by a special schooling and drilled, after appointment, into a perfected organization, with an appropriate hierarchy and characteristic discipline" (Wilson, 1887: 216). Perfection in administrative organization is attained in a hierarchically ordered and professionally trained public service. Efficiency is attained by the perfection of this structural arrangement. Wilson also conceptualizes efficiency in economic terms: "the utmost possible efficiency and at the least possible cost of either money or of energy" (Wilson, 1887: 197). Thus perfection in hierarchical ordering will maximize efficiency as measured by least cost expended in money or effort in realizing policy objectives.

Basic Propositions in the Wilsonian Paradigm

The basic propositions inherent in the paradigm that Wilson proposed to use in building a science of administration can be summarized as follows:

1. There will always be a single dominant center of power in any system of government; and the government of a society will be controlled by that single center of power.
2. The more power is divided the more irresponsible it becomes; or, alternatively, the more power is unified and directed from a single center the more responsible it will become.
3. The structure of a constitution defines and determines the composition of that center of power and establishes

the political structure relative to the enactment of law and the control of administration. Every system of democratic government will exalt the people's representatives to a position of absolute sovereignty.

4. The field of politics sets the task for administration, but the field of administration lies outside the proper sphere of politics.

5. All modern governments will have a strong structural similarity so far as administrative functions are concerned.

6. Perfection in the hierarchical ordering of a professionally trained public service provides the structural conditions necessary for "good" administration.

7. Perfection in hierarchical organization will maximize efficiency as measured by least cost expended in money and effort.

8. Perfection of "good" administration as defined above is a necessary condition for modernity in human civilization and for the advancement of human welfare.

If these basic propositions advanced by Wilson are representative of a paradigm used in constituting a scholarly tradition, we would expect other scholars to present similar theoretical formulations. We would also expect research efforts to be predicated upon these same theoretical foundations. To indicate the generality of the paradigm, I shall briefly consider the congruence of Wilson's paradigm with Max Weber's theory of bureaucracy [5] and with the governmental research and administrative survey tradition.

Weber's Theory of Bureaucracy

Congruence

Max Weber was concerned with the development of a general social theory that would provide an understanding of human civilization. Bureaucracy, for Weber, was a necessary condition, or an organizational means, for maintaining the legal, economic, and technical rationality inherent in modern civilization. Weber viewed the modern state as being "monocratic" or single-centered (Gerth and Mills, 1946: 214; Rheinstein, 1954: 349–350).[6] Rationality in administration depended upon a structure of hierarchical relationships. Weber's work sustains all of Wilson's essential theses. The congruence in their work is immediately revealed in a brief synopsis of some of Weber's key points of emphasis.

Bureaucratic organizations, for Weber, are technically superior to all other forms of organization—comparable to the technical superiority of a machine over nonmechanical modes of production. Precision, speed, knowledge, continuity, discretion, unity, strict subordination, and reduction of friction and of material and personal costs are the attributes of strictly bureaucratic administration. Bureaucracy emphasizes an "objective" organization of conduct according to calculable rules without regard to persons. A bureaucratic official conducts his office with formalistic impersonality applying the rule to the factual situation without hatred or passion. "Bureaucracy has a 'rational' character: rules, means, ends, and matter-of-factness dominate its bearings" (Gerth and Mills, 1946: 214, 215, 244).

Weber concurs with Wilson's position that perfection in bureaucratic administration depends upon rigorous exclusion of politics from the routines of administration. Bureaucracy depends upon the technical application of calculable rules of law to factual situations in a logically rigorous and machinelike manner. This rational character of bureaucratic administration led Weber, like Wilson, to associate bureaucratization with the development of modern civilization. "The nature of modern civilization, especially its technical-economic substructure," according to Weber, requires the "calculability of consequences" realized by bureaucratic organization: "Above all, bureaucratization offers the optimal possibility for the realization of the principle of division of labor in administration according to purely technical considerations, allocating individual tasks to

functionaries who are trained as specialists and who continu-
ously add to their experiences by constant practice" (Rheinstein,
1954: 350). The advance of modern civilization and the perfection
of bureaucracy, presumably, go hand in hand.

Anomalies

Max Weber's characterization of bureaucracy is largely associated with his specification of the **conditions** of bureaucratic
organization as an ideal type. When Weber goes on to consider
the social and political consequences associated with the **perfection** of bureaucratic organization, he presents some highly
anomalous themes.[7] "Where the bureaucratization of administration has been completely carried through," Weber anticipates
that "a form of power relationship is established which is virtually indestructible." It is an instrument that can be "easily
made to work for anybody who knows how to gain control over
it" (Gerth and Mills, 1946: 228). Bureaucracy, in effect, will serve
any political master. "Hence," according to Weber, "the bureaucratic machinery continues to function for the successful
revolutionaries or the occupying enemy just as it has been functioning for the legal government" (Rheinstein, 1954: xxxiv).

When viewed from the perspectives of the individual bureaucrat, the virtual indestructibility of the perfected bureaucratic
machine implies, in Weber's words, that "the individual bureaucrat cannot squirm out of the apparatus in which he is har-
nessed. The professional bureaucrat is chained to his activity by
his entire material and ideal existence. He is only a single cog
in an ever moving mechanism which prescribes for him an essentially fixed route of march. . . . The individual bureaucrat is
thus forged to the community of all the functionaries who are
integrated into the mechanism" (Gerth and Mills, 1946: 228).

The ruled are as powerless as the individual bureaucrat in
dealing with the fully developed bureaucratic apparatus. Once
perfected, the bureaucratic apparatus cannot, according to Weber, be dispensed with or replaced. "If the official stops working,

or if his work is forcefully interrupted, chaos results and it is difficult to improvise replacements from among the governed who are fit to master such chaos." More and more the material fate of the masses depends upon the operation of bureaucratic organizations. "The idea of eliminating these organizations," Weber concludes, "becomes more and more utopian" (Gerth and Mills, 1946: 229).

In the context of these observations, Weber notes that altering the course of conduct in a bureaucratic machine normally depends upon the initiative of those at the very top. He goes on, however, to indicate the powerlessness of those at the top: "Under normal conditions, the power position of a fully developed bureaucracy is always overtowering. The 'political master' finds himself in the position of the 'dilettante' who stands opposite the 'expert,' facing the trained official who stands within the management of administration." Weber contends that this powerlessness of the "master" holds whether the master is a "people," a "parliament," an "aristocracy," a "popularly elected president," or a "monarch." "The absolute monarch is powerless opposite the superior knowledge of the bureaucratic expert." Weber also anticipates a coalition of interest between the head of government and the bureaucratic apparatus as against desires of party chiefs operating within legislative bodies in a constitutional government (Gerth and Mills, 1946: 232–234).

From this portrait of a "fully developed bureaucracy" we can only conclude that the bureaucratic machine will place the professional bureaucrat in chains, will transform citizens into dependent masses, and will make impotent "dilettantes" of their political "masters." The dominance of a fully developed bureaucracy would render all forms of constitutional rule equally irrelevant. Bureaucracy becomes the exclusive political reality. So far as I know, Weber never attempted to resolve the anomaly or paradox implied by the conclusions he reached about the "full" development of his "ideal" form.[8] He does, however, indicate that the dominance of a bureaucracy depends upon its capacity to monopolize information behind a facade of secrecy, to preclude competitive rivalry among aspiring officials, and to monopolize the professional expertise available in a society (Gerth and Mills, 1946: 233–235).

The Research Tradition in American Public Administration

American scholarship in public administratio῾., ith a few exceptions, has had little concern for the picture that Max Weber portrayed of the fully developed bureaucracy.[9] Much of the research in American public administration has made little use of the predictive value of theory to derive hypotheses from theory and then use evidence to support or reject the hypotheses as a test of theory. American public administration is more preoccupied with theory as a prescriptive doctrine that can be used to rationalize and reorganize the structure of administrative relations in accordance with the principles of hierarchical organization. The principles are taken as eternal truths, which can "rescue executive methods from the confusion and costliness of empirical experiment" (Wilson, 1887: 210).

Research in the mainstream of American public administration is usually undertaken with explicit reference to some agency or unit of government, which becomes the unit of analysis. The precepts of the Wilsonian paradigm provide a conceptual yardstick to assess patterns of organization that do not measure up to those precepts. Recommended policy changes are usually made to bring organizational arrangements into conformance with those precepts. When a unit of government exercises general authority over the provision of numerous public services, the standard format of administrative surveys includes a diagnostic assessment of pathologies attributed to the proliferation of agencies, the fragmentation of authority, overlapping jurisdictions, and duplication of services. Duplication of services and overlapping jurisdictions are presumed, on prima facie grounds, to be wasteful and inefficient. The proliferation of agencies and the fragmentation of authority are presumed to provoke conflict and create disorder and deadlock.

When research in this tradition focuses on a community of people that is not organized as a unit of government, as in the case of a metropolitan region or a river basin, the axiomatics are simply pushed back a step. In such a case, any community of people must be constituted into a single unit of government with a single center of authority culminating in a unified command. A professionally trained public service organized into a chain of command responsible to a single chief executive will efficiently and responsibly discharge public policies in providing for the overall needs of the community.

Building upon the basic precepts in the Wilsonian paradigm, students of public administration gradually articulated several principles of administration. Such concepts as unity of command, span of control, chain of command, departmentalization by major functions, and direction by single heads of authority in subordinate units of administration are assumed to have universal applicability in the perfection of administrative arrangements. Strengthening of the government is viewed as the equivalent of increasing the authority and powers of the chief executive. General-authority agencies are preferred to limited-authority agencies. Large jurisdictions are preferred to small. Centralized solutions are preferred to the disaggregation of authority among diverse decision structures.[10]

The culmination of this research tradition is often identified with the work of the President's Committee on Administrative Management. The committee indeed affirms the essential theses in Wilson's theory of administration. Efficiency in government, according to the committee's *Report*, depends on two conditions: (1) the consent of the governed and (2) good management. The first condition is assured according to the committee's *Report* by the democratic character of the American Constitution.[11] The second condition, efficient management, however, "must be built into a piece of machinery." The principles of efficient management "have emerged universally wherever men have worked together for some common purpose, whether through the state, the church, the private association, or the commercial enterprise." The committee implied that principles of efficient management apply to all **associations** alike. The principles of management, summarized as "canons of efficiency," were assumed to require "the establishment of a responsible and effective chief executive as the center of energy, direction, and administrative management; the systematic organization of all activity in the hands of a qualified personnel under the direction of the chief executive; and to aid him in this, the establishment of appropriate managerial and staff agencies" (U.S. President's Committee, 1937: 3).

Similarity between the "canons of efficiency" and the traditional principles of hierarchical organization, however, conceals a basic discontinuity in the theory of organization used by the President's Committee in conceptualizing its work. This discontinuity was expressed best by Luther Gulick, a member of the committee and the author of a memorandum on the theory of organization prepared for the committee's use and for the guidance of its staff. That memorandum is often identified as a classical restatement of the traditional theory of public administration. Gulick's "Notes on the Theory of Organization," however, represent an anomalous orthodoxy, which deserves careful scrutiny (Gulick and Urwick, 1937: 3–45). While sustaining an argument on behalf of a general theory of organization, Gulick advances theses that challenge the very foundations of the traditional theory of public administration.

Gulick's Anomalous Orthodoxy

Gulick's essay on the theory of organization begins with a traditional statement of the problem of organization as arising from a need to coordinate work subject to a high degree of specialization and division of labor. Such coordination is attained through "a structure of authority [which] requires not only many men at work in many places at selected times, but also a single directing executive authority" (Gulick and Urwick, 1937: 7). The concept of unity of command, the notion that "one man cannot serve two masters," is central to Gulick's theory of organization (Gulick and Urwick, 1937: 9). It is the function of organization to enable a director to coordinate and energize all of the subdivisions of work so that the major objective or task may be achieved efficiently.

Principle of Homogeneity

Following this introduction to his analysis, Gulick presents a concept which he identifies as the principle of homogeneity. The principle of homogeneity implies that the means must be instrumental to the accomplishment of a particular task. Associating two or more nonhomogeneous functions would sacrifice technical efficiency in administration by mixing factors of production that would have the effect of obstructing or impairing the net social product. An educational program, for example, might be impaired if combined with a law enforcement program. Public welfare administration should, similarly, be separated from police administration. "No one," Gulick contends, "would think of combining water supply and public education, or tax administration and public recreation." Those functions are too heterogeneous to be combined in a single agency. Gulick also contends that "politics" and "administration" are heterogeneous functions that cannot be combined within the structure of administration without producing inefficiency (Gulick and Urwick, 1937: 10).

If there are limits upon the grouping of agencies which would impair technical efficiency, the central precepts in Wilson's theory of administration come tumbling down. Efficiency in administration measured in the accomplishment of work at least cost is not necessarily attained through perfection in hierarchical organization. There may be circumstances when hierarchical organization will violate the principle of homogeneity and impair administrative efficiency.

Reorganizing the Chief Executive

Gulick discussed the difficulty of attaining a hierarchical ordering among the municipal agencies of the city of New York under these circumstances. The Charter Commission of 1934 reached the conclusion that municipal agencies could not be grouped into fewer than twenty-five departments without a loss of efficiency from the grouping of heterogeneous functions. A solution was attained by reorganizing the mayor's office to include three or four assistant mayors. Gulick concluded that this arrangement solved the problem inherent in the conflict between the principles of span of control and of homogeneity "provided the assistant mayors keep out of the technology of the services and devote themselves to the broad aspects of administration and coordination as would the mayor himself" (Gulick and Urwick, 1937: 12). Gulick thus turns to the organization of the executive—meaning the exercise of management activities associated with "the job of the chief executive" (Gulick and Urwick, 1937: 13)—to solve the problems of executive control over agencies performing many heterogeneous functions.

Gulick invented the famous acronym POSDCORB to characterize **the work of the chief executive**. The acronym, as every student of public administration knows, stands for the following activities: planning, organizing, staffing, directing, coordinating, reporting, and budgeting. Gulick notes that several of these functions were being separately institutionalized through different agencies of the Federal government. Budgeting was organized through the Bureau of the Budget, planning through the National Resources Committee, and staffing through the Civil Service Commission. Each of these agencies was viewed by Gulick as "a managerial arm of the chief executive" (Gulick and Urwick, 1937: 14). Together these agencies might be organized as part of a managerial establishment in the Executive Offices of the President.

The Jungle Gym

Having introduced a series of management functions which he associated with **the work of the chief executive**, Gulick then analyzes the task of organizing the "work" units of government without violating the principle of homogeneity. He suggests that each activity can be classified in accordance with the major **purpose** being served, the **process** being utilized, the **persons or clientele** being served, and the **place** where the service is being rendered. He then suggests that each of these categories can be used as a basis for constituting work units and that one need not be exclusive of another. He thus speaks of vertical and horizontal departments by indicating that a particular department can be organized vertically to serve a major **purpose** such as the provision of public health services. Such activities may also have reference to **processes** requiring such diverse specialties as medicine, law, accounting, engineering, and personnel services, which can be organized into horizontal departments. The principle of "a single structure of authority" had somehow dissolved into a "fabric of organizational interrelations" with multiple networks of cross-departmentalization (Gulick and Urwick, 1937: Chart III, p. 19). The symmetry of a hierarchical pyramid was abandoned for the latticework of a "jungle gym" (Gulick and Urwick, 1937: 20).

Whether to rely primarily on one or another mode of organization in constituting departments or work units is a matter of calculating the relative advantages and disadvantages of each. Whichever mode is used as a primary basis of organization does not exclude the possibility of developing secondary, tertiary, or quaternary networks of organization to gain some of the residual advantage afforded by the other methods. "In an organization built on two or more bases of departmentalization," Gulick suggests, "the executive may use the process departments as a routine means of coordinating the purpose departments" (Gulick and Urwick, 1937: 34). One chain of command can, in effect, be used as a tool for coordinating alternate structures of command.

The Holding Company Idea

Gulick then introduces "the Holding Company Idea" to suggest that "a large enterprise engaged in many complicated activities which do not require extensive or intimate coordination may need only the loosest type of central coordinating authority.

Under such conditions, each activity may be set up, on a purpose basis, as virtually independent, and the central structure of authority may be nothing more than a holding company" (Gulick and Urwick, 1937: 24).The central coordinating authority in such circumstances could relax the primary structure of control and sustain coordination through secondary or tertiary organizations.

By analogy each department of government is likened to a subsidiary. The president is chief executive of the holding company. The Executive Offices of the President became the embodiment of the holding company idea. The managerial agencies of the government that performed the POSDCORB functions would be integrated into the holding company structure. Each would operate as one of several management bureaus. Gulick anticipated that in such a circumstance each department "would be given extensive freedom to carry on as it saw fit and the President at the center of the parent company would not pretend to do more than prevent conflict and competition" (Gulick and Urwick, 1937: 34).

One Master

Gulick argued that not all the activities of government can be appropriately departmentalized on the basis of a single plan of organization (Gulick and Urwick, 1937: 31–32). Different bases of departmentalization can be used, and the choice of which to use is calculated on the basis of relative advantage. The choice of one basis for the first order of departmentalization does not preclude the development of secondary or tertiary forms of organization. The organization of the executive can have recourse to multiple management processes and multiple control structures. A multiple command structure was clearly implied.

Yet Gulick poses his problem in traditional terms and reaffirms conventional wisdom. He is not prepared to abandon the maxim that "a man cannot serve two masters" (Gulick and Urwick, 1937: 31–37).The principle of unity of command presumably can be preserved if **everyone** serves but **one master**. The simple concept of hierarchy is replaced by a complex "fabric of organizational interrelationships" resembling a "jungle gym" but controlled by a single chief executive (Gulick and Urwick, 1937: 19–20). The management apparatus inherent in the holding company concept with its managing bureaus exercising control over operational agencies necessarily means that the management of each operating agency confronts a multiple command structure. The head of each operating agency might eventually find him or herself in a position comparable to a sergeant receiving commands from a platoon of officers. Unity of command is preserved if the jungle gym apparatus of the executive offices can be penetrated to gain access to the president as "the center of energy, direction and administrative management" (U.S. President's Committee, 1937: 3).

More than a half-century of intellectual effort in American study of public administration was predicated upon an assumption that perfection in the hierarchical organization of administrative arrangements is synonymous with efficiency. Luther Gulick introduced the principle of homogeneity to indicate limits on efficiency in the aggregation of administrative operations into ever larger units of organization. Gulick's effort to provide an alternative structure led him to consider alternative ways for aggregating work units and to suggest the possibility of primary, secondary, tertiary, and quaternary networks of organization. The principle of unity of command was retained by reference to the holding company concept, and Gulick returned from his speculative foray to reaffirm the conventional wisdom that "a man cannot serve two masters" (Gulick and Urwick, 1937: 9).

Simon's Challenge

Herbert Simon undertook the frontal attack which Gulick had avoided. Simon uses the criterion of efficiency as his basic tool to **define** what is meant by "good" or "correct" administration. "The criterion of efficiency," according to Simon, "dictates that choice which produces the largest result from the given application of resources" (Simon, 1965a: 179). Where output is specified, the criterion of efficiency determines which alternative form of organization is best.

Using the criterion of efficiency, Simon makes a critical examination of the traditionally accepted principles of administration and demonstrates that those principles do not necessarily hold. Increases in specialization as such will not necessarily increase efficiency. Only those increases in specialization that improve performance when the available resources are given would lead to an increase in efficiency.

Similarly, Simon takes Gulick to task for his return to the haven afforded by the principle of unity of command. A certain amount of "irresponsibility and confusion" might well ensue from relaxing the principle of unity of command, but Simon insists that such costs may not be "too great a price to pay" for the benefits to be derived from alternative modes of organization (Simon, 1965a: 24). If the benefits from relaxing the principle of unity of command exceeded the costs, the efficiency of an organization would be improved as a consequence of such relaxation.

In his effort to reconstruct a theory of administration, Simon endeavors to develop a theory of rational choice. He insists upon a fact-value distinction in the sense that factual circumstances are concerned with the calculation of probable consequences and evaluation is concerned with the calculation of preferences. The task in decision making is to consider different strategic alternatives, to anticipate the probable consequences that would follow factually from those alternatives. Given a complete and consistent set of factual premises and a complete and consistent set of value premises, the criterion of efficiency would imply that there is only one alternative that is preferable to all others (Simon, 1965a: 223). Only one decision would in such circumstances be consistent with rationality. A theory of rational choice under conditions of perfect information and a transitively ordered schedule of preferences permits no choice. The correct solution is fully determinate.

The essential problem in administrative organization is that of enhancing rationality in human choice, given the radical limits inherent in the psychology of choice (Simon, 1965a: 240–244).

Human capabilities for handling information, arraying preferences, and acting in relation to appropriate alternatives are subject to severe limitations. Cooperative teamwork requires that each member of an organization exercise discretion. Coordination of each individual's actions depends on the provision of appropriate factual premises and value premises to facilitate a rational choice in one's exercise of discretion.

The function of organization is to bound the rationality exercised by each person as a decision maker working within an organization. The bounding of discretion by the specification of factual and value premises leads Simon, following Barnard's pioneering work *The Functions of the Executive*, to conceptualize authority as being "zoned" (Simon, 1965a: 123–153; Barnard, 1938: 168–169). Presumably the specification of limits to areas of acceptance might derive from different sources of authority. An organization thus might reflect a composite of command networks rather than a single line of authority or chain of command.

The concepts of bounded rationality and zoned authority enable Simon to conceptualize an organization as being an equilibrium maintained within areas of acceptance established by its different constituent elements. He conceptualizes the constituent elements as "customers," "employees," and "entrepreneurs" (Simon, 1965a: 111ff.). The entrepreneur reflects the control group in an organization; the employment contract establishes the area of acceptance within which employees are willing to accept direction from management in guiding their actions. Customers in turn provide funds in exchange for products. These funds supply the incentives for the entrepreneur and the employees to function as a productive team or organization. Simon conceptualizes the legislature as being the equivalent of customers in supplying a public agency with its funds; but a legislature also functions as a control group (Simon, 1965a: 120–121). Simon does not attempt to untangle the implications for organizational equilibrium when a legislature simultaneously attempts to articulate consumers' preferences and to operate as a control group.

An equilibrium model of organization implies that the area of acceptance is derived by agreement among the persons involved in an organization. Basic issues that go beyond the areas of acceptance are subject to negotiation or to resolution by recourse to decision structures external to the organization. Simon's concept of organization as an equilibrium maintained within areas of acceptance has been used by James D. Thompson, for example, to express the concept of organization as a "domain consensus" (J. D. Thompson, 1967: 28). Administration becomes the management of interdependencies among the constituent elements within an organization in relation to opportunities and threats in a dynamic environment (J. D. Thompson, 1967: 34–38).

Within the context of a means-ends calculus inherent in purposive action, the problem of efficiency can be conceptualized as either minimizing the costs of production in relation to a particular output or of maximizing the output for a given level of expenditure. Simon recognizes the difficulty of establishing an explicit and measurable "social production function" when the service being rendered is the provision of police protection, the maintenance of public health, or some other public service (Simon, 1965a: 188–190). In view of this difficulty, Simon reaches the conclusion that "it is hard to see how rationality can play any significant role in the formulation of administrative decisions unless these production functions are at least approximately known" (Simon, 1965a: 189).

Simon's challenge to the Wilsonian tradition in the study of public administration was of radical proportion. The criterion of efficiency was used to reject the presumption that perfection in hierarchical organization is synonymous with efficiency. In pursuit of his analysis, he formulates a general theory of rational choice that might be applied to any aspect of social organization. Yet he curiously confines his analysis to something that he calls "an" organization or "the" organization.[12] The sets of events which Simon labels as an "organization" are uniformly characterized by a hierarchical ordering. Though rejecting unity of command as a logically necessary condition for efficiency in any and all circumstances, Simon repeatedly returns to face the fact of hierarchy in his discussion of administrative behavior.

In considering the function of social organization, Simon recognizes that "institutional arrangements are subject to infinite variations, and can hardly be said to follow from any innate characteristics of man. Since these institutions largely determine the mental sets of the participants they set the conditions for the exercise of . . . rationality in human society." He then goes on to indicate that "the highest level of integration that man can achieve consists in taking an existing set of institutions as one alternative and comparing it with other sets" (Simon, 1965a: 101). He does **not**, however, apply this principle to the problem of administrative behavior by comparing one set of organizations with other sets of organizations to establish the relative efficiency of different organizational arrangements.

In considering institutional arrangements in a democratic society, Simon indicates that "legislation is the principal designer and arbiter of these institutions" (Simon, 1965a: 101). But what theory of institutions is to guide legislators in their choice of designs for conceptualizing and formulating the institutional setting that establishes the basic premises for human rationality? By referring to legislation as the principal designer and arbiter of institutions, Simon is not giving serious attention to the constitutional level of analysis. Madison's distinction between a "constitution" and a "law" in *Federalist* 53 may be of fundamental importance in a constitutional democracy. Yet Simon's emphasis on rationality is of basic importance to the constitutional level of analysis.

By bounding his own theory of organization with a preoccupation for intraorganizational arrangements, Simon reduced the theoretical impact of his challenge. By leaving legislatures in the position of being the principal designers and ultimate arbiters of institutional arrangements, the traditional dichotomy of politics and administration is sustained. The criterion of efficiency becomes a tool for suboptimization.[13] A theory of bounded rationality without the appropriate institutional constraints can become a theory of bounded irrationality.[14] Administrative behavior is bounded by institutional constraints other than those internal to "the organization." Public administration requires reference to more than the theory of a firm.

Simon challenged, and his challenge stands. But having challenged, Simon returned to the world of bureaucratic organizations to pursue his work within the familiar constraints of a social universe dichotomized into the domains of politics and administration. Another community of scholars, concerned with conditions of institutional weakness and institutional failure in market economies, is pursuing similar interests in the study of nonmarket decision making. These scholars, many of whom are oblivious to the intellectual controversies in public administration, are fashioning the foundations for a new theory of public choice and collective enterprise. We shall turn to their work in the next lecture.

3 _____

The Work of the Contemporary
Political Economists

A persistent theme in the intellectual mainstream of American public administration is reference to efficiency as an essential criterion of "good" administration. Efficiency is conceptualized in two fundamentally different ways. One way views efficiency as being expressed through principles of hierarchical organization. The greater the degree of specialization, professionalization, and linear organization in a unitary chain of command, the greater the efficiency.[1] The other way views efficiency in terms of a cost calculus. The accomplishment of a specifiable objective at least cost or a higher level of performance at a given cost is the measure of efficiency. Wilson clearly assumed that perfection in hierarchical organization is equivalent to efficiency measured in a cost calculus (Wilson, 1956: 197. See also proposition 6, in Chapter 2, under "Basic Propositions in the Wilsonian Paradigm"). Wilson thus equated perfection in hierarchical organization with least-cost performance.

Gulick, at the very culmination of the administrative survey movement, challenged Wilson's assumption by specifying a principle of homogeneity as a limit to efficiency in hierarchical organization. Simon sustained that challenge and explicitly broke with the traditional theory of administration. Using the least-cost solution as his criterion of efficiency, Simon demonstrated that solutions based on perfection in hierarchical organization need not be the most efficient. Simon recognized that various institutional arrangements might be used to bound human rationality and affect the potential for attaining efficiency.

Simon chose, however, to confine his works largely to something that might be specified as "an" organization or "the" organization. "Organizations" in this sense became the primary focus for subsequent work on organization theory. This focus led to substantial emphasis on the problems of bounded rationality **within** an organization and to substantial neglect of different decision-making arrangements and of multiorganizational arrangements in administrative systems.

The challenge posed by Simon's work has been pursued by a community of scholars who use the criterion of efficiency to assess performance in the provision of public goods and services. Most of these scholars were trained as economists with specialized interests in agricultural economics, resource economics, public finance, public utilities, public regulations, and welfare economics more generally. Since their analytical tools derive from economic theory and their concern is with public decision making, I shall identify this group of scholars as contemporary political economists.[2]

Many early efforts of these political economists were largely oriented toward benefit-cost analysis. One facet of this work has evolved into the planning, programming, and budgeting system (PPB) for planning public expenditure decisions (U.S. Congress, 1969). PPB analysis, however, rests on theoretical presumptions similar to the traditional theory of public administration. Such analysts would find Leonard White's early definition of public administration as the *"management of men and materials in the accomplishment of the purposes of the state"* (White, 1939: 6; White's emphasis) appropriate if the term "nation" were substituted for "state." The PPB analyst takes the methodological perspective of an "omniscient observer."[3] Assuming that the PPB analyst knows the "will of the state," a program is selected for the efficient use of resources (i.e., men and material) in the accomplishment of those purposes. The assumption of omniscience may not hold; and as a consequence, PPB may involve radical errors and generate gross inefficiencies (Wildavsky, 1966).

In the last twenty to twenty-five years, other political economists have turned their attention to the relationship of institutional arrangements to economic performance in the public

sector. The presentation in this chapter will be confined to those
political economists who (1) use the individual as the basic unit
of analysis; (2) use the theory of externalities, common properties, and public goods to define the structure of events relevant
to public administration; (3) analyze the consequences of different organizational or decision-making arrangements on the output of public goods or services; and (4) evaluate these
consequences by whether the outcome is consistent with the
efficiency criterion or other measures of performance.

Model of Man

Work among most political economists is usually based on an
explicit model of man. They adopt a form of methodological
individualism which makes self-conscious use of the perspective
of a representative individual or set of representative individuals
in the conduct of analysis (Buchanan, 1966: 26ff.). The representative individual may be a member of a hypothetical community, an entrepreneur, a public employee, or some other
person whose interests are explicitly stated. Assumptions about
individuals normally include reference to (1) self-interest, (2)
rationality, (3) information, (4) law and order, and (5) the choice
of a maximizing strategy.

The assumption of self-interest implies primarily that each
individual has preferences that affect the decisions he or she
makes; those preferences may differ from individual to individual. Rationality is usually defined as the ability to rank all
known alternatives available to the individual in a consistent
manner (Downs, 1957: 4–6). Assumptions about information
usually have reference to three levels, which are defined as certainty, risk, and uncertainty (Knight, 1965). Under either certainty or risk an analyst can project a relatively determinate
solution to a particular problem. Under conditions of uncertainty, the determinateness of solutions is replaced by conclusions about the **range** of possible solutions.

Once uncertainty is postulated, a further assumption may be
made that an individual **learns** about states of affairs as he or

she develops and tests strategies (Simon, 1959). Estimates are made about the consequences of strategies. If the predictions follow, a more reliable image of the world is established. If predicted events fail to occur, an individual is forced to change his or her image of the world and modify his or her strategies (Shackle, 1961). When learning occurs, the assumption of rationality may also have to be modified to allow for a reordering of preferences as the individual learns more about the opportunity costs inherent in different alternatives.[4]

An assumption of uncertainty also implies that one of the essential considerations in the design of organizational arrangements is the development and use of information (Cyert and March, 1963). Planning and deliberation are activities that seek to clarify alternatives and the consequences that are likely to flow from those alternatives. An essential criterion of organizational arrangements is the extent to which relevant information is evoked or excluded and the effect that such organizational characteristics have on the error-proneness or error-correcting propensities of decision makers.

Classical economic theory postulates that economic man will act within the limits of "lawful" conduct. Most analysis by political economists is predicated upon some postulated condition of law and order in which basic definitions of rights, duties, liberties, and exposures exist in some form. An assumption may either be made that some basic constitutional settlement exists in the larger political environment or among segments of the domain being considered. In short, some political structure is assumed to provide a context for analysis. In the absence of any law-and-order assumption, it might be necessary to assume a Hobbesian state of war as the prevailing human condition.

The assumption that individuals will adopt a maximizing strategy implies the consistent choice of those alternatives which an individual thinks will provide the greatest net benefit as weighed by his or her own preferences. This can be expressed alternatively as the choice of the least-cost strategy and is equivalent to the efficiency criterion. Maximization under uncertainty is not possible in a formal mathematical sense. Yet it is possible to assume that individuals will attempt to maximize subject to uncertainty. In that case, an individual who pursues a maximizing strategy in the absence of knowledge of all alternatives and of the costs of learning about added possibilities would act **as if** he or she were "satisficing" (March and Simon, 1958: 140–141). I prefer to refer to an optimizing strategy on the presumption that human choice is always subject to constraints of one type or another.

Structure of Events

Political economists assume that "rational," self-interested individuals who pursue optimizing strategies will face a variety of situations.[5] The structure of events inherent in different situations can be characterized by their relative divisibility or indivisibility. The degree to which events can be subject to **control** by individual persons through **possession, exchange,** or **use** is the critical criterion in establishing their divisibility or indivisibility. Events that cannot be subject to possession, exchange, or use by individuals have the characteristics of involving interdependencies and commonalities in their possession and/or use.

Events involved in any decision-making situation can be arrayed on a continuum ranging from purely private to purely public (Davis and Whinston, 1967). Goods are events for which people have preferences; bads are events for which people have aversion. The potential demand for most goods will exceed supply, and goods will be scarce. The supply of most bads will exceed demand and thus require efforts to restrict or alter their supply. **Purely private goods** are defined as those that are highly divisible and can be packaged, contained, or measured in discrete units. Purely private goods are subject to provision under competitive market conditions where potential consumers can be **excluded** from enjoying the benefit unless they are willing to pay the price. **Purely public goods,** by contrast, are highly indivisible. Potential consumers **cannot** be easily excluded from enjoying the benefit once a public good is produced. Once public goods are provided for some, they are available for others to use or enjoy jointly without reference to who pays the cost (Samuelson, 1954: 387; Margolis, 1955). National defense is a classic example of such a good. Once it is provided for some individuals living within a nation, it is automatically provided for all individuals within the nation whether they pay for it or not.

Exclusion, jointness of use, measurability, noticeability, or other attributes can be used in conceptualizing different types of goods. Mancur Olson in *The Logic of Collective Action* (1965) places primary emphasis upon exclusion and gives some consideration both to jointness of use and noticeability. Vincent Ostrom and Elinor Ostrom in "Public Goods and Public Choices" (1977) use both exclusion and the failure of exclusion, and separable and joint use to construct a two-by-two matrix that has reference to private goods, toll goods, common-pool resources, and public goods. Measurability, degree of choice, and noticeability are factors of considerable importance, but multidimensional matrices are difficult to elaborate. These difficulties, however, should not detract from considering the nature of the good, or the set of events, and related technologies as being one of the most fundamental elements that needs to be considered in all forms of institutional and policy analysis. Most political economists refer variously to externalities, common-property resources, collective goods, or public goods, in contrast to private goods, as being associated with market weaknesses and market failures.

Within this range, the production or consumption of goods or services may involve **spillover effects** or **externalities** which are not isolated and contained within market transactions (Ayres and Kneese, 1969). Goods with appreciable externalities are similar to private goods to the extent that some effects can be subject to the exclusion principle. Other effects, however, are like public goods and impinge upon persons not directly involved. Water pollution is an example of a negative externality; the benefits other members of a community derive from a person acquiring an education would be a positive externality. A reduction in the cost of a negative externality and an increase in the yield of positive externalities are both equivalent to the provision of a public good.

Common-property resources have attributes somewhat analogous to public goods (Gordon, 1954; Christy and Scott, 1965: chap. 2). Common-property resources involve a jointness of supply and a separability of use so that individuals cannot be effectively excluded from access to the supply of a resource, but each individual makes a separable use of that resource. The use-unit is subject to separable use (Blomquist and E. Ostrom, 1985). A groundwater basin, for example, affords a common water supply, which is accessible to any overlying property owner. Once extracted, the water becomes available for the separable use of each overlying proprietor. Whenever the aggregate demand on such a resource exceeds the available supply, one person's increased demand will adversely affect the use of others. Beyond certain thresholds of supply, an exclusion effect will operate among users so that one person's use will impair use by others, but the supply of the resource continues to be subject to a high degree of interdependency and indivisibility. Spillover effects occur in relation to conditions of supply and may or may not occur in relation to conditions of use. The public-good contingency bears more upon consumptive or use aspects than upon conditions of supply.

Decision-Making Arrangements

The work of political economists is based on an assumption that self-interested individuals, who pursue optimizing strategies, will require reference to appropriate sets of decision rules or decision-making arrangements in dealing with different structures of events if the welfare potential of a community of individuals is to be enhanced. No single form of organization is presumed to be "good" for all circumstances.[6] Rather, any organizational arrangement can generate a limited range of preferred effects. Every organizational arrangement will be subject to limitations. Institutional weaknesses and failures will become apparent if those limits are exceeded. Thus any particular organizational arrangement will have certain capabilities and will be subject to sources of weakness or failure. The essential elements in the analysis of organizational arrangements are to (1) anticipate the consequences that follow when (2) self-interested individuals choose optimizing strategies within the structure of a situation that has reference to (3) particular organizational arrangements applied to (4) particular structures of events (goods) in the context of (5) some shared community of understanding. The optimal choice of organizational arrangements would be that which minimizes the costs associated with institutional weakness or failure (Buchanan, 1969).

The analysis made by political economists in assessing the consequences of decision rules on the choice of strategy in different situations will be applied to four different decision-making arrangements. The first application will examine the effect of decision rules allowing for individualistic choice related to a common-property or public-good situation. The second application will examine the effect of decision rules characteristic of large-scale bureaucratic organizations concerned with the full array of goods and services in the public sector. Given the problem of institutional weakness and institutional failure associated both with individualistic choice and with large-scale bureaucratic establishments, consideration will then be given to the choice of decision rules that would enable a community of people to reduce these costs by organizing a collective enterprise to develop a common-property resource or provide a public good. Finally, consideration will be given to the development of multiorganizational arrangements as a means of providing for a heterogeneous mix of diverse public goods and services.

Individualistic Choice and the Tragedy of the Commons

Individualistic choice occurs whenever each person is free to decide for oneself in the pursuit of one's own interest. Individualistic choice is characteristic of the market and occurs whenever the only requirement is the willing consent of those individuals who freely agree or contract with one another to exchange some good or undertake some action. If each is free to decide for oneself in the pursuit of one's own interest concerning a common-property resource or a public good, serious problems will occur. Each individual will presume to maximize one's own net welfare if one takes advantage of the common property or public good at minimum cost to oneself. In the case of a public good, the cost minimizer would have no incentive to pay his or her share of the costs for provision. Most public goods would not be provided if funds were collected strictly on a voluntary basis.

In the case of a common-property resource with a renewable yield or supply, like a common water supply, individualistic choice has great advantages in reducing the costs of entrepreneurship so long as supply exceeds demand. When the aggregate demand of all individual users exceeds the available supply of a common-property resource, however, an increase in demand will diminish supplies and increase costs for the community of users. Each person will calculate only his or her own individual cost and will ignore the social costs imposed upon others. Many individuals will choose a "dog-in-the-manger" strategy, pursue their own advantage, and disregard the consequences for others. Furthermore, some individuals will be motivated to conceal information about their intentions. Should others propose joint action, those who conceal information may remain free to take advantage of opportunities created by the joint actions of others. If voluntary actions are taken to curtail demand, some individuals will pursue a "holdout" strategy (Hirshleifer, DeHaven, and Milliman, 1960; Olson, 1965). The holdout will be free to capture a lion's share of the benefits derived from the voluntary joint actions of others. As long as each person is free to decide his or her own course of action, the probability of someone pursuing a hold-out strategy is high. The presence of holdouts will threaten the stability of any joint voluntary solution (V. Ostrom, 1968).

If the competitive dynamic is allowed to run its course, social costs will escalate to a point at which continued operations will yield an economic loss for the community of users. Individuals in weak economic positions will be forced out. The neighborhood effects that are generated may include poverty, deprivations, threats, and even violence. Individualistic decision making applied to common-property resources will lead inexorably to tragedy unless the common property can be partitioned into separable private properties or decision-making arrangements can be modified to enable persons to act jointly in relation to a common property. This eventuality has been characterized by Garrett Hardin as the "tragedy of the commons" (Hardin, 1968). Unrestricted individualistic choice in relation to common-property resources or public goods can generate destructive competition so that the greater the individual effort, the worse off people become.[7]

Because of this competitive dynamic, individuals cannot be expected to form **large voluntary** associations to pursue matters of common or public interest unless special conditions can be met (Olson, 1965). These conditions will exist only (1) when members can derive a separable benefit of a sufficient magnitude to cover the cost of membership or (2) when they can be coerced through some form of levy or taxation into bearing their share of the costs. Thus we cannot expect people to secure the development of a common property or the provision of a public good by relying upon purely voluntary arrangements with each individual free to decide for him or herself. Some form of collective choice is required. When individuals act with the legal independence characteristic of decision making in market structures in a situation dominated by externalities, common-property resources, or public goods, we can conclude that **institutional weakness** or **institutional failure** will occur. The magnitude of the weakness or failure will depend on the importance of the externality, or the degree of indivisibility occurring in the common property or public good.

Bureaucratic Organization

Bureaucratic organization is an alternative decision-making arrangement to that of individualistic choice. Bureaucratic organization implies reliance upon hierarchy requiring subordinates to defer to the commands of superiors in the selection of appropriate actions and subject to sanctions or discipline for failure to do so. Bureaucratic organization can reduce some of the costs associated with the use of individualistic choice. The exercise of governmental prerogative by public officials capable of central direction and control implies that effective sanctions can be mobilized to preclude the holdout strategy and to undertake management programs to develop a common-property resource or produce a public good.

In the organization of any management program, recourse to a hierarchical command structure will permit economic advantage to be realized whenever production processes require a pooling of efforts through a division of labor which takes advantage of common production facilities. This rationale applies to both private firms and public agencies. If a firm can conduct business under the management of an entrepreneur at a lesser cost than if each transaction were organized as a market transaction, both the entrepreneur and the employees of the firm can derive a benefit from agreeing to act in accordance with the decisions of the entrepreneur in allocating work assignments among several different employees (Coase, 1937). Bureaucratic organization is a method for enhancing efficiency in operations by minimizing decision or transaction costs within the limits or zones of authority provided by the employment contract and the competitive force of the product market.

When principles of bureaucratic organization are applied to the conditions prevailing in the provision of public goods and services, a number of sources for potential institutional weakness or institutional failure become apparent. In the absence of an exclusion principle, the competitive force of a product market will not exist for most public organizations (Downs, 1967: 29–30). As a consequence, entrepreneurs in such organizations will be less sensitive to diseconomies of scale that accrue from increasing management costs as the size of a public organization increases. We can anticipate that any organization might reach a point at which the management cost of supervising an additional employee would exceed the marginal value added by the employee's productivity. Beyond that point, a growth in organizational size would generate a net economic loss or yield a decreasing social return.

Gordon Tullock in *The Politics of Bureaucracy* (1965) analyzes the consequences that follow when rational, self-interested individuals pursue maximizing strategies in very large public bureaucracies. Tullock's "economic man" is an ambitious public employee who seeks to advance his or her career opportunities for promotions within a bureaucracy. Since career advancement depends on favorable recommendations by one's superiors, a career-oriented public servant will act so as to please his or her superiors. Favorable information will be forwarded; unfavorable information will be repressed. Distortion of information will diminish control and create expectations that diverge from events generated by actions. Large-scale bureaucracies will thus become error-prone and cumbersome in adapting to rapidly changing conditions. Efforts to correct the malfunctioning of bureaucracy by tightening control will magnify errors. A decline in return to scale can be expected to result. The larger the organization becomes, the smaller the percentage of its activities will relate to output and the larger the proportion of its efforts will be expended on management.

Tullock suggests that the limits on control in very large public bureaucracies will engender "bureaucratic free enterprise" (Tullock, 1965: 167) when individuals and groups within an organization proceed to formulate their own missions with opportunities for side payoffs, including graft and corruption. Goal displacement and risk avoidance motivated by individual self-interest will generate organizational dysfunctions as elaborate justifications are fabricated to cover potential exposures to the scrutiny of superior authorities. The social consequences generated by an organization become increasingly contradictory and unreal to an independent observer when compared with public rhetoric about organizational purposes and goals. Michel Crozier concluded his study of French bureaucracy by asserting that *"a bureaucratic organization is an organization that cannot correct its behavior by learning from its errors"* (Crozier, 1964: 187; Crozier's emphasis). Both Tullock and Crozier sustain an analysis of conditions giving rise to institutional weakness and failure in large bureaucratic organizations. Their analysis is fully consistent with Max Weber's portrait of the fully developed bureaucracy.[8]

Once a public good is provided, the absence of an exclusion

principle implies that each individual using such a good or service will have little choice but to take advantage of whatever is provided unless he or she is either able to move to another jurisdiction or wealthy enough to make separate provision (Tiebout, 1956). Under these conditions, the producer of a public good may also be relatively free to induce savings in production costs by shifting some of the burdens or costs of production to users or consumers of the service (Weschler and Warren, 1970). Shifting costs of production to users may result in an aggregate loss of efficiency if savings on the production side are exceeded by added costs on the consumption side. Public agencies rarely if ever, for example, calculate the value of a user's time and inconvenience when studying how to make better use of an employee's time. More efficient use of clerical time may be more than offset in the time spent by persons who stand in line waiting on their "public servants." A net loss in efficiency may occur (Weschler and Warren, 1970). If a citizen has no place else to go and is one in a multitude of other citizens, the probability of his or her interest being taken into account is negligible. The most impoverished members of a community are the most exposed to deprivations under these circumstances. From this theoretical perspective, an analyst would not be surprised to find a positive relationship between the professionalization of the public service and the impoverishment of ghettos in big cities.

The inability of users of public goods and services to sustain an arm's-length relationship with producers of public goods and services generates further problems when users' preferences are subject to change in relation to the available supply of public goods and services (E. Ostrom, 1971). **No one** can know the preferences of other persons unless they are given opportunities to express their preferences. If public agencies are organized in a way that does not allow for the expression of a diversity of preferences among different communities of people, then producers of public goods and services will be taking action without information about the changing preferences of the persons they serve.[9] Expenditures will be made with little reference to consumer utility. **Producer efficiency in the absence of consumer utility is without economic meaning.**

Similar difficulties are engendered when conditions of demand for a public good or service increase in relation to the available supply. When demand begins to exceed supply, the dynamics inherent in the tragedy of the commons may arise all over again. A congested street or highway, for example, will carry less and less traffic as the demand grows. What was once a public "good" may now become a public "bad" as congested and noisy traffic precludes a growing number of opportunities for alternative uses. In short, public goods may be subject to serious **erosion** or **degradation** as demands change. In the absence of a capability to respond with modified supply schedules and regulations for use, a public "good" may come to be a public "bad" and the tragedy of the commons can reach critical or explosive proportions (Buchanan, 1970).

The capacity to levy taxes, to make appropriate expenditure decisions, and to provide the necessary public facilities is insufficient for assuring optimal use of such facilities.[10] One pattern of use may impair the value of a common facility or a public good for another pattern of use. The development of water resource facilities, for example, will be insufficient to enhance welfare for members of a community of users without attention to basic rules and regulations controlling the use of such facilities by different sets of users. Use of streams for the discharge of waste, for example, can become a dominant use, which will force out other users.

Optimal use of public facilities, when each use is not fully compatible with each other use, requires the development of a system of rules and regulations establishing capabilities and limitations in the discretion that persons can exercise in using common facilities made available to them. The development of such rules and regulations is relevant both to the scheduling of production processes and to the ordering of use patterns by potential users and consumers. These rules and regulations, like any set of decision rules, are not **self-generating, self-modifying,** or **self-enforcing.** Thus we are confronted with the basic problems of **who** shall promulgate and enforce rules of conduct to govern relations among individuals who use common properties or public facilities in relation to what sets of interests. Administrative rules and regulations are, thus, **not** a matter of political indifference to the users of public goods and services.[11]

Although bureaucratic organization will contribute significant institutional capabilities in the organization of any enterprise or agency concerned with the control of externalities, the management of a common property, or the provision of a public good, such an organizational form is also subject to serious conditions of institutional weakness and failure. An optimal structure for a public enterprise will need to take account of diversities in users' preferences and in production economies, relationship of demand to supply, and relationships in which one pattern of use may impair other patterns of use. The very large bureaucracy will (1) become increasingly indiscriminating in its response to diverse demands, (2) impose increasingly high costs on those who are presumed to be beneficiaries, (3) fail to proportion supply to demand, (4) allow public goods to erode by failing to take actions to prevent one use from impairing other uses, (5) become increasingly error-prone and uncontrollable to the point that public actions deviate radically from rhetoric about public purposes and objectives, and (6) eventually lead to the point that remedial actions exacerbate rather than ameliorate problems. The circumstances that generate institutional weakness and failure in large-scale bureaucracies pose problems that require a reconsideration of the decision rules applicable to public enterprises.

The Constitution of Self-Governing Public Enterprises

If individuals are to surmount the problems inherent in the tragedy of the commons and are to avoid the pathologies of the fully developed bureaucracy, they are confronted with the task of conceptualizing alternative institutional arrangements for the organization of collective or public enterprises. The structure of events inherent in a common-property resource or a public-good situation provides us with a basis for conceptualizing the community of interests that needs to be taken into account in designing alternative institutional arrangements. An inchoate community is formed by the individuals who use or enjoy a common-property resource, or a public good. The domain of the common property or the public good defines and bounds the community of people who share in its joint use.

If the object of interest can be identified, courses of action can be examined to determine which alternatives will enhance the welfare of that community of individuals. If some form of joint action is available that would leave each individual better off, provided that all members of the community were required to contribute proportionately to that activity, each person will be motivated to devise and agree to a set of decision rules authorizing action on behalf of that community of individuals. Such rules would require some form of coercion to ensure that each individual will discharge a proportionate share of the burden.

"Bureaucratic free enterprise" need not be the vice that Tullock implied if (1) a bureaucracy is immediately accountable to the relevant community of interest for which it is acting, (2) the costs of providing a joint good are funded by the constituents in proportion to their benefit or in accordance with some comparable rule of equitable allocation, and (3) public facilities are subject to use under terms and conditions that are considered by the relevant community to be reasonably designed to advance their common welfare. If these conditions can be met, we can contemplate the possibility of organizing a self-governing collective enterprise with an organizational structure capable of internalizing decision-making arrangements appropriate to the community of interests associated with the management of a common property or the provision of a public good. Reliance upon external decision structures would be necessary only (1) if adequate remedies are not available for resolving local conflicts within the decision structures afforded by the constitution of such an enterprise or (2) if the operation of a public enterprise is conducted in a manner that causes injuries to others outside its boundaries. If such conditions are to be met, **the structure of public administration cannot be organized apart from processes of constitutional and political choice**, which provide means for (1) the expression of social preferences of individuals within the community being served; (2) the formulation, enforcement, and revision of the decision rules governing both performance of producers and conditions of consumer use; and (3) the articulation and enforcement of demands made by individual users in relation to the producers of public services.

In the production and exchange of purely private goods and services, money is a medium of exchange and can be used as a measure of value and an expression of consumer utility. Public goods are not subject to exchange, and market price cannot be used as an appropriate measure of user's preference. The constitution of public enterprises must depend instead on the development of political mechanisms such as voting, representation, legislation, and adjudication for people to express their interests by signaling agreements or disagreements as the basis for ordering their relationships with one another. Such mechanisms provide essential means for informing public entrepreneurs about their strategic opportunities and limitations.

The development of organizational arrangements, which provides opportunities for persons to signal their agreements and disagreements, can be conceptualized as a problem of constitutional choice (Buchanan and Tullock, 1962). Constitutional choice is simply a choice of decision rules that specify the terms and conditions of government. These can apply to both small and large collectivities. The organization of a public agency, when viewed as a problem in constitutional choice, is the choice or selection of an appropriate set of decision rules to be used in allocating decision-making capabilities among the community of people concerned with the provision of public goods and services under reasonably optimal conditions.

The rudiments of a theory of constitutional choice applicable to the organization of a public enterprise have been developed by James Buchanan and Gordon Tullock in *The Calculus of Consent* (1962). According to Buchanan and Tullock, a representative individual wanting to form an organization to provide a public good would need to take two types of costs into account: (1) external costs, which are defined as those costs an individual would expect to bear when decisions deviate from his or her preferences and still impose obligations to pay and (2) decision-making costs, which are defined as the expenditure of resources, time, effort, and opportunities foregone in decision making. Both types of costs are affected by the selection of decision rules specifying the proportion of individuals required to agree before future collective action is taken.

Expected external costs will be at their highest point when any **one** person can take action on behalf of the entire collectivity. Such costs would decline as the proportion of members participating in collective decision making increases. Expected external costs would reach zero when all were required to agree before taking collective action under unanimity. Expected decision-making costs, however, would have the opposite trend. Expenditures on decision making would be minimal if any **one** person could make future collective decisions for the entire group of affected individuals. Such costs would increase to their highest point with a rule of unanimity.

If a constitutional decision maker were a cost minimizer, and the two types of costs described above were an accurate representation of costs, we would expect the choice of a decision rule at the point where the two cost curves intersect. When the two cost curves are roughly symmetrical, some form of simple majority vote would be a rational choice of a voting rule. If expected external costs were far greater than expected decision-making costs, an extraordinary majority would be a rational choice of a voting rule. Such a rule of extraordinary majority would presumably apply to the problem of constitutional choice, where expected decision costs would be of minor magnitude providing that a reasonably optimal set of constitutional rules could be devised which would not impose high deprivations upon any particular element of the community. On the other hand, if the opportunity costs inherent in decision making were expected to be very large in comparison to external costs, reliance might be placed on a rule authorizing collective action by the decision of one person in the extreme case requiring rapid response (E. Ostrom, 1968).

If the basic decision rules of a public or collective enterprise allowed for effective articulation of community preferences within agreeable decision rules, advantage could be taken of any economies that might be realized through hierarchical control for organizing a production process capable of responding to community preferences. In turn, when collective provision of a public good of specifiable quality is undertaken, each individual in that collectivity might rationally be assigned authority to require that the individual demands of each user of that good be met. Such a rule would specify the authority of **anyone** to act in relation to his or her individual interest in the collective enterprise. An optimal set of decision rules for the constitution of public enterprises would be expected to vary with different situations. We would not expect to find one good rule that would apply to the provision of all goods and services.

The similarity of these rules with elements in the structure of municipal corporations, public districts, and various local government agencies will be apparent to any student of American local government. If the rationale for such rules is theoretically sound, an appropriate structure of decision-making arrangements would exist when those in administrative responsibility were required to meet an appropriate set of conditions for sustaining public entrepreneurship under reasonably optimal conditions.

The Development of Multiorganizational Arrangements

The development of a self-governing public enterprise may not be a sufficient solution to problems of common-property resources or public goods. Several problems remain which may be sources of institutional weakness or failure associated with such an enterprise. First, a public enterprise may generate externalities that impinge upon others **beyond its borders**. If the externalities are negative, means may be required to limit and control them. Second, common properties or public goods may come in many different shapes and sizes with significant elements of jointness or interdependency among the various uses that can be made. Water resource systems, for example, reflect a baffling array of problems associated with persistent interdependencies among many joint uses (V. Ostrom, 1968). Interdependencies among water-related uses may also be inter-connected with land use, energy supply systems, transport systems, and the like. But each use may also involve interdependencies so that provision of a particular service will require separate consideration on its own merit. Third, when conflicts arise, institutional facilities need to be available for processing conflict and searching out resolutions that will preclude the tragedy of the commons from working itself out at some new level of interdependency. Multiorganizational arrangements can be conceptualized as a fourth institutional arrangement. As such it will involve a wide variety of interagency agreements and mechanisms for coping with interagency conflicts.

Some political economists have suggested that the problems arising from a great variety of public goods and services having many different sizes and shapes can best be resolved by taking advantage of the overlapping jurisdictions and fragmentation of authority inherent in the American political system (Bish, 1971; V. Ostrom, Tiebout, and Warren, 1961; Tiebout, 1956; Tullock, 1969). Mancur Olson, for example, suggests: "Only if there are several levels of government, and a large number of governments, can immense disparities between the boundaries of jurisdictions and the boundaries of collective goods be avoided. There is a case for every type of institution from the international organization to the smallest local government. It is the merit of the present approach that it can help explain the need for both centralized and decentralized units of government in the same context" (U.S. Congress, 1969: 1:327).

This solution is the antithesis of that proposed in the classical public administration tradition. Instead of chaos and disorder, these political economists perceive a pattern of ordered relationships being sustained among diverse public enterprises.[12] Each different public enterprise is accountable to its relevant community of interests and functions essentially as a public firm in a much larger industrial complex (V. Ostrom and E. Ostrom, 1965; V. Ostrom, 1969). Benny Hjern and David O. Porter (1981) have developed similar concepts related to "implementation structures."

Where externalities spill over into a larger domain and affect other closely associated uses, second, third, and fourth levels of organization can be relied upon to take care of those externalities that spill over from small-scale public jurisdictions. The first-level agencies may, thus, operate as a small-scale producer and retailer in providing some public good or service to an immediate community of users. A second level of public agencies may function as intermediate producers and as wholesalers supplementing the operation of the first-level agencies. The third- and fourth-level agencies may become large-scale producers providing a complement of services relevant to a much larger public domain.

If the first-level agencies are constituted to articulate the preferences of the most immediate constituency of interests and are exposed to the demands of individual users, such agencies can be expected to reflect those interests in bargaining with second-, third-, and fourth-level agencies if substantial legal and political autonomy exists among the various public enterprises forming a public service industry.

Once we begin to look for new patterns of order among the multiorganizational arrangements existing in a public economy characterized by overlapping jurisdictions and fragmentation of authority, we can begin to see that the American system of public education, the American highway system, the American police system, the American water supply system, and many other public service systems are operated by thousands of enterprises functioning at different levels of government (V. Ostrom, 1969). Each of these public service industries maintains and operates facilities serving diverse communities of interest. Despite the diversity of agencies involved in the construction and maintenance of public roads, streets, and highways, for example, the American highway system is a highly integrated network that has surprisingly few discontinuous or duplicate facilities.

As long as ample overlap and fragmentation of authority exist, agencies at one level of government can take advantage of the capabilities of agencies operating at other levels (Landau, 1969). If economies of scale in the production of a public good can be realized by a larger agency, smaller-sized agencies can enter into contractual arrangements to buy services from the larger agency.

In such a circumstance small, local government agencies can operate as buyers' cooperatives on behalf of their constituents in arranging for the production of public services in accordance with the preferences of local inhabitants (V. Ostrom, Tiebout, and Warren, 1961). A wide variety of municipal services, including police services, are now being provided on a contract basis in different metropolitan regions. We might anticipate that bilateral and multilateral bargaining will generate a higher level of efficiency in the provision of police services, for example, than is available in the very large, highly centralized, big city police departments (E. Ostrom et al., 1973).

Conversely, if no economy of scale can be realized by increasing the size of the production unit, the interests of the larger community of users can be accommodated by having the larger unit of government contract with the optimal scale producer to modify its facilities and interests to accommodate the larger community of interests. The United States maintains an interstate highway system by contracting with state highway departments to plan, construct, and maintain highways in accordance with national standards and specifications. It is doubtful that the administration of this interstate system would be improved by nationalizing all aspects of highway planning, construction, and maintenance. Fiscal transfers can be made from one level of government to other levels when externalities accrue to a larger community of interest. Grants-in-aid are one method for accomplishing such transfers; smaller units such as school districts generate benefits that accrue to the nation as a whole (Wagner, 1971).

The industry characteristics of multiorganizational arrangements functioning in a public economy can be realized only when diverse public agencies are able to develop different economies of scale in response to varying communities of interest. Overlapping jurisdictions and fragmentation of authority thus are necessary conditions for public service industries, other than fully integrated monopolies, to exist. Centralization cannot be conceived as the converse of decentralization in the sense that we speak of centralization versus decentralization. In responding to problems of diverse economies of scale, elements of centralization **and** decentralization must exist simultaneously among several jurisdictions with concurrent authority.[13]

The work of contemporary political economists, based on a paradigm derived from economic theory, challenges many of the basic assumptions in the traditional theory of public administration. Yet their form of analysis and many of their conclusions have a familiar ring to most Americans. This familiarity derives from the circumstance that many of the classical American political theorists were political economists and used a similar mode of analysis (V. Ostrom, 1987). In the next lecture I shall use the intellectual perspective provided by contemporary political economists to examine the work of these traditional American political theorists. From this perspective, we shall discover that these traditional political theorists have provided us with the basis for a theory of democratic administration which stands in contrast to the theory of bureaucratic administration.

4

A Theory of Democratic Administration: The Rejected Alternative

One of the major conclusions derived from the political economists is that overlapping jurisdictions and fragmentation of authority can facilitate the production of a heterogeneous mix of public goods and services in a public economy. This conclusion is contrary to the basic presumption in classical public administration theory that overlapping jurisdictions and fragmentation of authority are the principal sources of institutional failure in American government.

The pioneer scholars in American public administration rested their political analysis upon a basic paradigmatic choice which explicitly rejected the political theory used in the design of the American constitutional system as being inappropriate for the study of political "realities." In this lecture, I shall attempt to clarify the paradigmatic choice Wilson made in pursuing his political analysis. I shall go behind that choice and examine the political theory he rejected. In doing so, I shall advance the thesis that Wilson rejected a theory of democratic administration while propounding a theory of bureaucratic administration as the one rule of "good" administration for all governments alike.

Some Anomalous Threads of Thought

Wilson based his analysis on a political science that derived its paradigm from Walter Bagehot's *The English Constitution* (1964). Wilson's reliance on Bagehot led him to look for a single

center of power in the American political system and to conclude
that Congress was "the predominant and controlling force, the
centre and source of all motive and of all regulative power"
(Wilson, 1956: 31) in American government. His search for a
single center of authority was based on the assumption that "the
natural, the inevitable tendency of every system of self-government like our own and the British is to exalt the representative
body, the people's parliament, to a position of absolute supremacy" (Wilson, 1956: 203). The exercise of "absolute supremacy"
in a single center of authority is the essential feature of Thomas
Hobbes's *Leviathan* (1960). Bagehot and Wilson used an analytical
paradigm similar to that of Hobbes for their political science.

Both Wilson and Bagehot, however, make anomalous allu-
sions to the American constitutional system that are somewhat
incongruous with the essential thrust of their analysis. Wilson,
for example, concludes his essay "The Study of Administration"
by reference to "the systems within systems" prevailing in
American government. Local self-government is interlaced with
self-government at the state and national levels. He then poses
the question: "How shall our series of governments within governments be so administered that it shall always be to the interest
of the public officer to serve, not his superior alone but the
community as well, with the best efforts of his talents and the
soberest service of his conscience?" (Wilson, 1887: 221). This
would imply that the decisions of a public officer are to be governed by his or her moral choice based on considerations of
conscience, the authority of political superiors, and the claims
of the community. Such officers would indeed be governed by
more than one master.

Bagehot, in turn, recognizes a basic difference in the conception of the English constitution as contrasted with the American
constitution: "In one the supreme determining power is upon
all points the same; in the other that ultimate power is different
upon different points—now resides in one part of the Constitution and now in another" (Bagehot, 1964: 215). The English
constitution was an example of the first type with "only one
authority for all sorts of matters." The American constitution,

by contrast, had "one ultimate authority for one sort of matter and another for another sort." Bagehot described the American political system as a "*composite*" form of government in contrast to the English system as a "simple" or unitary type (Bagehot, 1964: 219).

Bagehot's references to the American constitutional system reflect substantial ambiguity. He attributes the design of the American system to a misunderstanding of the English constitution, which the Americans had attempted to copy in fashioning their own constitution. He has substantial doubts about the long-term viability of the American political system. "The practical arguments and legal disquisitions in America" reminded Bagehot of the problem confronting trustees in discharging a "misdrawn will" (Bagehot, 1964: 218). But Americans, like sensible trustees, could, he believed, make any constitution work (Bagehot, 1964: 220). Yet he concluded the introduction to his second edition by observing that the English constitution and the American constitution provide the two leading forms of "government by discussion" (Bagehot, 1964: 310). Government by discussion was, for Bagehot, a necessary condition for the development of a first-rate political community.

Rather than assume, like Bagehot, that the American constitutional system was based on a misunderstanding of the English constitution, perhaps we should consider the possibility that the designers of the American constitutions knew what they were doing and deliberately sought to base their political experiments on alternative designs (V. Ostrom, 1987). In that case we would expect the American political system to reflect the particular assumptions and concepts inherent in its design. When those assumptions and concepts diverged from the English model, we would expect the American political system to generate different patterns of conduct from those generated by the English system. We might, for example, expect the federal structure of the American political system to be necessarily characterized by **overlapping jurisdictions**. We might also expect a system of government that was designed to enforce provisions of constitutional law as against those who exercise governmental prerogative to be necessarily characterized by a separation of powers among diverse decision structures in the national government and in other units of government. A federal political system with substantial **fragmentation of authority** at each of the different levels of government would then be expected to maintain a diversity of public enterprises, each concerned with securing the support of its clientele or constituency and exposed to a variety of legislative, executive, and judicial constraints. Together these diverse enterprises might be expected to develop multiorganizational structures analogous to public service industries. A federal system of administration would necessarily have recourse to overlapping jurisdictions where coordination would not be confined to command and control in a megabureaucracy but could be achieved by processes of cooperation, competition, conflict, and conflict resolution.

We find some confirmation for these conjectures about varying design characteristics for different political arrangements when we note that Max Weber associated bureaucratic administration with a system of rule based on a "monocratic" principle (Rheinstein, 1954: 350). A monocratic structure can be defined as one in which all functionaries are integrated into a hierarchy culminating in a single center of ultimate authority. Unity of command is most fully attained in a monocratic system.

Weber also makes passing reference to a form of public administration which he calls "democratic administration" (Rheinstein, 1954: 330–334) in contrast to "bureaucratic administration." The defining characteristics of democratic administration for Weber are (1) an egalitarian assumption that everyone is qualified to participate in the conduct of public affairs and (2) the scope of the power of command is kept at a minimum. Weber also indicates that "all important decisions are reserved to the common resolution of all." Common resolution is attained through assemblies or collegial bodies that constitute or represent the members of a community or an organization. The administrative functionaries in such a democratic organization, Weber further notes, occupy a position that is "always in suspense between that of a mere servant and that of master" (Rheinstein, 1954: 330).

Democratic administration for Weber is **not** a viable alternative to bureaucratic administration. He dwells upon the limitations of democratic administration by indicating that it can apply only to local organizations or organizations with a limited number of members. Democratic administration is identified as a "marginal-type case," which cannot be treated as a "**historical starting point** of any typical [or general] course of development" (Rheinstein, 1954: 331; my emphasis). Weber could not contemplate the possibility that democratic administration might be juxtaposed to bureaucratic administration as an alternative model for the organization of public administration in a democratic society.

Perhaps both Weber and Wilson erred in failing to consider democratic administration a viable alternative to bureaucratic administration. When Alexis de Tocqueville visited America, he was much impressed with the system of administration that he found embedded in democratic institutions.[1] Tocqueville undertook his study *Democracy in America* (1945) on the assumption that a great democratic revolution was sweeping through Western civilization.[2] He was concerned that this revolution would generate a new democratic despotism, which would enslave men and threaten the future of human civilization. Yet he saw hope in American democracy, especially in its structure of democratic administration.

Tocqueville recognized that if a new despotism were to be avoided, this democratic revolution would require a "new science of politics" to assist in the governance of democratic societies (Tocqueville, 1945: 1:7). He was concerned that individuals in a democratic society would "adopt the doctrine of self-interest" as their rule of action "**without understanding the science that puts it to use**" (Tocqueville, 1945: 1:11; my emphasis). If men understood the science of how to put the doctrine of self-interest to proper use in governing society, Tocqueville could contemplate a society

> in which all men would feel an equal love and respect for the laws of which they consider themselves the authors; in which the authority of the government would be respected as necessary,

and not divine; and in which the loyalty of the subject to the chief
magistrate would not be a passion but a quiet and rational persuasion. With every individual in the possession of rights which
he is sure to retain, a kind of manly confidence and reciprocal
courtesy would arise from all classes removed alike from pride
and servility. The people, well acquainted with their own interests, would understand that, in order to profit from the advantages of the state, it is necessary to satisfy its requirements. The
voluntary association of citizens might then take the place of the
individual authority of the nobles and the community would be
protected from tyranny and license. (Tocqueville, 1945: 1:9)

Tocqueville's vision for a democratic society suggests that the
American experiment might be viewed as a "historical starting
point," to paraphrase Max Weber, in the development of a general system of democratic administration. In a key transitional
paragraph at the end of his first chapter on the geography of
North America, Tocqueville observes: "In that land the great
experiment of the attempt to construct society upon a new basis
was to be made by civilized man; and it was then, for the first
time, that theories hitherto unknown or deemed impracticable,
were to exhibit a spectacle for which the world had not been
prepared by the history of the past" (Tocqueville, 1945: 1:25).
Three chapters later he contrasts European patterns of governance in which either a state rules over society or a system of
government is constituted so that "the ruling force is divided,
being partly within and partly without the ranks of the people."
But he goes on to observe, "But nothing of this kind is to be
seen in the United States; there society rules itself for itself"
(Tocqueville, 1945: 1:57).

Tocqueville is asserting that a series of political experiments
of Copernican proportions had occurred on the North American
continent, enabling a people to use principles of self-governance
to reach out and develop a democratic society of continental
proportions. All prior human efforts to create polities of continental proportions had been organized as empires. Wilson
draws upon the administrative structure fashioned by Napoleon
and Frederick the Great and his successors to create great em-

pires as his model of good administration. He demonstrates no awareness that Tocqueville perceived the possibility of a different system of administration developing in a highly federalized democratic society.

Using Weber's defining characteristics, slightly modified, we would expect democratic administration to be based on (1) an egalitarian assumption that everyone is qualified to participate in the conduct of public affairs, (2) the reservation of all important decisions for consideration by all members of the community and their elected representatives, (3) restriction of the power of command to a necessary minimum, and (4) modification of the status of administrative functionaries from that of masters to that of public servants. If a system of public administration having these characteristics can operate within a legal order subject to a rational rule of law and can provide public services as efficiently as a system of bureaucratic administration, then democratic administration need not be viewed as a "marginal-type case."

To be an **alternative** model to bureaucratic administration, democratic administration would also have to display characteristics that would make us willing to reject Wilson's basic thesis that there is but one rule of "good" administration for all governments. We would expect to find elements of bureaucratic organization, but we would not expect to find those elements to be the **dominant** characteristics in a system of democratic administration. Instead of a fully integrated structure of command, we would expect to find substantial dispersion of authority with many different structures of command. The exercise of control over the legitimate means of coercion would not be **monopolized** by a single structure of authority. Democratic administration would be characterized by **polycentricity** and **not** by **monocentricity**.

Our search for a democratic theory of administration will begin with the works that Wilson rejected in establishing the foundations for his political science. I shall look first at the essays by Alexander Hamilton and James Madison in The Federalist. I shall then examine Tocqueville's commentary on democratic administration as contrasted to the patterns of bureaucratic administration found in France. French bureaucracy is indicative of Wilson's model of "good" administration.

Hamilton and Madison's Theory of Democratic Administration

Both Hamilton and Madison use the term "democracy" in a much more restricted sense than we use it today. Madison, for example, defines democracy as a society consisting of a small number of citizens who can assemble and directly administer their affairs in person (*Federalist* 10). Both Hamilton and Madison make frequent reference to the term "popular" government. The word "popular" derives from a Latin root, *populus*, which has much the same meaning as the Greek root, *demos*, from which the term "democracy" derives. Both terms refer to people in the sense of a community of people. For our purposes, I assume that "popular" government is roughly equivalent to the modern meaning of "democratic" government. In this presentation, I shall use Max Weber's defining characteristics and measure the democratic theory of administration developed in *The Federalist* by those defining characteristics.

Most students of American public administration are thoroughly familiar with Hamilton's essay on the constitution of the executive department and on administration in *Federalist* 70 and 72.[3] Hamilton, in *Federalist* 70, contends that "energy in the Executive is a leading character in the definition of good government." He identifies unity in the executive as the first ingredient contributing to energy. By unity in the executive, Hamilton clearly means the exercise of control over the executive establishment in a single person as chief executive.

In *Federalist* 72, Hamilton addresses himself to the details of organization which fall within the province of the executive department. These include such operations as foreign negotiations, preparing plans of finance, spending public monies in accordance with general appropriations of the legislature, organizing the army and navy, and directing the operations of war. In the discharge of these operations Hamilton observes: "The persons . . . to whose immediate management these different matters are committed ought to be considered as assistants or deputies of the chief magistrate, and on this account, they ought to derive their offices from his appointment, at least from his nomination, and ought to be subject to his superintendence" (*Federalist* 72). In these discussions of the national executive department, Hamilton's analysis uses language that conforms closely to that of the traditional theory of public administration.

If, however, we do **not** confine American public administration to national executive instrumentalities, we discover a different approach to problems of public administration in other portions of *The Federalist*. Extended commentaries on public administration are also found in Hamilton's analysis of problems of defense, internal security, and taxation. These commentaries use a language that is surprisingly similar to that of contemporary political economists.

Concurrent Administration in a Federal System

Hamilton's analysis of defense identifies the problem as one shared in common by the states. Spanish and British territories surrounded the American states from Georgia to Maine. Both Spain and Britain were major maritime powers, and a future alliance between them was possible. The danger was a common problem—a common threat to the security of the several states.

Hamilton asks whether the common defense should be secured by separate provision of the several states or by the common provision of the Union as a whole. If required to act under "the plan of separate provisions, New York," Hamilton observes, "would have to sustain the whole weight of the establishments requisite to her immediate safety, and to the mediate . . . protection of her neighbors" (*Federalist* 25). Smaller states with less extensive commercial interests might in the short run rely for their security on the defense measures of a stronger neighbor. The states shouldering a disproportionately large share of the burden for defense, according to Hamilton, "would be as little able as willing, for a considerable time to come, to bear the burden of competent provision." If the larger states, then, acted to reduce their burden, insufficient provision for the common defense would follow. "The security of all would thus be subjected to the parsimony, improvidence, or inability of a part" (*Federalist* 25).

If the interests of the people in each state were purely defensive, the stronger states in providing for their own defense would assume a large part of the burden for protecting their weaker neighbors. The weaker neighbors, taking advantage of this opportunity, would make little provision for defense and gain a comparative advantage by enjoying the protection of others without bearing their proportionate share of the costs. The people in the larger states, perceiving their plight in assuming a disproportionate share of the burden, would reduce their expenditures for defense. Thus "the parsimony, improvidence, or inability" of each part to provide for the common good would lead to inadequate provision for the defense of the Union (*Federalist* 25).

If, however, two or three of the larger states were to assume a disproportionate share of the burden for defending American interests against external threat, those states need not limit their strategic opportunities to purely defensive actions. A disproportionately large military force in the command of two or three states might, Hamilton suggests, cause the other states to "quickly take alarm." Each would respond to the alarm by taking military countermeasures. Pretenses could easily be contrived to justify offensive action. "In this situation, military establishments, nourished by mutual jealousy, would be apt to swell beyond their natural or proper size; and being at the separate disposal of the members, they would be engines for the abridgement or demolition of the national authority" (*Federalist* 25).

This analysis leads Hamilton to the conclusion that the proper means for guarding against a common danger "ought . . . to be the objects of common councils and of a common treasury" (*Federalist* 25). Congress would serve as a common council to authorize the creation of an appropriate force to assure the common defense of the American Union from resources provided by a common treasury contributed to by people in each of the various states through uniform measures of taxation.

Hamilton also recognized that each of the states would require a militia for its own internal security. In *Federalist* 29, Hamilton assumes the posture of advising a Federal legislator from his own state, New York, regarding the establishment of an appropriate mix of forces if the proposed Constitution were ratified. Hamilton's optimal solution is a mixed force composed of (1) a select corps of well-trained militiamen in each state available (a) for the defense of that state, or (b) for mobilization by the United States for the common defense, and (2) a necessary complement of national forces to man frontier garrisons and to provide for the common defense of all the states. The common defense and internal security of the United States would thus be provided for by a combination of forces maintained by the coordinated actions of the state and national governments. This solution, Hamilton concluded, "appears to me the only substitute that can be devised for a standing army, and the best possible security against it, if it should exist" (*Federalist* 29).

Both Hamilton and Madison extend their argument to suggest that the existence of a militia in each of the states might also be used as a means of security against a military coup. Hamilton notes that people in a unitary or monocentric state, having no other institutions of government available to them, "can take no regular measures for defence" against a military coup: "The citizens must rush tumultuously to arms, without concert, without system, without resource; except in their courage and despair. The usurpers, clothed with forms of legal authority, can too often crush the opposition in embryo" (*Federalist* 28).

In a federal system of government with its overlapping jurisdictions, Madison anticipates a different outcome to any effort to usurp political authority by military force:

> The existence of subordinate governments, to which the people are attached, and by which the militia officers are appointed,

forms a barrier against the enterprises of ambition, more insurmountable than any which a simple government of any form can
admit. . . . Were the people to possess the . . . advantages of local governments chosen by themselves, who could collect the
national will and direct the national force, and of officers appointed out of the militia, by these governments, and attached
both to them and to the militia, it may be affirmed with the greatest assurance, that the throne of every tyranny in Europe would
be speedily overturned in spite of the legions which surround it.
(*Federalist* 46)

A federal system with its concurrent regimes or overlapping
jurisdictions provides Madison with the happy circumstances
that "the great and aggregate interests" of the American people
could be organized in relation to a national government and the
local and particular interests could be organized into numerous
state and local governments. Madison was persuaded that "it is
only in a certain sphere that federal power can, in the nature of
things, be advantageously administered." Presumably "the nature of things" reflects events of diverse sizes and shapes. Jurisdictions of different scales can advantageously administer
programs capable of dealing with different sized events. "The
federal and State governments are . . . but different agents and
trustees of the [same] people, constituted with different powers
and designed for different purposes" (*Federalist* 46). Madison is
not especially disturbed about the prospect of a rivalry between
Federal and state agencies for popular support: "If . . . the people should . . . become more partial to the federal than to the
State governments, the change can only result from such manifest and irresistible proofs of a better administration as will overcome all their antecedent propensities [to favor the states]. The
people ought not . . . be precluded from giving most of their
confidence where they may discover it to be the most due" (*Federalist* 46).

Hamilton is generally persuaded that in a federal system, with
its concurrent structures of governmental authority, the people
can be masters of their own fate by using one system of government to check the usurpations of the other: "The people, by

throwing themselves into either scale, will infallibly make it preponderate. If their rights are invaded by either, they can make use of the other as the instrument of the redress" (*Federalist* 28).

In his analysis of the concurrent powers of taxation shared by the state and national governments, Hamilton rejects the assumption that a fully duplicate and separable system of tax administration will be established. Instead, he suggests that the national administration will work out cooperative arrangements with the states so that each can gain the advantage of joint action and avoid the prospects of mutually exclusive rivalry. Thus he anticipates that "the national legislature can make use of the *system of each State within that State*" (*Federalist* 36; Hamilton's emphasis). The use of the system internal to each state as an adjunct to national administration becomes readily available so long as each state does not possess a formal veto on national programs and so long as the national legislature has the independent authority to devise its own system of administration. Both are free to consider cooperative arrangements so long as each is free to consider alternative forms of action. Hamilton clearly anticipated the possibility of fiscal transfers occurring between different units of government to facilitate coordinated arrangements so one unit of government could take advantage of the capabilities afforded by other units of government (*Federalist* 36).

Principles of Self-Government

The system of administration which Hamilton and Madison envisioned in the American federal system was to operate in the context of a political system in which **all** units of government were to be fashioned upon principles of self-government (*Federalist* 39). Although Hamilton and Madison do not in any one place specifically enumerate the principles of self-government, the following principles discussed at various places in *The Federalist* might be included as among the principles of self-government applicable to each unit of government:

1. The terms and conditions of government derive from the right of the people to establish and alter those terms and conditions (*Federalist* 40).

2. The right of the people to establish and alter the terms and conditions of government is expressed through processes of constitutional decision making which require action by extraordinary decision rules. These decision rules have more demanding requirements than those necessary to enact ordinary legislation (*Federalist* 39).

3. The terms and conditions of government specified in a constitution or a charter are legally binding upon those who exercise governmental authority and are unalterable by those governmental authorities (*Federalist* 53).

4. The terms and conditions of government specified in a constitution or a charter assign both authority to act on behalf of the commonweal and limitations upon that authority. Limitations upon the authority of public officials to take collective action are specified as correlative to the rights of persons which establish constitutional grounds for individual actions against the usurpation of public authority (*Federalist* 78).

5. Each unit of government acts in relation to a defined constituency and exercises its jurisdiction in relation to persons as individuals. The selection of principal governmental officials responsible for taking legislative or executive action is based upon either direct or indirect election of constituents (*Federalist* 10, 16, 35, and 57–59).

6. The internal structure of each unit of government is devised so that collective decision making is allocated among diverse positions or decision structures. All important decisions are subject to consideration by the common council of those who depend upon election by members of the community. Dispersion of authority among diverse decision structures in any one unit of government is a necessary condition if the rules of constitutional law are to be enforceable as against those who exercise governmental authority (*Federalist* 47 and 80).

7. The authority allocated to the diverse decision structures

in the larger units of government is so divided that each is able to exercise potential veto power in relation to the authority allocated to others. Collective action thus depends on the operation of concurrent majorities exercised by decision structures composed of members who are related to their constituencies through varying terms of office, modes of representation, and differently sized constituencies (*Federalist* 51–52, 56–58, and 73).

8. The legal and political competence of each unit of government is limited in relation to the legal and political competence of other units of government. Each person is a constituent member of several units of government. Local and state officials will act in relation to national problems; national officials will act in relation to state and local problems. If the domain of a smaller unit of government is insufficient to take account of the common interest among interdependent events, reference can be taken to the next larger unit to secure an appropriate scale of decision making (*Federalist* 10, 16, 46, and 51).

9. Conflicts over jurisdiction among units of government, conflicts over constitutional limits upon the exercise of public authority, and conflicts over the provision of public services are all subject to judicial remedies before the regular courts of law (*Federalist* 80).

These principles of self-government are highly consistent with Max Weber's defining characteristics of democratic administration. Weber's egalitarian assumption that everyone is qualified to participate in the conduct of public affairs is reflected in the presumption that members of the community at large have an important voice in constitutional decision making, to elect public officials, and to hold those officials individually accountable for expressing the essential interests of constituents in major decisions. Individuals also have the prerogative to press for the enforcement of demands upon public officials through administrative, legislative, judicial, political, and constitutional remedies. Important decisions are reserved for consideration by members of the community and by their elected representatives.

The power of command is severely restricted by the scrutiny of officials in diverse decision structures within any particular unit of government, by the allocation of authority among different units of government, and by the presumption that the exercise of all governmental authority is limited by the terms and conditions specified in constitutional law. Finally, these various control mechanisms imply that administrative officials are obliged to **serve** members of the community rather than function as their masters.

In general, we might conclude that the principles of self-government discussed in *The Federalist* provide for a system of administration which is thoroughly embedded in a complex structure of democratic decision making. The American experiment can be viewed as a "historical starting point" for a generic type of administration to be characterized as "democratic" administration in contrast to "bureaucratic" administration. Hamilton's theory of administration in *Federalist* 70 and 72 might then be considered as a **special** theory of administration applicable to the Federal executive structure but **not** to the American system of government as a whole. The general conditions of hierarchical ordering within a bureaucratic system of administration can be significantly relaxed if public administration is organized in relation to the specific constituencies being served and if mechanisms of popular control, legislative surveillance, and judicial remedies are substituted for mechanisms of bureaucratic control. Processes of democratic administration necessarily depend upon mechanisms for democratic control being operable in the conduct of any public enterprise.[4]

Tocqueville's Analysis of Democratic Administration

Tocqueville in *Democracy in America* focuses his attention primarily upon the conditions of political organization within what he called the American "republics." His concern is primarily with the American states and with the systems of government within each state. He gives relatively less attention to the constitution of the national government and to its place in American society. Tocqueville's work thus provides an important complement to *The Federalist* in elucidating the political relationship of the Union to the states.

Tocqueville recognizes that the American tradition of self-government grew out of the townships, took possession of the states, and then fashioned a national constitution predicated upon those republican principles which were current in the entire community before the constitution existed. The American constitution is a complex system, which, according to Tocqueville, "consists of two distinct social structures connected, and, as it were encased one within the other; two governments, completely separate and almost independent, the one fulfilling the ordinary duties and responding to the daily and indefinite calls of a community, the other circumscribed within certain limits and only exercising an exceptional authority over the general interest of the country. In short, there are twenty-four small sovereign nations, whose agglomeration constitutes the body of the Union" (Tocqueville, 1945: 1:59).

Tocqueville characterizes the political and administrative affairs of each state as being "centered in three foci of action": the township, the county, and the state (Tocqueville, 1945: 1:59–60). Each is governed on the principle that "everyone [i.e., every individual] is the best and sole judge of his own private interest, unless they are prejudicial to the common weal or unless the common weal demands his help" (Tocqueville, 1945: 1:64). The township in turn is independent in all that concerns itself alone and is subordinate to the state only in those interests that are shared in common. These principles are applicable to each of the several foci of action or centers of authority, which are available to each citizen in governing the diverse communities of interests that are shared with others in a town, a county, a state, and a nation.

The reiteration of the principles of self-government in each different unit of government means that public administration is confined to circumstances that keep centralization and hierarchy to a minimum. Instead of a single hierarchy of public functionaries, Tocqueville found that "the executive power is disseminated into a multitude of hands" (Tocqueville, 1945:

1:81). People participate in the execution of their laws by the choice of public executives as well as in the making of their laws through the choice of legislators. Political responsibility is secured **more** by the principles of election than by accountability to central authority through a single hierarchy of control. Popular political control pervades both the government **and** its administration.

Tocqueville recognizes that the use of popular elections to choose public officers, who are responsible for the execution of the law and for the discharge of public services, creates a problem of how to compel popularly elected officials to conform to the law. He found that conflicts among independently elected administrative officials are resolved by adjudication in the courts of law. "The courts of justice . . . alone can compel the elected functionaries to obey, without violating the rights of the electors." When elections, instead of the authority of command in a single administrative hierarchy, are the primary method for the control of administration, Tocqueville concludes, "The extension of judicial power in the political world ought to be in the exact ratio as the extension of the elective power; if these two institutions do not go hand in hand, the state must fall into anarchy or into servitude" (Tocqueville, 1945: 1:74).

As republican institutions are replicated in multitudinous units of governments serving as many different communities of interest, a rule of law can be sustained as conflicts between individual citizens and public officials or among public officials in different jurisdictions are adjudicated by courts of law. As Tocqueville noted, "In no country in the world does the law hold so absolute a language as in America; and in no country is the right of applying it vested in so many hands" (Tocqueville, 1945: 1:71). Thus the legal basis of a rational social order can be sustained by reliance upon the offices of the judiciary as an alternative to administrative functionaries in a Weberian bureaucracy.

The mandate of executive leadership can thus be constrained by popular election, legislative surveillance, and judicial remedies. Under such circumstances, elected executives can be required to function as public servants in their communities rather than as the political masters over those communities. Americans have recourse to some eighty thousand hierarchies of diverse sizes rather than to a single overarching hierarchy of public authority. The essential spirit of American democracy, for Tocqueville, is reflected in a system of democratic administration organized primarily by principles of voluntary association and of self-government. As a European observer, Tocqueville noted, "The appearance of disorder which prevails on the surface leads one to imagine that society is in a state of anarchy" (Tocqueville, 1945: 1:89). But a deeper look revealed an underlying order in the bustle of activity:

> In America the power that conducts the administration is far less regular, less enlightened, and less skillful, but a hundredfold greater than in Europe. In no country in the world do the citizens make such exertions for the common weal. I know of no people who have established schools so numerous and efficacious, places of public worship better suited to the wants of the inhabitants, or roads kept in better repair. Uniformity or permanence of design, the minute arrangement of details, and the perfection of administrative system must not be sought for in the United States; what we find is the presence of a power which, if it is somewhat wild, is at least robust, and an existence checkered with accidents, indeed, but full of animation and effort. (Tocqueville, 1945: 1:91–92)

The uniformity of design, the minute arrangement of detail, and the perfection of administration associated with centralized administration in France had the opposite effect: "It excels in prevention but not in action" (Tocqueville, 1945: 1:90). The citizen in a centralized state would rather become "a passive spectator than a dependent actor in schemes with which he is unacquainted" (Tocqueville, 1945: 1:91). Perfection in centralized administration will lead to tranquillity without happiness, industry without improvement, stability without strength, and public order without public morality (Tocqueville, 1945: 1:90). In such circumstances ordinary citizens become indifferent to the interest of the community in which they live (Tocqueville, 1945: 1:44).

If egalitarian conditions of life characteristic of democratic societies were combined with a highly centralized system of administration, Tocqueville anticipated that such societies would include "an innumerable multitude of men, all equal and all alike, incessantly endeavoring to procure the petty and paltry pleasures with which they glut their lives. Each of them, living apart, is a stranger to the fate of the rest; his children and his private friends constitute to him the whole of mankind. As for the rest of his fellow citizens, he is close to them, but he does not see them; he touches them, but he does not feel them; he exists only in himself and for himself alone" (Tocqueville, 1945: 1:318). Above this multitude of men Tocqueville sees

> an immense and tutelary power which takes upon itself alone to secure their gratification and to watch over their fate. That power is absolute, minute, regular, provident and mild. . . . It chooses to be the sole agent and the only arbiter of [their] happiness; it provides for their security; foresees and supplies their necessities, facilitates their pleasures, manages their principal concerns, directs their industry, regulates the descent of property, and subdivides their inheritance: what remains, but to spare them all the care of thinking and all the trouble of living. . . . It compresses, enervates, extinguishes and stupefies a people, till each nation is reduced to nothing better than a flock of timid and industrious animals, of which the government is the shepherd. (Tocqueville, 1945: 1:318–319)

Such is Tocqueville's view of democratic society with a centralized government and a bureaucratic administration. The fully developed bureaucracy in a democratic society will generate, as Tocqueville foresees, a "species of oppression" which "is unlike anything that ever before existed in our world; our contemporaries will find no prototype of it in their memories" (Tocqueville, 1945: 1:318).

Tocqueville would certainly have rejected Wilson's presumption that there is but one rule of good administration for all governments alike. An "ultra-monarchial form of administration" combined with a republican constitution could only be a short-lived monster for Tocqueville (Tocqueville, 1945: 1:321). Mass societies dominated by highly centralized bureaucratic structures were the essential attributes of a new species of oppression that Tocqueville envisioned for the future of mankind.[5]

Tocqueville was persuaded that a large democratic society could be free **only** if men comprehend the **utility** of political forms or structures in the constitution of democratic systems of governance. He would certainly have agreed with Weber that a democratic system of administration in a free society must be based on (1) an egalitarian assumption that everyone is qualified to participate in the conduct of public affairs, (2) the reservation of all important decisions for consideration by all members of the community and their elected representatives, (3) restriction of the power of command to a minimum, and (4) modification of the status of administrative functionaries from that of masters to that of public servants.

Such possibilities can be realized only when careful attention is given to political forms that allow for concurrent action in several overlapping jurisdictions or concurrent foci of action: "Municipal institutions constitute the strength of free nations. Town meetings are to liberty what primary schools are to science: they bring it within the people's reach, they teach men how to use and enjoy it" (Tocqueville, 1945: 1:61). Under these circumstances, Tocqueville indicated that in a free democratic society "every man is daily reminded of the need of meeting his fellow men, of hearing what they have to say, of exchanging ideas, and coming to an agreement as to the conduct of their common interests" (Tocqueville, 1945: 1:xiv).

Restriction of the power of command also depends upon the fragmentation of authority among decision structures if the discretion of officials is to be limited by a rule of law. The power of the courts, in particular, must grow in proportion to the increase in popular control if democratic administration is to be the basis for a rational legal order (Tocqueville, 1945: 1:74). In short, Tocqueville anticipated that liberty could be sustained in an egalitarian society only if a system of public administration were developed which would meet the defining criteria used by Max Weber in characterizing democratic administration. **Democratic administration cannot be separated from the processes of popular control inherent in democratic politics.**

The work of Hamilton and Madison and of Tocqueville involves the articulation of a theory of democratic administration when measured by the criteria specified by Max Weber. The American experiment, based on a theory of democratic administration, can thus be viewed as a turning point in pioneering a new course of human development. Democratic administration, through a system of overlapping jurisdictions and fragmentation of authority, acquired a stable form that provides an alternative structure for the organization of public administration. Democratic administration need not be a "marginal-type case" confined only to local organizations with a limited number of members. A democratic theory of administration is the approach that Wilson rejected while propounding a bureaucratic theory of administration as being universally applicable to all systems of modern government. I shall pursue some of the implications of a theory of democratic administration for the study of public administration in the next chapter.

5

The Choice of Alternative Futures

Some Opportunity Costs in the Choice of Paradigm

In the course of these lectures, I have examined the study of public administration from an assumption that the persisting intellectual crisis is a paradigmatic one as conceptualized by Thomas Kuhn in his *Structure of Scientific Revolutions* (1964). I have argued that Woodrow Wilson and his contemporaries made an explicit paradigmatic choice in rejecting the political theory articulated by Hamilton and Madison in *The Federalist*.[1] The political theory in *The Federalist* was dismissed as having no analytical relevance for understanding the "realities" of American politics except to explain the source of some of the pathologies in American government. That theory, according to Wilson, had "**proved mischievous** just to the extent that it had succeeded in establishing itself as realities" (Wilson, 1956: 187; my emphasis).

Wilson's analytical theory assumed that the natural and inevitable tendency in any system of government is to have recourse to some sovereign body that will exercise "ultimate supremacy" and have the last say in making collective decisions. It is in this sense that we speak of a government as having a monopoly over the legitimate exercise of authority and use of force in a society. Indeed, much of contemporary political science is based on this presumption.

In such a theory, the distinguishing feature of a democratic or republican form of government is whether ultimate authority is exercised by a representative assembly selected by vote of the people. Thus Wilson took it for granted that "the representatives of the people are the proper ultimate authority in all matters of government, and that the administration is merely the clerical part of government" (Wilson, 1956: 181). Wilson saw good administration as a single hierarchical arrangement generic to all forms of government. The constitutions of different governments might vary in form; but the pattern of good administration would always be of the same form.

The choice of a paradigm in public administration depends on the relative advantage that can be derived from relying on one or another approach. To estimate the relative advantage inherent in different approaches, we must clarify basic assumptions about the nature of political organization and determine the consequences that are likely to follow from relying on differently designed structures or organizational relationships. If our calculation of these consequences is well founded, then each person can estimate the costs that are inherent in the opportunities that would be foregone by taking one or another approach.

A Theory of Sovereign Prerogative

The basic theory of sovereignty inherent in Wilson's political science was formulated by Thomas Hobbes. Hobbes reasoned that, in the absence of some superior power, the natural condition of man was a state of war in which each man was potentially exposed to acts of violence by every other man. In order to enjoy the felicity of a state of peace, men must be prepared to forego some options and agree to carry on relationships under terms and conditions that would not cause harm or injury to others. Hobbes was able to conceptualize the axioms for a felicitous order or a state of peace. He argued, however, that these axioms were insufficient for a stable commonwealth in the absence of a commanding power to enforce such axioms as rules of law. In Hobbes's words, "covenants, without the sword, are but words" (Hobbes, 1960: 109). Laws, to be effective, depend on mechanisms for their enforcement.

For there to be one society there must in Hobbes's theory be one system of law. For there to be one system of law, there must be but one source of law. Since the substance of law is established by its enforcement, there can be only one ultimate source of authority in both the formulation and the enforcement of law. Thus Hobbes envisioned a unification of the offices of legislation, administration, and adjudication in relation to a single sovereign with ultimate authority over all governmental prerogatives. A unitary sovereign exercising a unity of power was, he assumed, a necessary condition for maintaining a lawful and stable commonwealth. Such a sovereign is the source of law and cannot be held accountable by other persons to a rule of law. Thus the sovereign is above the law. The price of peace is deference and obedience to the authority of an absolute sovereign. Obedience is the essential virtue for good administration in a Hobbesian commonwealth.

Wilson's adherence to a unitary theory of sovereign prerogative led to his rejection of *The Federalist* as a political theory based on division of authority or separation of powers. In rejecting *The Federalist*, Wilson was rejecting the theory that was used to articulate the design of the American political system. An appropriate theory of design is necessary to understand both how a system will work and how modifications or changes in a system will affect its performance. To use one theory of design to evaluate the characteristics of a system based on a different theory of design can lead to profound misunderstandings. To use one theory of design to reform a system based on a different theory of design may produce many unanticipated and costly consequences. A Volkswagen is not a Ford. To evaluate one by the design criteria of the other or to repair one by using the parts of the other would not be reasonable procedures.

A Theory of Positive Constitutional Law

The theory of design used by Americans in fashioning their constitutions was of a radically different magnitude than the theory of design that Wilson used in his evaluation of that system. Americans sought to fashion systems of government in which those who exercised the prerogatives of government would have limited authority subject to the terms and conditions of constitutional law. The design for the American political system was based on a theory of positive (i.e., enforceable) constitutional law.[2] Hobbes considered such a theory to be repugnant to the nature of commonwealths (Hobbes, 1960: chap. 25, and 212–213). Who is to enforce the law upon those who have the ultimate authority and exercise a monopoly over the legitimate use of coercive capabilities in a society? The sovereign is the source of law and cannot be held accountable to law.

Perhaps in light of two centuries of experience, we can really begin to contemplate the possibility that the American experiment was not a fundamental error or misunderstanding based on "paper pictures" or "literary theories" (Wilson, 1956: 31). Instead, the American experiment reflects a different theory of design than Hobbes's *Leviathan* (V. Ostrom, 1987). A key to understanding the design of the American political system is to specify the logically necessary conditions for a system of positive constitutional law which is enforceable as against those who exercise governmental prerogatives.[3]

Several conditions would appear to be logically necessary for a system of positive constitutional law:

1. A system of positive constitutional law will necessarily depend upon processes of constitutional decision making which exist, at least in part, outside the competence of governmental authorities who are subject to its provisions. A positive constitution must be *unalterable* by governmental authorities acting upon their own motions if such authorities are to be limited in their decision-making capabilities (*Federalist* 53).

2. A system of legally enforceable constitutional law will necessarily depend upon an explicit formulation of the constitutional authority of persons in terms of rights which are not subject to alienation (that is, cannot be alienated, transferred, or taken away) by governmental authorities.

The constitutional authority of persons creates correlative limits upon the authority of those who exercise governmental prerogatives. Persons will then be able to exercise constitutional authority in asserting their claims as against governmental decision makers.

3. A system of positive constitutional law will necessarily depend upon a separation of powers so that each set of governmental decision makers will act in relation to limits placed upon their authority by other sets of governmental officials (Vile, 1967: 310). Some form of separation of powers, or fragmentation of authority, thus, is a logically necessary condition for enforcing provisions of constitutional law as against governmental decision makers (*Federalist* 47).

4. A system of positive constitutional law will also depend upon citizens who are prepared to pay the price of civil disobedience in being willing to challenge the constitutional validity of any law or official action and face punishment and official displeasure if their cause is not affirmed. Persons in a constitutional republic must be able to initiate and sustain causes of action in the protection of their constitutional rights and in the imposition of limits upon governmental authorities. The constitutional office of **persons** assumes substantial significance in the maintenance of a lawful constitutional order. We might, then, assume that the ultimate authority to deal with the jurisdiction of government rests broadly in all of those who function as members in such a political community and share a common theory of constitutional design.

5. A positive constitutional law will depend upon the existence of alternative political regimes each with its own charter or constitution so that individuals can have access to different units of government to articulate diverse communities of interest. Each individual will have access to alternative regimes and to the political, judicial, and constitutional remedies afforded by those diverse regimes. Conflicts of interest can be articulated in diverse forums.

The action of officials in each regime will serve to establish
limits upon the exercise of discretion by those who act on
behalf of other regimes.

Specification of logically necessary conditions for a positive
constitutional law does **not**, however, provide us with both the
necessary and sufficient conditions for a positive constitutional
law. The choice of political arrangements is within the domain
of choice. Human discretion can be exercised at variance with
decision rules. Madison recognized this condition when he observed, "In every political institution, a power to advance the
public happiness involves a discretion which may be misapplied
and abused" (*Federalist* 41).

The selection of decision rules for inclusion within a constitution is based on estimates of the probable consequences that
constitutional decision makers expect to flow from different decision rules. The success of constitutional decision making thus
depends on a knowledge of the probable consequences that will
flow from different decision rules. Such knowledge will always
be subject to conditions of risk and uncertainty. The long-term
viability of the American constitutional system will depend on
the capability of the American people to (1) provide remedies
against those who usurp authority and abuse their public trust
and (2) reform the structure of government so as to maintain
the essential equilibrium of a system of constitutional rule.

The successful reform of the American constitutional system
requires a continued knowledge of the probable consequences
flowing from different decision rules. This knowledge must include an assessment of the costs as well as the benefits which
are necessarily associated with any particular constitutional design. Such costs can be minimized but never eliminated. It is
not possible to gain the benefits of constitutional rule without
reaping its disadvantages as well. An absence of knowledge
about the costs inherent in the design of any particular political
system may lead individuals to attempt reforms that are aimed
at eliminating those costs. Attempts to eliminate costs inherent
in the design of any system may lead to its impairment and to
elimination of the benefits accruing from that system.

Some Necessary Costs of a System of Positive
Constitutional Law

A political system designed to enforce a system of positive
constitutional law as against one designed to articulate the exercise of a unitary sovereign will necessarily involve costs in
delay, open controversy, and complex relationships. Hamilton,
for example, recognized that the power "of preventing bad
laws" inherent in the exercise of veto capabilities also involves
the power "of preventing good ones." He also contends that
"the oftener [a] measure is brought under examination, the
greater the diversity of situations of those who are to examine
it, the less will be the danger of those errors which flow from
want of due deliberation" (*Federalist* 73). Thus the costs of delay
need to be weighed against the costs of errors engendered by
hasty action. Similarly, the costs of open controversy must be
weighed against the costs of secret cabals.

Tocqueville is also explicit in warning his European compatri-
ots about the complexity of the American political system and the
relatively high level of knowledge required to pursue strategic
opportunities in that system. Yet that cost must be weighed
against the danger that simple solutions will lead to the concentration of political power in a single center of authority. Tocqueville would have concurred with Justice Joseph Story's
observation: "In proportion as a government is free, it must be
complicated. Simplicity belongs to those only where one will
govern all . . . where law is not a science but a mandate to be
followed and not to be discussed."[4]

A Science of Association as Knowledge of Form and Reform

Tocqueville has suggested that the danger of democratic despotism engendered by the search for simple solutions in a centralized state can be avoided if a democratic people give proper
attention to political science as a "science of association." He

views a science of association as being "the mother of sciences" in democratic countries: "The progress of all else depends upon the progress it has made" (Tocqueville, 1945: 2: 110). A science of association will enable men in a democratic society to "comprehend the utility of forms" (Tocqueville, 1945: 2: 325) for putting the doctrine of self-interest to proper use as a rule of action for organizing and sustaining collective enterprises (Tocqueville, 1945: 1: 10). Tocqueville observes, "If men are to remain civilized or to become so, the art of associating together must grow and improve in the same ratio in which the equality of conditions is increased" (Tocqueville, 1945: 2: 110). A science of association is a necessary ingredient for advancing civilization in democratic societies and is the basis for Tocqueville's conclusion: "A new science of politics is needed for a new world" (Tocqueville, 1945: 1: 7).

It is precisely this science of association and the art of associating together that is the critical issue in the study of public administration. Those who study, teach, and practice public administration must come to some basic resolutions about the essential relationship between conditions and consequences for constituting and reforming human associations. Must the science of association used in public administration be built on a Hobbesian theory of sovereignty? Or can a science of association also be built on a theory of limited constitutions on the assumption that political structures can be devised in which those who exercise the extraordinary prerogatives of government are subject to the rule of constitutional law?

Some Common Assumptions

It can be argued that both Hobbes's theory of sovereignty and the American theory of a limited constitution are based on some common initial assumptions. Hamilton and Madison rely on a model of man that is fully consistent with Hobbes's model of man as formulated in his essays "Of Man" in *Leviathan*. Both view social organization as being grounded in a structure of enforceable legal relationships. The distinguishing characteristic of government is its power to enforce law. To that extent, both are based on a common science of human association. The assumptions common to both include the following:

1. Individual human beings are assumed to be the basic material or units that form any political system. No government will exist without reference to individual human beings. Each person, in the final analysis, is assumed to be the judge of his or her own self-interest and can be expected to act in a way that will enhance his or her net welfare potential.

2. Decision rules are the basis for ordering relationships in any association. Decision rules are propositions assigning decision-making capabilities to those who participate in social relationships. Limiting the field of choice by recourse to decision rules is a necessary condition for establishing predictability in social relationships. Discretion exercised in accordance with decision rules will allow pursuit of some possibilities and exclude other possibilities. If actions injurious to others can be excluded from the domain of choice, human welfare would be enhanced by the pursuit of lawful possibilities.

3. Decision rules are neither self-generating nor self-modifying but depend on individual persons who take account of others to formulate, enforce, and alter rules. If persons are to act consistently and productively in relation to one another, means must be available for constraining and resolving conflicts that arise from actions taken in accordance with existing decision rules and for devising new decision rules to comprehend new social conditions.

4. Decision rules are not self-enforcing but depend on the assignment of extraordinary powers to **some** persons to enforce decision rules in relation to other members of a community. Such powers include the capacity to impose coercive sanctions and thus involve the potential use of lawful decision-making capabilities to impose deprivation upon others.

5. Given the conditions specified in the above assumptions,

we must necessarily conclude that any form of organization capable of establishing and enforcing ordered social relationships among a large community of persons will necessarily depend on a **radical inequality** in the assignment of decision-making capabilities to those who exercise the prerogative for allocating and controlling the decision-making capabilities exercised by others. **Conditions of political inequality must necessarily exist in any political association.** (V. Ostrom, 1987: 50)

Two Different Solutions to the Problem of Political Inequality

Hobbes's theory of sovereignty and the American theory of the limited constitution depart from each other by providing **different** solutions to the problem of political inequality. Hobbes accepts absolute inequality as a necessary and sufficient condition for the organization of any commonwealth: there must be a commanding power! There must be a single center of authority capable of exercising **absolute** sovereignty if a stable and peaceful commonwealth is to be maintained. The price of peace is obedience; the sovereign is above the law.

The Americans were concerned with the problem of whether societies of men could, by reflection and choice, institute a system of government that could use constitutional law to enforce limits upon those who exercise the prerogatives of government. The condition of political inequality need not be absolute but only sufficient to maintain the enforceability of commonly accepted rules of law. Power can be divided and arranged among the several offices of government in such a manner that each will be a check on the other. By connecting the interest of the man to the constitutional authority of the office, ambition can be made to counteract ambition. Agreement will prevail when benefits accrue from mutual advantage. Conflict will intervene when some seek an advantage at the expense of others. Political structures are but a method for encapsulating conflict while due deliberation is sustained until human reason can search out new and improved solutions. The American constitutional system is an effort to chain Leviathan by a system of rules with rulers themselves subject to the rule of law.

If we assume that each theoretical formulation has the potential for being logically sound and operationally feasible, we would expect the two formulations to reflect different design characteristics. We would further expect those design characteristics to be organized through different decision structures and to give rise to different sets of consequences when implemented in an operable system of government (V. Ostrom, 1987). These consequences will include both benefits **and** costs. Every choice has its price.

From this analysis, we would expect Wilson's theory of administration to be relevant for a political system with a highly centralized monocentric decision structure. His theory would be appropriate for understanding and reforming the French and Prussian political systems or those having similar structural characteristics. Conversely, we would not expect Wilson's theory to apply to a highly polycentric political system with substantial overlapping of jurisdictions and fragmentation of authority. We would then be led to reject Wilson's thesis that there is but one rule of good administration for **all** governments alike. We would also entertain the possibility that the American experiment represents a "historical starting point" of major significance in the development of a system of democratic administration. Democratic administration as a general form of public administration can be juxtaposed to bureaucratic administration as an alternative type.

Basic Proposition in a Paradigm of Democratic Administration

The basic propositions inherent in the paradigm that Wilson proposed to use for building a science of administration were summarized in the second lecture (see Chapter 2, "Basic Propositions in the Wilsonian Paradigm"). The basic propositions relating to a science of democratic administration inherent in a paradigm that grows out of the work of modern political economists and that of the early democratic theorists can be summarized as follows:

1. Individuals who exercise the prerogatives of government are no more nor no less corruptible than their fellow citizens.

2. The structure of a constitution allocates decision-making capabilities among a community of persons; and a democratic constitution defines the authority inherent in both the prerogatives of persons and the prerogatives of different governmental offices so that the capabilities of each are limited by the capabilities of others. The task of establishing and altering organizational arrangements in a democratic society is to be conceived as a problem of constitutional choice.[5]

3. The exercise of political authority—a necessary power to do good—will be usurped by those who perceive an opportunity to exploit such powers to their own advantage and to the detriment of others unless authority is divided and different authorities are so organized as to limit and control one another.

4. The provision of public goods and services depends on decisions taken by diverse sets of decision makers and the political feasibility of each collective enterprise depends on a favorable course of decisions in all essential decision structures over time. Public administration lies within the domain of politics.

5. A variety of different organizational arrangements can be used to provide different public goods and services. Such organizations can be coordinated through various multiorganizational arrangements including trading and contracting to mutual advantage, competitive rivalry, adjudication of conflicts, and the power of command in limited hierarchies.

6. Perfection in the hierarchical ordering of a professionally trained public service accountable to a **single** center of power will reduce the capability of a large administrative system to respond to diverse preferences among citizens for many different public goods and services and to cope with diverse environmental conditions.
7. Perfection in hierarchical organization accountable to a **single** center of power will **not** maximize efficiency as measured by least-cost expended in time, effort, and resources.
8. Fragmentation of authority among diverse decision centers with multiple veto capabilities within any one jurisdiction and the development of multiple, overlapping jurisdictions of widely different scales are necessary conditions for maintaining a stable political order that can advance human welfare under rapidly changing conditions.

A theory of democratic administration does not preclude a theory of bureaucratic administration. But acceptance of a theory of democratic administration does imply a rejection of the assertion that a theory of bureaucratic administration is the only theory of good administration for all governments alike. The existence of two theories of public administration still poses a serious problem for American students and practitioners of public administration. What theory and mode of analysis is appropriate to the practice of American public administration?[6]

What happens when a highly polycentric system of democratic administration is modified to conform to the precepts of a monocentric system of bureaucratic administration? Is there a possibility that such alterations and reforms will exceed the limits for maintaining an enforceable system of constitutional rule? Are we prepared to pay that price? Will there be a threshold beyond which the price of peace is one of servitude in a bureaucratic despotism? Some of these questions have led me to entertain the outlandish hypothesis which I introduced in the first lecture: Dare we contemplate the possibility that the contemporary malaise in American society may have been derived, in part, from the teachings of public administration? Have our reform efforts to eliminate fragmentation of authority and overlapping jurisdictions so altered the basic structure of American government that many of its benefits have been eliminated as well? If we continue to use one theory of political design to reform a system based on another theory of design, may we confront a vicious circle in which the more we do the worse off we become? Without an appropriate theory of political organization, we shall be unable to discern the causes of our misery, and we shall suffer ills of which we are ignorant (Tocqueville, 1945: 1: 239–240).

The Use of Different Approaches to Policy Analysis

In continuing our inquiry into these different approaches to the study of public administration, I propose that we begin to explore the implications that each will have for the solution to some contemporary problems confronting the American people. A choice of paradigm can be expected to influence our diagnosis of sources of institutional weaknesses that give rise to social pathologies. Proposals for reform will also be derived from a choice of paradigm. Once we become more fully aware of the significance attached to a choice of paradigm, we can become more critical of our own work as scholars and of the implications that our work has for the practice of public administration in a democratic society. The use of different paradigms may indeed lead to alternative designs for alternative futures.

Policy Analysis of Institutional Arrangements in Urban Areas

The power and persistence of the Wilsonian paradigm is reflected in its continued use as a basis for policy analysis and for proposals of institutional reform. The prestigious Committee for Economic Development (CED), for example, drew upon that paradigm in preparing its report *Modernizing Local Government* (1966). Its more recent report *Reshaping Government in Metropoli-*

tan Areas (1970) adheres less rigorously to that paradigm but continues to use the language of the traditional paradigm. Similar proposals for metropolitan reform continue to be expounded in the late 1980s.

The diagnostic assessment of the conditions of institutional weakness and failure contained in the first CED report (1966) are based on the following findings:

[1.] Very few of the local units [of government] are large enough—in population, area, or taxable resources—to apply modern methods in solving current and future problems. Even the largest cities find major problems insoluble because of the limits on geographic areas, their taxable resources, or their legal powers.

[2.] Overlapping layers of local government—municipalities and townships within counties, and independent school districts within them—are a source of weakness. . . . This [overlapping] impairs overall local freedom to deal with vital public affairs; the whole becomes less than the sum of its part.

[3.] Popular control over government is ineffective and sporadic, and public interest in local politics is not high. . . . Confusion from the many-layered system, profusion of elective offices without policy significance, and increasing mobility of the population all contribute to disinterest.

[4.] Policy-making mechanisms in many units are notably weak. The national government [by contrast] has strong executive leadership, supported by competent staff in formulating plans that are then subject to review and modification by a representative legislative body. . . .

[5.] Antiquated administrative organizations hamper most local governments. Lack of a single executive either elective or appointive is a common fault. Functional fragmentation obscures lines of authority. . . . The quality of administration suffers accordingly. (CED, 1966: 11–12)

This analysis stresses the existence of numerous units of government, overlapping jurisdictions, and fragmentation of authority to infer that such events are causally linked to problems of institutional failure in urban communities. A monocentric political system with a hierarchically ordered administrative structure accountable to a single chief executive is used as a yardstick for ascertaining the preferred solution. The principal recommendation included in the CED report *Modernizing Local Government* includes the following:

[1.] The number of local governments in the United States, now about 80,000, should be reduced by at least 80 percent.

[2.] The number of overlapping layers of local government found in most states should be sharply curtailed.

[3.] Popular elections should be confined to members of the policy-making body and to the chief executive in those governments where the "strong mayor" form is preferred to the "council-manager" plan.

[4.] Each unit should have a single chief executive, either elected by the people or appointed by the local legislative body, with all administrative agencies and personnel fully responsible to him or her; election of department heads should be halted. (CED, 1966: 17)

Focusing on the cost of overlap and complexity, the CED report completely discounts **any** costs associated with institutional weakness and failure in large-scale public bureaucracies. No recognition is given to the substantial literature in organization theory on the problem of goal displacement and bureaucratic dysfunctions. The concept of bureaucracy as an ideal-type solution pervades the CED analysis.

Citizens in a democratic society will run a very substantial risk if they are asked to stake their future upon ideal-type formulations. Anyone offering perpetual-motion machines for sale would be exposed to a potential charge of fraud. Perhaps it is a reflection upon the contemporary state of political science that a distinguished group of businessmen advised by a distinguished group of political scientists can recommend that 80 percent of the units of local government should be eliminated without making any effort to assess the opportunity costs inherent in such a solution. Sixty thousand units of local government represent a major investment by the American people in decision-making facilities. Their elimination would be destructive of the basic infrastructure of American democratic administration. Can we afford to pay that price?

And what would we be buying at the cost of eliminating most of the infrastructure of American democratic administration? Tullock's analysis of institutional failure in large-scale bureaucracies suggests that we would be buying increasing measures of corruption associated with bureaucratic free enterprise. The prevalence of corruption in big-city police forces can hardly be ignored. Big-city police departments systematically fail to respond to demands for public security. Employment of private guards and private security forces is assuming substantial magnitude.[7] Such expenditures clearly indicate that people are willing to pay for public services which police departments fail to render.

Among the less prosperous segments of the population in big cities, we observe a similar increase in demand for public security, which is being met by the organization of neighborhood patrols and escort services through neighborhood improvement associations, churches, and other voluntary groups. In addition, many urban gangs function essentially as mutual protection societies. Some of these organizations are evolving into the equivalent of "soldier societies" capable of protecting their own domain or "turf" and of levying sufficient tribute to maintain viable organizations.

Aggressive rivalry between organized police and organized "soldier societies" is developing to the point that covert warfare is manifest by sporadic outbreaks of overt violence. The modern police tactic of "aggressive patrol" conducted by special task forces is no less than a military strategy to impose collective sanctions upon urban neighborhoods (Graham, 1968). The peace of democratic communities depends on the goodwill and helping hand of the individuals who live in those communities (Jacobs, 1961). Law and order maintained by the commanding power of an alien force is in fundamental violation of the most basic precepts of democratic administration.

Claims of efficiency in large-scale bureaucratic organizations can be supported only as long as ideal performance is postulated for a bureaucratic machine. Much of the literature in public administration pervasively ignores the problem of size even though the principle of span of control implies a radical constraint on organizational size. The notion that "there is little hard economic evidence of what **the** optimal size should be" (CED, 1970: 20; my emphasis) is valid only as long as **a single optimum** is presumed. The theory of externalities, common properties, and public goods would postulate the criterion that the domain of a public agency should coincide with boundaries of the appropriate field of effects so that substantial interdependencies are internalized within the jurisdiction of an appropriate agency (V. Ostrom, Tiebout, and Warren, 1961; Olson, 1969). Optimal size will vary with the boundary conditions of **different** fields of effects inherent in the provision of **different** public goods and services. Under these conditions, optimality can be attained only by reference to multiple agencies with overlapping jurisdictions (Tullock, 1969).

Economists do not anticipate that a single optimal size will exist for the different services produced for **any one** industry. Instead, economic provision of the services rendered by a particular industry will require a complex of agencies of many different sizes. A firm capable of producing automobiles at the lowest marginal cost will vary in size from a firm capable of repairing automobiles at the lowest marginal cost. Similarly, we would expect that the size of a police agency capable of facilitating optimal movement of automobile traffic through a metropolitan area will be different from one capable of optimally satisfying the demands of neighborhood residents for public security on neighborhood streets (E. Ostrom and Whitaker, 1973).

Economists would expect different economic activities to reflect different economies of scale. Some services are produced more efficiently by large-scale enterprises. The converse is also true: some services are produced more efficiently by small-scale enterprises. When capital costs in plants or physical facilities are proportionately large, economies of scale will accrue if those costs can be spread over a large number of users. Conversely, if labor costs or personnel services constitute a large proportion of the budget in the provision of a public service, economies of scale will be exhausted by smaller-sized organizations. Public agencies that are user-oriented in providing services to satisfy the diverse interests of individuals and members of households will be subject to very limited economies of scale. Neighborhood government and community control would be appropriate mechanisms to use in the provision of some public goods and services within big cities (Altshuler, 1970; Kotler, 1969).

Werner Hirsch (1964; 1968), in reviewing different studies of economies of scale among public sector agencies, indicates that the opportunities for improving efficiency through increased size are exhausted for many services in communities that reach a size of 50,000 to 150,000 population. Exceptions to this conclusion are capital-intensive utility services such as water supply, transportation, and sewage disposal. Even then, factors relative to the resource base may lead to radical variations in economies of scale.

Urban populations of 50,000 to 150,000 are small in size when compared to the major metropolitan areas of the United States. The diseconomies of scale associated with the large-scale organization of many urban services has led George Stigler to conclude:

> If we give each governmental activity to the smallest governmental unit which can efficiently perform it, there will be a vast resurgence and revitalization of local government in America. A vast reservoir of ability and imagination can be found in the increasing leisure time of the population, and both public functions and private citizens would benefit from the increased participation of citizens in political life. An eminent and powerful structure of local government is a basic ingredient of a society which seeks to give the individual the fullest possible freedom and responsibility. (Stigler, 1962: 146)

Serious problems of institutional failure would occur if **only** small units of government were relied on to perform functions of local government. The problem of "balkanization" in local government can be resolved, however, by an appropriate overlapping of local governmental jurisdictions so that significant interdependencies of a regional character can be handled by regional authorities. Tullock has suggested that the Buchanan and Tullock cost calculus is applicable to a choice of the optimal amount of overlap in a highly federalized political system (Tullock, 1969). Stigler's solution is viable only if advantage can be taken of the presence of overlapping jurisdictions in metropolitan areas.

The CED's most recent report, *Reshaping Government in Metropolitan Areas* (1970), reflects a major shift in emphasis by recognizing some variations in scale economies. A two-level arrangement is called for with a general unit of government for each metropolitan area and numerous community districts within each metropolitan area. This report indicates a willingness to sacrifice "neatness and symmetry" for greater "effectiveness and responsiveness" (CED, 1970: 19). A case is made for centralization and decentralization as accruing concurrently in a two-level structure. The report calls for "a genuine sharing of power over functions," without explicitly recognizing that such a condition **necessarily** requires fragmentation of authority and overlapping jurisdictions, furbished in the usual phrases about a "fragmented system of government" and "overlapping local units" as forming "a confusing maze" (CED, 1970: 10). The present system is reported to work better for suburbanites than for residents of central cities without deriving any conclusion that institutional failure may accrue from **the absence of overlapping jurisdictions and fragmented authority within central cities**.

More than a shift of emphasis is called for in our analysis of urban problems. Streets can no longer be kept clean in many areas of the great city of New York. School administrators can no longer cope with cockroaches in the city of Los Angeles *Los Angeles Times*, August 13, 1971). The technologies have long existed for cleaning streets and controlling cockroaches; but modern, professional administrators are somehow unable to mobilize the means to perform simple but essential tasks at appropriate times and places. When the **possible** becomes **impossible**, we have reason to believe that problems of institutional failure have reached serious proportions.

Perhaps we should begin to explore some of the **opportunities** that exist among overlapping jurisdictions in metropolitan areas (Tiebout, 1956; V. Ostrom, Tiebout, and Warren, 1961; Warren, 1964; 1966; Bish, 1971). In southern California, for example, many cities are taking **advantage** of overlapping jurisdictions by contracting for the provision of different public goods and services. Under this arrangement a municipality may function as a buyers' cooperative with its chief administrative officer serving as a purchasing agent to search out the most favorable alternative for procuring a public service. If citizens have complaints about services rendered, the chief administrative officer will represent their interest in demanding performance from the vendor. The vendor must strive to meet community demands or be confronted with the possibility that the city as a buyers' cooperative will contract with another vendor or establish its own services.

Competitive rivalry among diverse public agencies operating within an urban public economy composed of jurisdictions capable of tending to diverse communities of interest may offer an alternative approach to the realization of efficiency in government. In approaching a choice of institutional arrangements for the organization of government in metropolitan areas, contemporary political economists would attempt to examine different alternatives and recommend the one that would render individuals the best service for their money and efforts. The recommended solution based on the criterion of efficiency is the alternative that would give individuals the greatest net advantage. Perhaps we need to be more attuned to the principle of relative advantage in our policy analyses than to the logic of ideal forms.

Policy Analysis of the Administration of National Affairs

Similar paradigmatic problems exist in the analysis of public policy relative to the conduct of national public affairs. Since the formulation of Luther Gulick's anomalous orthodoxy in preparing the report for the President's Committee on Administrative Management, the thrust of policy analysis in national affairs has focused largely on strengthening the president as chief executive. Herbert Emmerich in his Alabama lectures on Federal reorganization, for example, defines reorganization as "a change in the size, distribution, and nature of executive functions, or their staffing and financing and particularly when these changes measurably affect the ability of the head of the executive branch—the President—to supervise and direct the manner in which these functions are exercised" (Emmerich, 1950: 7). For Emmerich, reorganization "envisions goals that necessarily transcend the objectives of efficiency and economy" (Emmerich, 1950: 8). These goals relate to the strengthening of the office of the president: "The Presidency is the focal point of any study of reorganization" (Emmerich, 1950: 7).

James L. Sundquist of the Brookings Institution follows in this tradition to suggest that Federal coordination of **community assistance programs** necessarily depends upon presidential direction:

> The facts of bureaucratic life are that no Cabinet department has ever been able to act effectively, for long, as a central coordinator of other departments of equal rank that are its competitors for authority and funds. Nor does coordination spring readily from the mutual adjustment of Cabinet-level equals within the federal hierarchy. **It must be induced, overseen, managed, and directed from the supra-cabinet level—in other words, from the Executive Office of the President, where the authority exists to identify problems that need settlement, expedite discussion, referee disputes, make binding decisions, and issue orders.** Voluntary bargaining among Cabinet departments of equal rank is no substitute for a decision-making structure led by a presidential staff officer who carries the authority and the governmentwide perspective of the President. (Sundquist, 1969: 244–245; my emphasis)

Sundquist, like so many other policy analysts, does not consider the costs associated with the addition of new coordinating and directing structures in the Executive Offices of the President. Sundquist fails to identify how coordinating agencies, in the absence of operating responsibilities, are to identify problems needing settlement, expedite discussions, referee disputes, and make binding decisions in **community assistance programs** from the Executive Offices of the President unless those who are elected to the presidency and those who are appointed to the executive offices are presumed to be both omniscient and omnicompetent.

Presumptions of omniscience and omnicompetence cannot hold in the design of national institutional arrangements any more than presumptions of frictionless motion can hold in applied mechanics. Reliance on such presumptions will generate a rhetoric based on concepts that are inappropriate to the resolution of policy problems. The community assistance programs were generated in President Lyndon Johnson's rhetorical "war on poverty." Some problems may be tractable to a massive mobilization for a frontal onslaught; but human poverty is not one of them. The notion that a commander in chief will mobilize an integrated and comprehensive effort by **all** agencies of government in **attacking** the multitudinous causes of poverty while simultaneously sustaining numerous other wars, campaigns, and crusades may be politically expedient rhetoric, but it will **not** solve the problems of poverty, eliminate pollution, stop crime in the streets, or ameliorate the urban crisis. Expenditure of massive amounts of public funds on the assumption that spending money will solve **any** problem is also destined to fail.

Once a president becomes rhetorically committed to a "war on poverty" or a "war on crime" we might reasonably infer that subordinates will facilitate the transmission of favorable information. Thus the hierarchy of command in the Executive Offices of the President will induce a multiplier effect in generating and transmitting misinformation. The larger the executive establishment in the executive offices becomes, the less accessible the president will be to those outside the executive offices, including members of Congress, officials in the various departments and bureaus of the national government, and persons outside the formal structure of the national government. The more insulated the president becomes, the more prone to error presidential decision making will be.

Measures taken to solve problems by the rhetoric of warfare and crisis politics will exacerbate rather than alleviate many problems. Performance will radically diverge from expectations, and the illusion of perpetual crisis will permeate public affairs. If the illusion gives way to skepticism, the credibility gap will become an institutionalized feature of American public life. The rhetoric of warfare, crisis politics, and credibility gaps are unfortunate ingredients in the public life of people living in a potentially dangerous world. The rhetoric of crisis, like the cry of "wolf," will not be heeded if frequently used in inappropriate circumstances.

Reiterating the prescription for strengthening presidential prerogative as a major remedy for dealing with community assistance programs, rural development activities, the quality of the environment, poverty, law and order, and urban affairs comes close to articulating a slogan of "All Power to the President." If all such recommendations were to be implemented, what consequences would we predict for the future of American democracy?

It is the exigencies of national defense that peculiarly require a system of one-man rule inherent in the prerogatives of commander in chief—not the exigencies of community assistance programs, rural development, poverty, or the public security of neighborhood streets. The advantage of surprise in a military attack requires utmost speed and dispatch in mobilizing defenses against an attack. Speed and dispatch can be facilitated by reducing the number of decision makers to a minimum of one. But a decision rule of one also gives strategic opportunities for that one decision maker to pursue preemptive strategies that foreclose due deliberation regarding the opportunity costs inherent in collective choice. The rhetoric of supreme sacrifice— of sustaining action "at all cost" or "at any price"—is the mark of preemptive leadership. Tragedies ensue when **supreme sacrifices** are exacted for trivial interests or misconceived objectives.

The office of president is an **essential element** in the American constitutional system. There are circumstances when decision costs must be minimized and critical actions must be taken with speed and dispatch. Such circumstances can at most involve a small number of decisions. A president cannot proceed with equal speed and dispatch in treating all the problems of some 240 million people. An overloaded president with a large executive establishment exercising control from the Executive Offices of the President can become a critical source of institutional failure in the American system of government. Institutional failure in the American presidency will be marked by an increasing proneness to error and dilettantism. Using the rhetoric of warfare and of crisis politics to dabble with such difficult and persistent problems as human poverty can only engender profound skepticism and cynicism regarding the efficacy of American public administration.

If we are concerned about human poverty, community assistance programs, rural development, the public security of neighborhood streets, and the quality of the environment, should we proceed on an assumption that these are all **national problems** requiring **national solutions**, which can be solved only by presidential intervention? Or should we proceed on the assumption that these problems are but names for a multitude of difficulties confronting human beings in different circumstances? **Similar problems need not be common problems.**

If we approach the problems of poverty and crime in the street from a science of association inherent in a theory of democratic administration, we would search for solutions that would minimize a strict subordination in command structures. We would avoid the rhetoric of warfare in mobilizing **all** resources of the nation for a **comprehensive attack** on either poverty or crime as **national** problems. Instead, we would be concerned with allocating decision-making capabilities so that discretion can be exercised to take mutual advantage of joint opportunities available to the persons involved.[8]

Democratic administration depends on avoiding the presumptions of monopoly power in the conduct both of public policy analysis and of public affairs. Using Max Weber's criteria of democratic administration, policy analysts in that tradition would be concerned with how to enhance citizens' participation in community development, social welfare, and public order. Voluntary action by citizens in providing for the common welfare of fellow citizens has a place in democratic societies which can never be fully replaced by paid functionaries and mass mobilization campaigns. Policy analysts in the tradition of democratic administration would show a preference for small-scale enterprises over large-scale enterprises if such scales are appropriate to the domain of particular public goods and services. They would also be concerned to proportion costs to benefits so that individuals can have a sense of reality about the opportunity costs inherent in collective action. They would seek to establish decision structures that would require public officials to maintain a due dependence on their constituents and their representatives in making important decisions. Democratic administration depends on elections, representation, and open deliberation in common councils for reaching collective decisions.

The task in fashioning a system of democratic administration is how to restrict the power of command to a minimum and substitute structures of economic, political, and judicial control rather than relying on a single overreaching bureaucracy to coordinate all human efforts. Such controls should be devised so that public servants as public entrepreneurs are exposed to the necessity of taking account of an appropriate cost calculus, the preferences of their constituents, and the legal constraints of constitutional and public laws that bear upon the organization and conduct of collective enterprises. Such controls can sustain viable enterprises capable of substantial efficiency when public entrepreneurs are oriented toward serving their constituents rather than becoming political masters.

In the administration of national affairs, presidential prerogative is of critical importance for dealing with the exigencies of warfare. These exigencies, however, will in the long run be destructive of constitutional rule in a democratic society.

Hamilton once observed:

> Safety from external danger is the most powerful director of national conduct. Even the ardent love of liberty will, after a time,

give way to its dictates. The violent destruction of life and property incident to war, the continual effort and alarm attendant on a state of continual danger, will compel nations the most attached to liberty to resort for repose and security in institutions which have the tendency to destroy their civil and political rights. To be more safe, they at length will become willing to run the risk of being less free. (*Federalist* 8)

Hamilton also recognized that the exigencies of war will lead people "to strengthen the executive arm of government, in doing which their constitutions would acquire a progressive direction toward monarchy. It is the nature of war to increase the executive at the expense of the legislative power" (*Federalist* 8).

The American solution of 1787 was an effort to fashion a political system in which all our political experiments would be predicated upon the capacity of mankind for self-government (*Federalist* 39). The search for political solutions among communities of people sharing interdependent interests in the collective security of nations is an alternative to allowing the logic of warfare—of accident and force—to dominate the constitution of human societies. The task of constraining presidential prerogative depends on the constitution of diverse international communities capable of tending to limited problems of common concern. The future of the free world depends on more overlapping jurisdictions and fragmentation of authority, not less.

Conclusion

Thus I would conclude that Hobbes was right in fashioning a constitution appropriate to a garrison state capable of functioning with reasonable effectiveness in a world plagued by recurrent warfare. I would also contend that Hamilton and Madison were right in presuming that societies of men are capable of establishing good government by reflection and choice where constitutional rule can be enforced in a political system characterized by substantial fragmentation of authority and overlapping jurisdictions. Such a constitutional system is capable of maintaining democratic administration as a general form of public administration in contradistinction to bureaucratic administration. The threat of recurrent warfare can be potentially resolved by appropriate recourse to federal principles of organization.

If I am correct, practitioners and students of public administration will need to rethink both the theory and the practice of their science of administration. If practitioners of American public administration are to contribute to the viability of a democratic society, they must be prepared to advance and serve the interests of the individual persons who form their relevant public.[9] Their service is to individual persons as users or consumers of public goods and services, not to political masters. They respect the authority of governmental officials who define and limit the scope of public endeavors. They sustain a reasoned contention on behalf of interests they perceive to be essential. They use their knowledge to serve others; and in the course of doing so, they and others join in mutual efforts to enhance their common weal.[10] The value of the knowledge that they profess and use as tools of analysis and as guides for action is measured by its usefulness for enhancing the welfare of discrete human beings.

Public servants in a democratic society are not neutral and obedient servants to their master's command. They will refuse to obey unlawful efforts to exploit the commonwealth or to use coercive capabilities to impair the rights of persons, but they will use reason and peaceful persuasion in taking such stands. Each public servant in the American system of democratic administration bears first the burden of being a citizen in a constitutional republic; and citizenship in a constitutional republic depends on a willingness to bear the costs for enforcing the rules of constitutional law against those who exercise the prerogatives of government.

Fashioning the architecture for a system of democratic administration will require different concepts and different solutions from those that can be derived from Wilson, Goodnow, W. F. Willoughby, White, and Gulick. Instead, a new theory of democratic administration will have to be fashioned from the works of Hamilton, Madison, Tocqueville, Dewey, Lindblom, Buchanan, Tullock, Olson, William Niskanen, and many others.

The theory of externalities, common properties, and public goods; the logic of collective action and public enterprise; the concepts of public service industries; and fiscal federalism will have prominent places in that theory. Attention will shift from a preoccupation with the organization to concerns with the opportunities individuals can pursue in multiorganizational environments. Policy analysis will focus on problems of institutional weakness and failure inherent in any organizational structure or institutional arrangement. Policy recommendations will be presented with greater emphasis on the opportunity costs inherent in different organizational arrangements.

A democratic theory of administration will not be preoccupied with simplicity, neatness, and symmetry but with diversity, variety, and responsiveness to the preferences of constituents. A system of democratic administration depends on an ordered complexity in social relationships. In such a system, it is the task of scholars to formulate a science of association that will enable communities of people to fashion organizational arrangements that will put individual self-interest to proper use as a rule for action in advancing human welfare. A new political science is needed for a new world if the human potential of democratic societies is to be realized through a system of democratic administration. Success depends on a knowledge of both the capabilities and limitations of diverse organizational forms, which can be used to minimize the power of command and yield services to enhance the welfare of people.

6

The Continuing Constitutional Crises in American Government
Vincent Ostrom and Barbara Allen

Watergate as a Crisis in Constitutional Government

In the last chapter, I warned of the problems that can arise when one theory of organization is used to make alterations in governmental structures based on a different theory of organization: "An appropriate theory of design is necessary to understand both how a system will work and how modifications or changes in a system will affect its performance. To use one theory of design to evaluate the characteristics of a system based on a different theory of design can lead to profound misunderstandings. To use one theory of design to reform a system based on a different theory of design may produce many unanticipated and costly consequences." The basic conflicts over contending theories which evoke intellectual crises among communities of scholars can also be the source of political and constitutional crises when those theories are used in organizing human actions.

The Watergate affair was initially revealed as an episode in partisan politics when several Republican partisans were arrested for unlawful entry into the headquarters of the Democratic National Committee. Subsequent investigations provided substantial evidence that the arrests at Watergate were only a minor episode in the abuse of executive authority. Each of the individuals arrested had had associations with the Special Investigations Unit in the Executive Offices of the President or with the Central Intelligence Agency. Other members of the White House staff had been indicted for charges associated with burglarizing the offices of a psychiatrist to procure information about a former government employee.

Testimony in the Watergate hearings indicated that large sums of cash, not subject to public accounting, had been available to top White House personnel. A former police officer, employed through a private law firm, was used to conduct investigations for the staff of the Domestic Council. "Enemy" lists were formulated to include persons not in favor at the White House. Strong circumstantial evidence suggests that Federal tax audits and criminal justice procedures had been used to harass persons actively opposed to the administration. Thin threads of evidence suggest that killings without due process of law had been practiced against Black Panthers.

The vice-president had been convicted of a felony associated with the unlawful receipt and use of funds paid for bribery. Two former cabinet officers were under indictment for charges associated with irregular payments of funds. In the midst of these irregularities the president claimed executive immunity for withholding evidence pertinent to proceedings in grand juries, trial courts, and congressional committees. Presidential prerogative was asserted to limit the scope of criminal investigations in relation to high officials in the Executive Offices of the President. Whether a president may lawfully use the cloak of his office to impede such proceedings became a critical constitutional issue. A constitutional crisis of major proportions was provoked over issues involving executive authority.

The Constitution of an Omnipotent Executive

The constitutional crisis associated with the Watergate affair can be viewed as the consequence of a long series of efforts to "strengthen" the executive[1] and to center all control over Federal administration in the Executive Offices of the President. These efforts reflect a central tenet of American scholarship in public administration: unity of command. The Brownlow Committee in the Roosevelt administration formulated the basic design. The articulation of that design was published in the *Report* (1937) of the President's Committee on Administrative Management. That design was further explained in Luther Gulick's "Notes on the Theory of Organization" (Gulick and Urwick, 1937). Those explanations were further elaborated in Herbert Emmerich's *Essays on Federal Reorganization* (1950). The subsequent experiments in strengthening the Executive need to be viewed in light of Gulick's anomalous orthodoxy discussed in Chapter 2. The recommendations have been reiterated by the Hoover commissions, the Ash Council, and countless other reorganization efforts. Substantial success has been attained in these efforts to strengthen a reified Executive.

Following the work of the Brownlow Committee and the Hoover Commission, Congress in the Administrative Reorganization Acts of 1939 and 1949 extended authority, as recommended, to the President as the reified head of the Executive to promulgate reorganization plans that would have the force of law, subject to a legislative veto within a sixty-day period. By these acts, Congress conveyed substantial lawmaking authority to the President to reallocate executive authority for the conduct of the Federal government. On the basis of this authority, President Richard Nixon submitted, on March 12, 1970, "Reorganization Plan No. 2 of 1970," to go into effect on July 1 of that year in the absence of adverse legislative action. Congress did not act. That reorganization plan contained much of the essential structure for creating a legally omnipotent Executive. In *INS* v. *Chadha* (1983), the U.S. Supreme Court held that "once Congress makes its choice in enacting legislation, its participation ends. Congress can thereafter control the execution of its actions only indirectly—by passing new legislation." The prerogatives of the President are further enhanced.

The presidential message transmitting Reorganization Plan No. 2 stated the basic rationale for that effort. Two basic functions of government were identified as "policy determination" and "executive management." These two functions, according to the message, involved questions of "(1) what Government should do and (2) how it goes about doing it" (*U.S. Codes*, 1970: 6316).

The legal architecture inherent in Reorganization Plan No. 2

was a basic conveyance of authority. All functions vested by law in the Bureau of the Budget or in the director of the Bureau of the Budget were transferred to the President. The old Bureau of the Budget was designated as the Office of Management and Budget (OMB). The director of OMB was assigned responsibility to perform "such functions as the President may from time to time delegate and assign thereto" (U.S. Codes, 1970: 6320). The President is the effective **director** of OMB; the appointed executive director is his administrative assistant.

The Domestic Council, as the body to decide "what Government should do," was to be composed of the president, the vice-president, several cabinet officers, and such other offices of the executive branch as the President may direct. The council was to perform "such functions as the President may from time to time delegate and assign thereto." An assistant to the president designated by the President to serve as executive director of the Domestic Council was to direct the council's staff in the performance of "such functions as the President may from time to time direct" (U.S. Codes, 1970: 6321). Again the legal structure of the Domestic Council implied that decisions about "what Government should do" were to be taken at the direction of the President.

Woodrow Wilson, by contrast, presumed that Congress had the prerogative to decide "what shall be done" and that the president "is plainly bound in duty to render unquestioning obedience to Congress" (Wilson, 1956: 181). But who is to enforce that duty if the President commands the entire Executive establishment?

The accompanying message indicated that OMB was to perform management functions beyond those previously exercised by the Bureau of the Budget. OMB was assigned responsibility for executive personnel in policy positions and in the top ranks of the civil service. Control over top-level executive personnel became a new OMB management tool. In addition, OMB was responsible for "Washington-based coordinators" who would coordinate interagency relationships at operating levels "throughout the country" (U.S. Codes, 1970: 6318). Presumably, these "Washington-based coordinators" were to assist in coordinating intergovernmental relationships among state and local governments as well.

Reference was also made to the improvement of government organization and the development of new information and management systems as being major functions of OMB. The message anticipated that "resistance to organizational change is one of the chief obstacles to effective government" and implied that such resistance must be overcome to ensure that "organization keeps abreast of program needs" (*U.S. Codes*, 1970: 6318).

Reorganization Plan No. 2 presumes that the President as Chief Executive has ultimate authority over the entire executive establishment. Decisions about **what** government should do and **how** it is done are within his prerogative. If basic authority to exercise a unified command over the Federal Executive establishment is to reside in the President, several implications follow about the legal force of Presidential instructions, channels for command over the Executive establishment, and mechanisms for enforcing compliance.

Presidential Instructions as Effective Law?

The most general provision of the U.S. Constitution, defining the authority of the president as chief executive, is contained in the clause "he shall take care that the laws be faithfully executed" (Article II, Sec. 3). The emphasis here is on the enforcement or execution of law. The president need not be the exclusive executive. He may see that "the laws be faithfully executed" when that authority is delegated to other executive instrumentalities. The lawmaking functions of government are identified with Congress within the constraints provided by the more fundamental law laid down in the Constitution itself. A separate and independent judiciary was established to determine conflicts and render judgment in controversies over the application of law.

When the functions of policy determination and executive management are fully integrated in a unified command structure exercised in the office of President, discretion for determining the legal force that will be given to public law resides with the

President. The attorney general is his subordinate as are all employees within the Justice Department and other agencies of the Federal government. Subordinate employees are subject to dismissal for failure to defer to Presidential orders. Prosecutors who proceed too diligently in matters of potential embarrassment to the President are subject to dismissal. In his dismissal of Archibald Cox as special prosecutor, for example, President Nixon observed in a letter to the acting attorney general: "In his press conference today . . . Cox made it apparent that he will not comply with the instructions I issued to him, through Attorney General Richardson, yesterday. Clearly the government of the United States cannot function if employees of the executive branch are free to ignore in this fashion the **instructions** of the President. Accordingly, in your capacity as acting attorney general, I direct you to discharge Mr. Cox immediately" (*Sunday Herald-Times*, Bloomington, Ind., Oct. 21, 1973, p. 1; my emphasis).

In this case Presidential instructions override considerations of whether Prosecutor Cox was lawfully and diligently discharging his responsibility to proceed with criminal investigations of possible felonies committed by members and former members of the President's White House staff and the Executive Offices of the President. If the grounds for dismissal are failure to conform to Presidential **instructions** and not failure to discharge his **legal responsibilities under law**, then Cox's dismissal implies that **Presidential instructions prevail over other provisions of law**.

No presumption exists that Presidential instructions will be publicized as the public acts of a public authority. Instead, they can be secret, protected by executive immunity. The internal affairs of an omnipotent Executive are always cloaked in a passion for anonymity. Max Weber, in his discussion of domination, refers to what he calls the "law of small numbers." A small ruling circle can easily dominate larger masses of people. The smaller the number of a ruling circle who have the capacity to command authoritative action, the greater the ease of pursuing preemptive strategies. A "monocratic" structure in which "all functionaries are integrated in a hierarchy culminating in a single head" has the greatest advantage in pursuing preemptive strategies. Weber goes on to observe: "Another benefit of the small number is the ease of secrecy as to the intentions and resolutions of the rulers and the state of their information; the larger the circle grows, the more difficult or improbable it becomes to guard such secrets. Wherever increasing stress is placed upon 'official secrecy,' we take it as a symptom of either an intention of rulers to tighten the reins of their rule or of a feeling on their part that their rule is being threatened" (Rheinstein, 1954: 334).

On the basis of the "law of small numbers," a President will always have a preemptive advantage in dealing with Congress. Congress can reduce this preemptive advantage by assigning executive authority to the level of an agency with responsibility to discharge public actions according to the standards of public law. The president can then discharge his executive responsibility to take care that "the laws be faithfully executed." When all executive authority is vested in the President to command the entire Executive establishment, his exercise of that authority will require secrecy as to his intentions and resolutions. Such secrecy is inimical to public accountability under rules of public and constitutional law in a democratic society.

Thomas Hobbes long ago recognized that "covenants without the sword are but words" (Hobbes, 1960: 109). The force of law depends critically on executive discretion and action. Enforcement is an essential condition of effective law. Unless enactments by Congress explicitly establish standards that are to apply to specific executive instrumentalities in the implementation of particular laws, those instrumentalities cannot be held accountable for their discharge of executive functions. As responsibility for "policy determination" and "executive management" over the Federal administrative establishment are centralized in the office of President, the meaning of statutory law will turn increasingly upon Presidential instructions. Policy decisions taken by reference to statutory provisions can be overridden by Presidential instructions, which, under such circumstances, become effective law.

When Presidential instructions become effective law, enactments by Congress will serve only as general statements of principles or purposes. In Hobbes's terms, acts of Congress would then be mere "words." Legislation will become "positive morality," in John Austin's language, not "positive law" (Austin, 1955). When legislation becomes positive morality, not positive law, Congress will be relegated to the performance of ceremonial functions in proclaiming moral platitudes about public life.

A New Presidential Executive Service?

Alexis de Tocqueville, in his study of the *ancien régime*, reports how the management of internal affairs in France was organized through a single official—a controller-general—who exercised authority through Paris-based coordinators, called intendants, who assumed responsibility for coordinating interagency relationships throughout France. Tocqueville quotes the following observation made by a former controller-general: "Until I held the post of Controller-General I would hardly believe that such a state existed. Believe it or not the French kingdom was ruled by thirty Intendants. Your parlements, Estates and Governors simply do not enter into the picture" (Tocqueville, 1955: 36). The system of intendants remained intact through the French Revolution. They emerged as "prefects" organized in a general administrative service which exercises executive authority in coordinating all other public instrumentalities in the French administrative system.

The constitution of OMB contains the necessary elements for the creation of a new Executive service, apart from the civil service, analogous to the French administrative service. The director of OMB is equivalent to the old controller-general. The Washington-based coordinators are the intendants or prefects and superprefects in a new Executive service. A separate command structure responsive to Presidential direction is interposed into the structure of other administrative services to assure that Presidential instructions are effectively transmitted and enforced throughout the administrative apparatus. An Executive service becomes the president's new management system—a duplicate chain of command—for attaining control over all levels of administration throughout the country.

If proposals by Congressman Henry S. Reuss to use revenue-sharing as a "catalyst" (i.e., a management tool) for reorganizing state and local governments (Reuss, 1970) and by James L. Sundquist to use Presidential surrogates to coordinate intergovernmental relations were acted upon, we might contemplate that the new Executive service would also become a command structure to "make federalism work" in a "coordinated" way (Sundquist, 1969). State and local authorities, as in the case of the French "parlements, Estates and Governors," would become the superfluous facade of government. In Bagehot's terms, they would become the "dignified" part of the government, distracting the attention and maintaining the allegiance of the uninformed masses while the "efficient" part—the Executive operating by Presidential instructions—proceeds with the actual work of government (Bagehot, 1964: 59–65).

A New Secret Police?

A highly integrated Executive structure in which the power of command is fully centralized in a single chief executive will be subject to substantial problems of institutional failure (see Chapter 3, section "Bureaucratic Organization"). The creation of a duplicate command structure inherent in a specialized Executive service as the equivalent of the French administrative service can attempt to overcome some of the impediments to communication and control, but the personal costs associated with demands for action in accordance with Presidential instructions and orders can be expected to create resistance to Executive authority. This resistance will become "one of the chief obstacles to effective government" centered in a fully integrated Executive.

If a new Executive establishment is to cope effectively with this obstacle it will become necessary to create a Special Investigations Unit to maintain Executive secrecy and exercise discipline over recalcitrant government employees. Efforts to tighten the screws of administrative control will cause bureaucratic pipelines to leak like sieves. Plumbers will be needed to stop the leaks. No chief executive can "master the Federal bureaucracy and make it do his will" (*Newsweek*, December 12, 1972; my emphasis) without access to new information and enforcement systems. The new information system will require secret intelligence provided by secret police. Were the "plumbers" the beginnings of a new system of secret police in the American system of government?

Conclusions

The Administrative Reorganization Acts of 1939 and 1949 offer extensive opportunities for those who seek to strengthen Executive authority. They provide the Executive with substantial authority to legislate. Administrative organization is a key to control over the enforcement apparatus of government. Laws depend on mechanisms for enforcement to become effective. Otherwise, laws are mere "words." If Executive instructions can be interposed to direct enforcement practices apart from the prescriptions of general law, then Executive instructions become effective law.

Reorganization Plan No. 2 thus contains the essential legal architecture for a radical alteration of the American constitutional system. Executive authority can displace congressional authority by substituting Executive instructions about **what** government should do. A system of administrative jurisprudence based on additional reorganization plans can be organized within the Executive to displace judicial authority. Control over the essential functions of government can be encompassed entirely within the Executive establishment. Thus control over a new administrative state can be organized within the Executive Offices of the President. Among the essential elements for the governance of the new administrative state would be a National Security Council to assist the President in his responsibility for world affairs, a Domestic Council to assist the President and deciding what government should do in domestic affairs, an Office of

Management and Budget to assist the President in the management of internal affairs including interagency and intergovernmental relationships throughout the country, a Special Investigations Unit to provide the President with a secret information system so that he can eliminate obstacles to "effective" government, and, finally, a Council of State, like the French Conseil d'Etat, to adjudicate the grievances of citizens subject to Presidential instructions. The Executive Offices of the President would then become the "efficient" part of the government; the Congress, the courts, the statehouses, and the other centers of authority would become the "dignified" parts of government relieved of their other burdens of work so that they can devote themselves largely to the ceremonial functions of government.

If this vision of the strong Executive stirs misgivings among students and practitioners of public administration, we should give high priority to rethinking the intellectual grounds upon which the science and practice of public administration stand. A system of constitutional rule depends on establishing limits to authority. Alexander Hamilton long ago recognized that strengthening the executive implies that governments "acquire a progressive direction toward monarchy" (*Federalist* 8). An unqualified concern for strengthening Executive authority will lead to absolutism and despotism. A passion for strengthening the executive is inimical to the survival of democratic institutions.

We have developed habits of thought which view the Executive as a single aggregate structure controlled by a single chief executive. Enactments of Congress then apply to the aggregated Executive rather than presuming that specific legislation entails standards applicable to particular executive agents, for example, the director of selective service in administering legislation authorizing a draft for recruiting military manpower in wartime. The abandonment of methodological individualism in conceptualizing the architecture of law and in the study of systems of governance and administration means that we no longer see executive functions in a configuration of relationships involving human beings as discrete individuals who are entitled to fundamental respect. Habits of thought in which symbols are reified and words stand for aggregated social entities, such as the Executive, mean that we cannot think in ways that are consonant with the requirements of liberty, justice, and mutually respectful human relationships.

There is logic to a system of constitutional government which presumes that all exercises of governmental authority must be subject to limits. When those limits are abandoned, constitutional government is also abandoned. Woodrow Wilson's presupposition that there is but one form of good administration that applies to all governments alike is in error. The study of public administration in a democratic society cannot be confined to management with a presupposition that an integrated bureaucratic system of superior-subordinate relationships provides the appropriate structure for the operation of management systems in the exercise of Executive authority. It is a serious error to presume, as Leonard White (1948: xiii) did, that "the study of administration should start from a base of management rather than the foundation of law."

Extending Prerogatives and Abandoning Responsibilities

Executive Responsibility and Deniability

The Watergate affair flared and faded from the American political horizon. Richard M. Nixon resigned from the office of president of the United States under the threat of impeachment proceedings when it appeared that the "smoking gun" had been found. Spiro Agnew, the vice-president, had earlier resigned from office in connection with criminal proceedings unrelated to the Watergate affair. Gerald Ford, president pro tem of the Senate, succeeded to the presidency and extended a pardon to Nixon for any criminal wrongdoings that he may have committed while occupying that office. The former attorney general and several former top White House officials, including the former director of the Domestic Council, were convicted of criminal offenses and served prison terms in relation to the Watergate affair. Changes of personnel in the operation of government have occurred, but the basic erosion of constitutional law has continued. The validity of Presidential instructions remained unchallenged.

As these words are being put on paper, the Iran-Contra affair has become the focus of congressional hearings and judicial proceedings. Again, the issue is one of Executive prerogative and privilege. Extending Executive prerogative always involves the testing of limits, and asserting Executive privilege always has the potential for shielding inquiry about the abandonment of responsibility. This time, the focus is on the discharge of Executive prerogative through the National Security Council rather than the Domestic Council. The key question is whether legislation enacted by Congress applies to the discharge of ordinary executive functions or whether a President can discharge the authority of his office to command the entire Executive establishment by reference to a command apparatus which is put in place by those who act or presume to act upon his instructions.

There is evidence that career officers, who were assigned to the National Security Council, functioned in a chain of command that zigzagged its way through Gulick's jungle gym to carry on operational missions through clandestine channels and freewheeling agents. The secretary of state and the secretary of defense have also become a part of the formal facade of government who know not what their subordinates do. Those instructed to pursue clandestine operational missions exercise substantial discretion so that the President can maintain **deniability** with regard to formal channels of responsibility. The extension of Executive prerogative is thus accompanied by assertions of Executive privilege, which forms a protective shield for the abandonment of responsibility. Officials can no longer be taken at their word, and public trust is sacrificed to distrust, suspicion, and innuendo. There is no rational solution to the liar's paradox.

If the erosion of executive accountability were the only source of serious constitutional difficulty, other instrumentalities of government might be relied upon to undertake the necessary measures to place appropriate limits on executive authority. This, however, is unlikely to occur. The affairs of the legislative and judicial instrumentalities of the national government are in serious disarray (U.S. Advisory Commission on Intergovernmental Relations, 1987b).

Legislation and Administrative Rule-Making

During the course of the last half-century, the Supreme Court has virtually abandoned its efforts to maintain constitutional limits on the substantive powers of Congress. Congress has, therefore, become, as Wilson anticipated, the ultimate source of legislative authority on all matters of government. Even speed limits on American highways and byways are now the subject of national legislation. The enumerated powers in Section 8, Article l, of the U.S. Constitution have been stretched so far that there is no longer any aspect of American life that does not come within the scope of "interstate and foreign commerce" or "the general welfare of the United States."

Although members of Congress can presume to exercise authority in all matters of American life, they are still limited by the hard constraint that human beings can listen to and understand only one speaker at a time (V. Ostrom, 1987: chap. 5). What Congress can do and do well is subject to extreme limits. As a consequence, any deliberative body that concerns itself with everything must necessarily become superficial in much that is done. We observe these tendencies at the very core of legislative responsibilities in the American national government.

The rationale for legislation is to establish public standards of law that apply to the exercise of executive authority. Yet the increasing tendency is for Congress to rely on the loosest terminology such as "clean air" or "pure water" to establish legislative standards and then assign the elaboration of rules and regulations to executive instrumentalities. The administrative reorganization acts imply that fundamental rulemaking authority is transferred to the Executive. Legislative enactments of Congress become more like positive morality than positive law. Under these circumstances, critical debate in a legislative process is sacrificed to the celebration of moral virtue.

Transferring rulemaking authority to the Executive means that law is no longer formulated by those who are required to address citizens as constituents. Instead, professional or administrative criteria become paramount and the standards to be implemented are set by enforcers rather than with the consent of the governed. When applied to multiple aspects of life having to do with health, safety, the elimination of poverty, a normal life for the handicapped, the preservation of life, pure water, clean air, and other such contingencies, the maximization of each value creates circumstances that defy rational calculations. Human beings cannot achieve the best of all possible worlds. Conditions of scarcity and constraint imply that to secure more of something always involves costs, a willingness to sacrifice something else.

Placing rulemaking in the hands of enforcers rather than legislators, who face citizens as constituents, is yielding a transformation in the nature of law. Law always has reference to norms or criteria that distinguish the forbidden (prohibited) from the permitted and required. The bias of enforcers is to constrain the discretion that is available to those who are subject to law. The domain of the permitted is squeezed out by an increasing emphasis on the forbidden and the required. The constraint in law is emphasized at a sacrifice of the choice of alternative means to achieve policy objectives. Enforcers too easily presume that their way to health, safety, and other social values is the only way. People find themselves trapped in circumstances in which the requirements of law become increasingly absurd. The "informal" economy grows, and the "formal" economy stagnates. Life in American society begins to move "underground."

In the meantime, the overwhelming preoccupations of members of Congress become that of representatives processing the complaints of their constituents while simultaneously acting as brokers for their constituents in deriving tax or trade advantages and procuring a bigger bite of the national treasury. Tax measures, terms of trade, and the appropriation of funds become embodied in omnibus legislation, often denominated as "comprehensive," which presumes that everyone gets something without having to endure costs or sacrifices. Members of Congress trade their votes for the best ostensible deal they can secure for themselves and their constituents in each omnibus offering. Such a Panglossian view of the world is a fool's paradise that may last for a while, drawing on accumulated capital, but awaits either corrective measures or inevitable disaster.

Important indicators to be watched are the escalating obligations (articulated as entitlements), debt structures, and the costs of servicing obligations and debts. Congress has demonstrated an inability to control expenditures and obligations and has given preliminary indication in the adoption of the Gramm-Rudman-Hollings resolution of an intention to transfer control over expenditure limits to the Executive. The Supreme Court has indicated that such authority cannot be exercised by the comptroller general as an agent of Congress. Presumably, Congress as the body vested with "all legislative Powers" under the Constitution is free to vest those powers with the Executive, however paradoxical that may seem.

If the Executive is to control expenditure limits that apply to the use of funds from the national treasury, appropriations enacted by Congress become little more than hunting licenses. Congress would be free to appropriate without limit, and the Executive would then decide what to spend. Acts "appropriating" funds would not "appropriate." They would merely authorize the Executive to make payments within some other more restricted fiscal limit established by the Executive.

Legislation as positive morality and appropriations as illusory commitments of funds imply that the legislative process in Congress increasingly takes on the characteristics of a public theater acting out a drama that is more fiction than reality. Actors in that drama are more concerned with their public images than with their capacity to cope with public problems. This is what some political scientists currently refer to as "symbolic" politics.

In the meantime, the importance of symbols in human communication is neglected. The evening news becomes a soap opera offering a new chapter in the lives of Ronald and Nancy or whoever the personalities of the day may be. Words in the realm of intelligent political discourse lose their meaning, and public life becomes theater.

Congressional usurpation of authority in presuming to exercise supremacy in all matters of government is then marked by a correlative abandonment of responsibility. This is what happens when fallible human beings of limited capabilities presume to be omniscient and omnipotent. Beyond the limits of some threshold, variable among human beings, to do more means doing other things less well. Human beings who have not learned this fundamental constraint in life cannot be responsible either to themselves or to others.

Judicial Default and Activist Thrusts

Similar problems have afflicted the judiciary. In this case, we come to the core of the American system of **constitutional** government as conceptualized in the U.S. Constitution and explained in *The Federalist*. In discussing the judicial department in *Federalist* 78, Alexander Hamilton indicates that the concept of a limited constitution depends on the "complete independence of the courts of justice." Limitations on legislative authority, Hamilton argues, "can be preserved in no other way than through the medium of the courts of justice, whose duty it must be to declare all acts contrary to the manifest tenor of the Constitution void. Without this, all the reservations of particular rights or privileges would amount to nothing." Hamilton conceived legislative powers to be broadly synonymous with government. He defined government as "the power of making laws" (*Federalist* 15); but he also recognized that laws to be effective must be enforced, requiring reference to executive authority. The judiciary is, thus, concerned with the proper application of law. Executive efforts to enforce law are subject to judicial scrutiny to assure that law is properly applied.

The key issue, then, is what constitutes valid law: the enactments of a legislature, or a constitution, if a legislature acts beyond the scope of constitutional authority? Hamilton rejects the presumption that a legislative body is the proper judge of its own **constitutional** authority. Rather, he argues:

It is far more rational to suppose that the **courts** were designed to be an intermediate body between the **people** and the **legislature**, in order, among other things, to keep the latter within the limits assigned to their authority. The interpretation of the law is the proper and peculiar province of the courts. A constitution is, in fact, and must be regarded by the judges as fundamental law. It therefore belongs to them to ascertain its meaning, as well as the meaning of any particular act proceeding from the legislative body. If there should happen to be an irreconcilable variance between the two that which has the superior obligation and validity ought, of course, to be preferred; or, in other words, the Constitution ought to be preferred to the statute, the intention of the people to the intention of their agents. (*Federalist* 78; my emphasis)

If the contrary principle were to prevail, Hamilton asserts, "would be to affirm, that the deputy is greater than his principal; that the servant is above his master; that the representatives of the people are superior to the people themselves; that men acting by virtue of powers, may do not only what those powers authorize, but what they forbid" (*Federalist* 78).

As a consequence of such a formulation, the American judiciary has come to play an important role in constitutional jurisprudence. Following *Marbury* v. *Madison*, the Supreme Court accepted this formulation and took on the role of attempting to maintain the integrity of the Constitution as fundamental law establishing the terms and conditions of the American national government and its relationship to the federal system of government.

Following controversies over the constitutional standing of New Deal legislation during the 1930s, the U.S. Supreme Court virtually abandoned efforts to maintain limits with respect to the exercise of congressional authority. In *Garcia* v. *San Antonio Metropolitan Transit Authority* (1985), Justice Harry Blackmun, speaking for the majority of the Court, could find no criterion to place discrete limits on the substantive powers that apply to the scope of national legislative authority. The meanings of the commerce clause, the general welfare clause, and the necessary and proper clause have been construed so broadly that the Supreme Court has abandoned its responsibility to function as an arbiter in determining the meaning of the substantive powers to be exercised by the national government (U.S. Advisory Commission on Intergovernmental Relations, 1987b).

The exception pertains to the specific prohibitions on the exercise of government prerogatives contained largely in what is commonly referred to as the Bill of Rights reflected in the first eight amendments and the thirteenth, fourteenth, and fifteenth amendments to the Constitution. In this realm the Federal judiciary has radically extended its prerogatives while abandoning its responsibilities to maintain limits with regard to the substantive powers of the national government. This extension of judicial prerogative has mainly been directed against state and local governments, strongly reinforcing tendencies toward the nationalization of American government.

The key transformation in the judicial process has been the reliance upon constitutional provisions about individual rights to decree mandatory remedies pertaining to such provisions as equal protection of the laws. The earlier presumption in constitutional jurisprudence was that any act by an instrumentality of government beyond its constitutional competence did not have legal standing and was therefore null and void. The potential immunity of an official arises only from lawful action. If an official acted beyond the scope of valid authority, he or she did so as an individual without lawful authority and that individual was personally liable for any wrongdoing. Beginning with the school desegregation cases, the Federal courts have gone beyond the earlier forms of judicial relief, holding an offending statute, or regulation, to be invalid and without legal force, to a mandatory form of relief requiring a positive program of actions to remove the offending practice and substitute a conforming remedy. Furthermore, remedies were presumed to be available for racial segregation as a de facto wrong. Affirmatively mandated programs to desegregate schools and to apply constitutional standards to many other situations have been the subject of rapidly escalating judicial proceedings. The Federal courts have, for example, established themselves as monitors exercising rulemaking and enforcing powers over many penal institutions of state and local governments. A variety of basic constitutional difficulties arise from these conceptions of the judicial process.

The most serious difficulty arises when court decrees usurp the prerogatives of legislative bodies, executive instrumentalities, and the constitutional authority of citizens that properly reside with state and local units of government. Court decrees impose rules. They constitute judicial legislation. They are subject to enforcement by contempt proceedings. Judges in these circumstances are rulemakers, rule enforcers, and rule adjudicators in the application of judicial decrees to state and local instrumentalities of government as collectivities. In such circumstances, judges violate a basic maxim of justice that no one is a fit judge of his or her own cause of action in relation to the interests of others.

This is especially serious inasmuch as the application of mandatory decrees to units or instrumentalities of governments, as collectivities, violates another basic requirement of justice. This circumstance was the subject of analysis by Alexander Hamilton in *Federalist* 15 and 16 in identifying the basic failure of government under the Articles of Confederation. Rules and sanctions applied to collectivities as such do not serve as a basis for distinguishing between wrongdoers and innocent bystanders. Justice cannot be done when sanctions are applied to collectivities as a whole.

The problem can be best illustrated when applied to a private corporation. Let us assume that individuals acting through the instrumentality of a corporation have violated laws subject to criminal sanctions. If the corporation is found guilty, fined, or assessed an equivalent "civil" penalty, the obligation is discharged by payment from the corporate treasury. The burden is passed on either to shareholders, to customers of the corporation, or to both, and those who committed the offense are shielded from individual criminal liability by the presumption of corporate liability. The same principle applies to units of government as public corporations. The presumption of corporate liability of a school district, for example, does not address the question of who acted beyond the scope of valid authority to violate the basic constitutional rights of persons or citizens.

This problem is compounded when judicial remedies are extended to remedies for de facto wrongs without engaging in a judicial inquiry about the de jure source of that wrong. Segregation as among neighborhoods may not have derived from policies pursued by school districts. It is at least plausible to anticipate that a major source of segregation derives from the practices of realtors and realty boards. Reliance on court decrees mandating the busing of schoolchildren to achieve racial balance may be imposing costs upon others without addressing the basic source of the difficulties. The courts in such circumstances treat the symptoms of injustice but neglect the sources of that injustice.

Government by Mutual Accommodation

These patterns of abandoning judicial responsibility on one hand and radically extending judicial prerogative on the other leave the constitutional integrity of the American national government to a pattern of mutual accommodation among the legislative and executive instrumentalities of government with no one raising basic questions about proper constitutional limits on the exercise of national authority. Congressional and judicial inquiries about Watergate and the Iran-Contra affair point to wrongdoing on the part of discrete individuals. This is also an important function of legislative and judicial processes. The search at this level of analysis is for the "smoking gun." There is, however, a deeper question of constitutional significance. Do these individual failings reflect circumstances in which proper limits and patterns of accountability have so eroded that effective public scrutiny and control can no longer be maintained? Such a question implicates the constitutional level of analysis. What happens when pervasive problems of institutional failure begin to afflict the American national government and issues bearing on limits to the substantive authority of the instrumentalities of the national government can no longer be raised as basic constitutional matters requiring attention at the constitutional level of deliberation?

The tendency on the part of the national government to expand authority has been strongly reinforced by the presuppositions held among students and practitioners of public administration, the press, public interest groups, and the population at large that all problems can be resolved by turning to Washington. As promises increasingly diverge from expectations and the burdens of obligations and debts become increasingly difficult to meet, we can anticipate that basic questions of a constitutional character will rank high on the future political agenda in American society. It is difficult to believe that Americans will acquiesce in the death of democracy and celebrate the achievement of the ultimate in Presidential Government: one-man rulership. How to reestablish the integrity of constitutional government will need to be addressed.

A New Millennium

Today, at the start of a new millennium, the author who holds an earlier view of federalism is likely to be characterized as an "idealist." The continuing buildup of executive powers in a "unitary executive," the dismal state of congressional oversight and the exercise of lawmaking authority, the sloganeering of a "global war on terrorism," the militarization[2] of urban spaces, and the continuing centralization of power pose threats to constitutional governance.

It is not the case, of course, that clean air and water, a jurisprudence of obligation along with a jurisprudence of right, or a world characterized by tranquility and trust rather than terrorism are undesirable or impossible. Nor should we ignore the moral orientation of such desires as we engage in democratic self-*governance*. The opposite is true. Such engaged thinking and doing must be based, however, on more than generalities. It must allow the critical scrutiny of logical analyses. Those who recommend federalism or polycentricity as a framework for democratic administration and as a requisite for self-government recognize the practical and theoretical necessity of overlap among governing functions or across arenas of governance.

Federalism, as described by *The Federalist* and worked out from colonial covenants and charters through the practices of the 1789 Constitution to the present day, involves shared powers as well as the notions of limited and distributed authority (V. Ostrom, 2007; Lutz, 1988; Elazar, 1995–1998; Allen, 2005). Thus, for example, judges will play a part in lawmaking not only in interpreting the meaning and proper application of legislative and constitutional provisions and protections but in additional forms of prescription and oversight. In equity proceedings or mediation, for instance, judges make "rules" and oversee their execution. Judges consider the effects of these rules and call for adjustments as necessary to achieve a particular objective under law.

The key elements distinguishing equity jurisprudence from "judge-made law" described in the analysis of *Garcia* is an emphasis on the application of principle to *particular circumstances*, and the possibility of challenge if an equity court exceeds fundamental law. The problem with structures of command and control—whether they concentrate rule making, enforcement, and adjudication in a legislature, executive, or court—is simply that such consolidation ultimately negates the distinction between constitutional choice and ordinary lawmaking. The "government" conceived in this unitary form may alter itself by itself. This is an affront to liberty and self-governing capacities. The starting point for such consolidation is very often the simplistic belief that a rule fit for some particular circumstance may be effectively universalized as a mandatory affirmative remedy for a diversity of wrongs and a complexity of attendant effects.

In current public parlance, attributions like "judge-made law" have also become fodder for polemicists, leaving citizens to pick their ways across an ideological minefield of generalities and name-calling. Yet, democratic citizenship implies institutional and intellectual capacities and commitment to consider basic principles; undertake diagnostic assessments of distinct social, political, and economic conditions; and engage in public reflection and choice to ameliorate shared problems or enhance shared understandings. In terms of the open society—the *res publica*—

necessary to such critical thinking and acting on the part of citizens and citizen-officials in *government*, conditions have worsened as we have turned the page on the twentieth century.

In 2000, supporters of greater executive power described in a doctrine dubbed the "New Paradigm" by its primary architects, Vice President Dick Cheney and his chief of staff David S. Addington, claimed a variety of presidential prerogatives meant to restore authority that Congress, in their view, had unduly diminished in post-Watergate legislation. During the next two presidential terms, the doctrine, which had been instituted before the September 11, 2001 attacks, advanced legal theories justifying numerous well-known, widely debated enhancements of power for the president as commander in chief in the War on Terror. The Bush administration asserted executive authority to act outside the 1949 Geneva Conventions and the U.S. Constitution to designate persons accused of acts of terrorism or conspiracy to commit terrorism (including U.S. citizens seized in the United States) as "unlawful enemy combatants," and detain, interrogate, and try such suspects according to procedures decided by the president.

Beginning in 2001, hundreds, including an untold number of children under the age of eighteen, were denied access to counsel and detained for years at U.S. installations at Guantánamo Bay, Cuba, without charges being brought against them. Denying some claims of the New Paradigm, the U.S. Supreme Court ruled in *Rasul v. Bush* (2004) that the federal courts did have jurisdiction over Guantánamo and that detainees must be allowed to challenge their detention. Congress, the same year, overwhelmingly voted to ban "cruel, inhumane and degrading" treatment of the prisoners over the strong objections of President Bush and Vice President Cheney. Two years later, in *Hamdan v. Rumsfeld* (2006), the Supreme Court again challenged the Bush administration's view of executive powers, ruling that the president's effort to create a unique system of justice for Guantánamo detainees violated the standards set by Congress in the Uniform Code of Military Justice, that the Geneva Conventions Common Article 3 applies to the detainees, and that these latter standards, too, may be invoked in U.S. courts.

In addition to these highly publicized moves to increase presidential powers dramatically, supporters of the Cheney-Addington New Paradigm have also promoted broad use of less well-known "presidential signing statements." These are declarations of the "unitary executive's" intention to execute congressional legislation only as the president wills, eliminating the need for a presidential veto—and public debate—while providing a de facto, subterranean method of eschewing congressional intent (Van Alstine, 2006). Adversaries decry the usurpation of congressional lawmaking authority; advocates enumerating the various forms of executive lawmaking capacities—executive orders, proclamations, and directives—note that even George Washington saw fit to use such mechanisms (Boaz, 2005; Dean, 2006; Egelko, 2006). Admirers of the "imperial presidency"—an epithet coined in the Watergate years (Schlesinger, [1973] 2004) and recently rehabilitated as an institutional virtue—cite phrases from Alexander Hamilton to justify such presidential egress into legislative arenas as essential to protect "the community against foreign attacks" (Yoo, 2003; Hamilton, *Federalist* 70). Among the legislation revamped by a presidential signing statement was the "Detainee Treatment Act," passed in 2004 to ensure the humane treatment of detainees, in defiance of the New Paradigm's denial of "illegal combatant" rights, including Geneva Convention provisions.

Authors of *The Federalist*, Alexander Hamilton, John Jay, and James Madison, bearing the name Publius, hoped to balance "energy" or capacity in government against "stability" in government (Hamilton, *Federalist* 37, 69, and 70). Madison and Hamilton (and Thomas Jefferson among many others) found the most immediate instance of too much "energy" or power and too little stability in the newly minted state governments, whose institutional designs had in several cases given rise to oligarchies. As Publius noted in language used first by Jefferson, the legislative, executive, and judicial functions had been concentrated into the same hands forming an "elective despotism" where *"no barrier was provided between these several powers."* Further, in state governments, "executive powers had been usurped" and injudicious appeals were made to the passions rather than the reason of the public that threatened rights and security (Hamilton or Madison, *Federalist* 49, ML 324, original italics). Madison also observed that "the executive department [of some states] had not been innocent of frequent breaches of the constitution," naming the necessities of war, complicity of the legislature, or poor constitutional design as the causes of such failures. All of this led Publius to conclude: "that a mere demarcation on parchment of the constitutional limits of the several departments, is not a sufficient guard against those encroachments which lead to a tyrannical concentration of all the powers of government in the same hands" (Madison, *Federalist* 48, ML 326). Hamilton was also concerned with the instability resulting from inadequate efforts to distribute and share governing capacities or distinguish constitutional and ordinary lawmaking.

If Hamilton's often-cited remarks on an energetic executive from *Federalist* 70 are continued to their conclusion, we find that such power and authority "is essential to the protection of the community against foreign attacks; it is not less essential to the steady administration of the laws; to the protection of property against those irregular and high-handed combinations which sometimes interrupt the ordinary course of justice; to the security of liberty against the enterprises and assaults of ambition, of faction, and of anarchy" (Hamilton, *Federalist* 70, ML 454). In short, energy in the executive could address many of the shortcomings experienced in the state governments and in other historical cases cited by Publius as examples of unbalanced and unchecked legislative power.

A more detailed analysis of Publius's thoughts on the considerable design problems associated with the aims of liberty and self-government is beyond the scope of the present discussion and is taken up in other work (V. Ostrom, 1991; 1997; 2007; Lutz, 1988; 2006; Allen, 2005). Here, it is enough to point out that the principle, voiced by Publius in the context of confederal and state governments that had failed to assure republican government for their citizens, was not that of an imperial presidency. It was, rather, one of *separation* of powers—in a design characterized by the limited, distributed, and shared constitutional powers to be achieved in a *compound* and extended republic.

Instead of repeating Hamilton and Madison's logic as a fait accompli justification for command and control, we may wish to conduct a deeper diagnostic assessment of current events beginning, perhaps, with questions about the present generation's acceptance of a curtailment of civil liberties in "wartime" or, more basic yet, about the effects of such characterizations as a "war on terrorism" describing a state of war without end.

We have recently amended the Foreign Intelligence Surveillance Act of 1978 (FISA). The Act was originally designed by Congress to ensure accountability in intelligence-gathering following the Watergate Crisis and the misappropriation of government surveillance instrumentalities for presidential use against *his* enemies to expand the use of "warrantless" searches and seizures against U.S. citizens and others. The Patriot Act (2001) has dropped the requirement that a warrant for surveillance must have as its sole purpose the aim of gaining foreign intelligence; revelations in 2004 of secret domestic surveillance on thousands of U.S. citizens have been justified by the Department of Justice. As former deputy assistant attorney general in the Office of Legal Counsel at the Department of Justice John Yoo explained to a U.S. House of Representatives Permanent Select Committee on Intelligence:

> [t]he Fourth Amendment's warrant requirement does not apply to surveillance and searches undertaken to protect the national security from external threats. Surveillance of terrorists could be undertaken within two distinct legal regimes. The first is the regular criminal justice system, in which the government may seek a warrant to conduct surveillance of a terrorist suspect's voice or electronic communications by presenting sufficient evidence of probable cause to an Article III judge. Surveillance undertaken in this manner would be no different than that used against organized crime groups or drug cartels operating within the United States. A second method, however, could present itself when terrorists undertake direct operations within the territorial United States. During wartime, the military engages in searches and surveillance without a warrant . . . if al Qaeda forces organize and carry out missions to attack civilian or military targets within the United States, government surveillance of terrorists would not be law enforcement so much as military operations. In such circumstances, when the government is not pursuing an ordinary

criminal law enforcement objective, the Fourth Amendment requires no search warrant. (Yoo, 2003: 4)

In sum, search and surveillance under the Patriot Act now require the government to certify only that gathering foreign intelligence information is a "significant purpose" of its agents. In wartime, such search and surveillance may be presumed to be military operations requiring no warrants. In this exposition, Yoo also contends that the barrier erected by courts and the Justice Department between foreign intelligence-gathering activities and law-enforcement activities in the aftermath of Watergate (or, framed differently, the maintenance of Fourth Amendment protections against searches and seizures lacking probable cause or failing to specify the object sought or place and person to be searched) has rightfully been dismantled by the Patriot Act. The Patriot Act has also expanded the scope of FISA warrants to a national scope and now permits the granting of a warrant for multiple communication devices associated with any individual, rather than requiring the specification of individual phone numbers or other individual communication portals.

The story of Supreme Court rulings and congressional legislation under the New Paradigm continues to unfold. Writing for the 5-to-3 majority in *Hamdan v. Rumsfeld,* Justice John Paul Stevens said, "In undertaking to try Hamdan . . . the executive is bound to comply with the rule of law that prevails in this jurisdiction" *(Hamdan v. Rumsfeld,* 2006: 80). The ruling, which cited (as the flaw in the New Paradigm practice) the executive's failure to gain congressional authorization for its procedures in detaining unlawful combatants, may signal a rebuke of the imperial presidency, encouraging further reevaluation of warrantless search activities and presidential signing statements. Alternatively, if the portrayal of the entire world as a battlefield in an unbounded war on terror is convincing, Congress may one day concede the powers claimed by a commander in chief who believes he can ignore laws that appear to limit his authority to conduct such a war.

The tools available to Watergate plumbers have been enhanced. If history (or the logic of Hamilton and Madison) is an indicator, there is little reason to think such tools will not be put to use. While much has been written about the potential "to misapply or abuse" these powers, far less has been said about the increasing use of military forces in urban places, the declining institutional outlets for legitimate dissent and protest, increasing proclivities of mass media and other opinion leaders to represent legitimate mass protest as akin to a terrorist threat, the weakening demarcation between law enforcement and military engagements and, within the realm of military vernacular and action, the blurring of distinctions between wartime and other-than-war operations (Warren, 2004). Those lacking voice to influence—or failing that, to protest against—various policies in the new global economy, for example, are also prohibited from challenging lawmakers, lobbyists, corporate leaders of the World Trade Organization, the World Bank, the G-8, and so forth. The leaders of these organizations are sequestered in virtual fortresses protected by encamped military units, missiles, and other large and small armaments. In these contexts, what are we to think of the chances for democratic public administration?

In the latter half of the twentieth century, it seemed that metropolitan areas as significant sites of associational life and political learning were endangered by reformers who adopted the logic of bureaucratic administration and consolidation as the *only way*. Opportunities for public economies and entrepreneurship in providing public goods in a polycentric order were described as obstacles to rational development as theories and practices of polycentricity came under attack. By 1970, it had become common to think of a myriad of problems confronting most societies as necessitating a war plan for the commander in chief who would strike down poverty, homelessness, drug abuse, and so forth, in an all-out, centralized campaign. Americans once fearful of monarchists accepted the appellation of a Drug Czar with powers commensurate to the name. At the turn of the century, the designation "czar" was applied to the commander of forces engaged in public education.

As former deputy assistant attorney general Yoo explained, it is only logical to apply the tools for a "war on drugs" to a "war on terror." That similar tools, including the Racketeer Influenced and Corrupt Organizations Act (1970)—RICO, with its problematic statute of limitations and claims-accrual baggage—have been used against a variety of unlikely targets, including anti-abortion protestors, terrorists, and law enforcement agencies is perhaps also only logical. No one doubts that conspiracy, corruption, crime, and terrorism are inimical to democracy or that poverty, ignorance, and substance abuse destroy individual and communal resources requisite for a voluntaristic society. Yet the blurring of metaphoric wars, the consequent mental stance of a people who view themselves as under siege, and the fond hope of deliverance, as Tocqueville indicated, through a tutelary force transcending their general depression cause us to ask along with Alexander Hamilton whether we can long endure as a society constituted on the basis of reflection and choice.

The extraordinary prerogatives of the president as commander in chief may create incentives to engage in warfare, rather than to exercise public entrepreneurship to build federal constitutions of order for communities at local, national, and international levels. What we identify as the United States of America could be an initial model for building a North American Union analogous to the European Union, rather than fencing off and fortifying national borders (for further discussion, see V. Ostrom, 2007). Instead of being rushed into enacting Declarations of War, Congress should create a joint council of inquiry to consider peaceful alternatives for the resolution of conflict among those engaged. The next millennium will realize its potential only if we answer in the affirmative Alexander Hamilton's query as to whether societies of men and women can learn to create good government from reflection and choice. The study of public administration needs to draw on the full range of social sciences and humanities to approach problem-solving as a matter of *inquiry* by focusing on the role of public entrepreneurship in building creative civilizations in a world of great ecological diversity.

7

Intellectual Crises and Beyond
Vincent Ostrom and Barbara Allen

The American Intellectual Crises

If we wish to open ourselves to new frontiers of inquiry, Thomas Kuhn's concept of a paradigm and of a paradigm shift in scientific revolutions is a useful beginning. A Copernican conception of a solar-centered planetary system has, for example, many incommensurabilities with an earth-centered concept of the universe. The earth, the moon, the planets, and the sun have continued to move in relation to each other in patterns that have remained stable for millennia of millennia. It is we as human beings who, by virtue of our intellectual vision of that reality, can think differently about relationships with reference to day and night, the tides of the oceans, the phases of the moon, the seasons of the year, the wandering stars, and other heavenly bodies. These ideas opened a host of new opportunities and today make ventures in space possible.

How we think profoundly effects what we see and do. We need to look critically at the way we think. The only way we can do this is to become aware that there may be other ways of thinking about familiar problems. Until this possibility is taken seriously and we begin to explore what would be implied by using different conceptualizations and computational logics to address familiar problems in a different way, we cannot critically assess habituated ways of thinking.

In my own experience, what I (Ostrom) have referred to as the work of contemporary political economists has better enabled me to understand the way that multiorganizational arrangements in overlapping jurisdictions could function as *viable systems of order* in the governance of metropolitan areas, the operation of public service industries, the organization of public economies as essential complements to market economies, and the functioning of a highly federalized system of administration. Instead of being solely dependent upon the command and control structures of a bureaucracy, coordination can be attained by processes of cooperation, competition, conflict, and conflict resolution occurring among multiple independent public jurisdictions. Such an approach enables one to understand how systems of public administration can be put together in different ways other than relying primarily on the principles of bureaucratic organization, which had been accepted as the core organizing concept in the traditional teachings of American public administration.

Having shifted perspectives and used a different approach, I also discovered that I could go back and re-read Alexis de Tocqueville's *Democracy in America* (1945) and the essays in *The Federalist* with an altogether different level of understanding. A basic paradigm shift had taken place in the late nineteenth and early twentieth centuries, and Woodrow Wilson's work explicitly articulated such a break from earlier traditions with a commensurate shift in perspectives and modes of inquiry. I had been nurtured on the "behavioral" presuppositions of "modern" scholarship and had earlier read *The Federalist* and *Democracy in America* with puzzlement about their "gems of wisdom" and "penetrating insights" about American society. It took a paradigm shift grounded in the work of political economists for me to appreciate that the writings of Hamilton, Jay, Madison, and Tocqueville were thoroughly grounded in the use of theory as an analytical tool for thinking about the constitution of order in human societies. Reasoned analyses were being articulated, not flashes of insights or intuitions.

As a student, I (Allen) benefited from these insights linking the political economy of metropolitan governance with these much earlier ideas about institutional design and political culture. Concepts like polycentricity informed my thinking about the pacts, covenants, charters, and constitutions comprising federal systems that invariably developed from the ground up. In thinking about the meaning of federalism for self-governance and democracy, the covenant idea has taken center stage. Covenants, as we shall detail below, demand reciprocity and an orientation to perpetuity in relationships that, it follows, tend toward increasing equality and responsibility among the parties who enter these voluntary agreements. Covenant-based political relations, or *foederal* systems (taking *foederal*, the Latin term for covenant), require polycentric arrangements that institutionalize the conditions of limited and shared authority necessary to actualize the normative aim of self-government. Given the covenantal roots of American federalism, such insights were second nature to constitutional framers including James Madison and early constitutional analysts like John Adams.

The idea of *foederalism*, if somewhat foreign to the experience of Alexis de Tocqueville, was nevertheless recognized as one of the pillars of American constitutionalism and *administrative practice.* Tocqueville even noted its effects in the relatively more "centralized" administrative practices of Alexander Hamilton's New York. Beyond the connections between the modern concept of polycentricity and the early roots of *foederal* institutions, the paradigmatic shift that Ostrom describes changed the way we think about the theory and practice of institutional design. The institutional arrangements described by Madison and Hamilton and analyzed by Tocqueville were understood as artifacts of human imagination and design—experimental efforts to address enduring problems of human society through constitutional choice.

As conceptions whose meanings were conveyed by language, the institutions of governance represented facts of a different order from the "brute facts" of nature (Searle, 1969). These were differences understood by constitutional framers who had long considered how changes in time and place could modify the terms and conditions of political order. Institutional facts could be analyzed, but the science necessary to that task differed radically from the science applied to the physical world. As Tocqueville insisted, a new science of politics is needed for a new world.

According to Tocqueville, the members of a self-governing political community must develop a "science of association" enabling them to create shared understandings to inform their collective and constitutional choices. As with the institutional analysis offered in *The Federalist*, Tocqueville's science emphasized experimentation: iterations of reflection, deliberation, choice, action, outcome, learning, and amendment. The institutional requirements and the mental stance of a people embarking on a perpetual experiment in self-government set a high bar; Tocqueville and American constitutional framers assumed political capacity and enlightenment to be attributes of any people taking on the challenge. Nothing less than an engaged open society with limits on all manner of authority, however difficult it may be to design and maintain such a polity, would produce the "science" they required. The study of constitutions based on principles of experimentation and association—and the interpretation of the political relations and societies such constitutions produced—might also call for something new. Instead of searching for the ultimate center of power, the health of association-based or polycentric systems must be measured by the strength of relationships among their constituent parts (V. Ostrom, 1997; Elazar, 1998; Allen, 2005). Undertaking such an evaluation requires that we see the world differently (Herzberg, 2005; Wagner, 2005).

In contrast to conceptions of political science imagined by Tocqueville, as well as by Madison and Hamilton, Wilson—like Bagehot before him—sought to go behind the facade of what he conceived to be political formalities and address himself to political "realities." The works of practitioners and thinkers like Adams, Hamilton, or Madison were portrayed as "literary theories" and "paper pictures." Both Bagehot and Wilson presumed that they could directly perceive political reality. Wilson was explicit in viewing the task of an observer to "escape from theory and attach himself to facts, not allowing himself to be confused by a knowledge of what that government was intended to be, or led away into conjectures as to what it might one day become, but strove to catch its present phases and to photograph the delicate mechanism in all its characteristic parts exactly as it is today; an undertaking all the more arduous and doubtful of issue because it has to be entered into without guidance from acknowledged authority" (Wilson, 1956: 30).

In view of such presuppositions, no self-respecting scholar

could devote him- or herself to the study of forms when the fundamental task was to understand reality. Those who devoted themselves to a study of forms were open to ridicule; the "realists" conceived of themselves as the true scientists. These new realists turned to their conception of the physical sciences as offering the appropriate perspectives and methods for the study of political phenomena. A new science could be developed, it was presumed, by focusing on behavioral regularities, generating and testing hypotheses about behavioral regularities, and gradually aggregating theories of human organization while rejecting prior traditions of scholarly inquiry.

We now face a serious puzzle. If human beings create their own social realities to some significant degree, can one understand that reality without reference to the theoretical conceptions used to design and create it? The authors of *The Federalist* had written some eighty-five essays to explain the design of the most critical experiment among the various American experiments in constituting different units of government in a popular or democratic system of governance. It would seem that the results of these practical experiments to design a system of governance should be construed in light of the theory that was used to inform that design. Instead, Wilson and many twentieth-century scholars in political science and public administration had relied on a theory of a unitary state and bureaucratic administration to form their presumptions about political reality. These presumptions were the antithesis of the theory articulated by Hamilton and Madison in *The Federalist* (V. Ostrom, 2007).

Since intellectual traditions of the past were categorically rejected, a new theoretical conception was being implicitly drawn on to undertake new efforts at governmental reform and administrative reorganization in the twentieth century. These efforts were viewed less as experiments than as doing what appeared to be obviously necessary to correct a series of misconceived efforts and crazy-quilt patterns that had accrued from a series of historical accidents.

The perspective of the naive realist forsakes a critical awareness of the place of language in human thought and the importance of a critical awareness of language as an intellectual tool for what can and cannot be said about reality. Human beings are not endowed with infallible vision. The effort to understand reality is more difficult than painting word pictures of what one presumes to see. No one has "seen" something called "the government." What we presume to see is an intellectual construction; and we must rely upon the language and computational logic of a theoretical apparatus to enable us to understand the nature of any pattern of organization as a social reality.

Though purporting to address themselves to reality, the administrative, legal, and political realists allowed themselves, like Wilson, to be informed by presuppositions about that reality ("there is always a centre of power") and to make their general assessments of reality with reference to models of parliamentary government and bureaucratic administration as ideal types. This method is not appropriate for scientific inquiry. Eucken (1951: 173) demonstrates that we can, by analyzing and abstracting significant characteristics of the world we experience, develop "ideal types" that can be used as intellectual constructs. These cannot purport to be pictures of actual life: each construct represents but an aspect in the manifold forms of social reality.

The nineteenth-century conception of the sovereign nation-state may be such an intellectual construct and one that today stands in opposition to the many self-governing enterprises that exist. The ideal of sovereign states reflects an ontology at odds with the understanding of limited, distributed, and shared constitutional authority and power at the heart of federalism. The ideal of absolute sovereignty has plagued post-colonial societies in Africa, much of Southeast and Western Asia, and Central and South America, as polities whose governing traditions often included a degree of polycentricity, if only in the local networks of communal problem solving, before these societies adopted the mentality of nineteenth-century empire builders. In such societies, the powers amassed for the imagined sovereign state provided individuals who exercised prerogatives of command over military force to engage in coup d'états to create autocracies, subjugate would-be citizens, enrich themselves by plundering the "State's" natural resources, and create dependencies by destroying village life (Sawyer, 1992; 2005; Kaul, 1996; Olowu and Wunsch, 2004;

Gellar, 2005; Agrawal, 2005; Shivakumar, 2005). In the twenty-first century, the influential collective and, in some cases, *constitutional* choices made by "non-state actors" has raised questions about the practical meaning of state sovereignty. The emergence of a global economy with features of complex public economies as well as market economies has also challenged the idealization of the unitary state actor in actual international relations, even if not always in the models proposed by experts in that academic specialty.

Yet the ideology of the sovereign state persists. The perversities and lack of perfection existing in human experience for Wilson and many later social scientists and politicians called forth prescriptions urging that reality be made to conform more closely to ideal types. Perfection is sought by what Hans-Günter Krüsselberg (1983: 61) refers to as an "incantation of state omnipotence." Human experience, when compared to ideal types, or what Harold Demsetz (1969) has called Nirvana models, will always be found wanting. The proper basis for making comparisons in assessing the performance of practical experiments in human governance based on different design concepts is the realm of practical experience, not Utopian ideal types, Nirvana models, or images of diabolical machines.

We thus need to consider the many levels of analysis *explicitly* when we think about systems of administration and their associated systems of governance in human societies. First, it is essential to distinguish between languages as symbol systems, the different uses that can be made of languages, and the events that are the referents, objects, or topics of communication. When the events that are the object of inquiry are themselves artifacts that may be based on different design concepts, a second level of complexity arises. If, further, those artifactual constructions manifest themselves in the way that people think, make choices, and act, we have added complexities about how conceptualizations, theories, and practices work themselves out at different levels of choice and are reflected in human conduct.

A theory that presumes a unitary system of government with a single center of power that has ultimate authority (the last say) in the governance of society brings all aspects of life in a society within the jurisdiction of that authority. What happens in a unitary state is internal to an all-encompassing unit of government. All other units have a subordinate and derivative status.

By contrast, a highly federalized system of governance has many autonomous units of government. To understand how such a system of government operates, it is necessary to refer to multiorganizational relationships that have the internal dynamics applicable to single organizations plus the dynamics of interorganizational arrangements. Given a system of separation of powers internal to each unit of government, it is again necessary to recognize that each unit of government is in itself a polycentric order having reference to independently operating legislative, executive, and judicial instrumentalities. All of these instrumentalities of government operate within the context of an open public realm constitutionally maintained by such traditions as freedom of speech, freedom of assembly, the separation of secular and religious affairs, freedom of contract and voluntary association, and rights to property and to due process of law.

Each unit of government in a constitutional federal republic is a polycentric order operating within larger sets of multiorganizational arrangements. These orderings are maintained primarily with reference to open public realms where the law applicable to particular communities of relationships can become publicly knowable. The standards inherent in a rule of law apply alike to those who are citizens and to those citizens who as representatives may for a time, subject to institutional limits, exercise legislative prerogatives of setting standards, executive prerogatives of enforcing standards, and judicial prerogatives of judging the application of standards. Citizens, in turn, judge the performance of officials in light of the basic constitutional prerogatives exercised by citizens. These constitutional prerogatives are not "private" rights. Basic constitutional rights pertain to the function of persons and citizens in an open public realm. Such a realm exists for the purpose of developing a critical civic consciousness about the accountability of those representatives—that is, those who exercise diverse prerogatives in the maintenance of a public order with regard to many communities of interest.

The constitutional prerogatives of officials who exercise authority—or, in the words of Hobbes, *author* the actions of citizens whom they represent—and the responsibilities and rights of citizens who must monitor and enforce limits if officials exceed their authority are only part of a self-governing order. Joined to this picture of a representative, *federal* republics are the myriad responsibilities of citizens to solve many commonly encountered problems *directly*. The public dimension of individual rights is paramount in a system based on a science of association. Participants in such a polity are expected to perform many roles: as authors of the actions of associations they may represent (e.g., as legislative representatives from a legally defined geographic space or "district"); as individuals who monitor such representatives' behavior and accept the potentially costly burden of enforcing limits on officials through court challenges or acts of civil disobedience; and as persons who work with others to address shared concerns through direct action. In short, such a system places a very high premium on each person's agreement to judge and be judged in the myriad activities of governance.

Such systems then operate in processes of cooperation, competition, conflict, and conflict resolution rather than through command and control by an overarching hierarchy of officials. These systems may have equilibrating tendencies using power to check power, as Montesquieu recognized. The basic design principle, as Madison asserted in *Federalist* 51, is to rely on "opposite and rival interests" with powers distributed "in such a manner as that each may be a check upon the other—that the private interests of every individual be a sentinel over the public rights." In federal systems of government, this principle is then extended to "the distribution of the supreme powers of the State." This was a way of resolving Hobbes's dilemma in which the sovereign who exercises the ultimate power to govern is the source of law, above the law, and cannot be held accountable to law by other human beings for the discharge of sovereign prerogatives. Sovereigns cannot have the last say and still be accountable to others. Something is wrong with the logic we use if we want it both ways. To have it both ways is incoherent, wishful thinking.

Any such system of governance, then, depends on further distinctions in levels of analysis to include constitutional choice, collective choice, and operational levels of analysis. The constitutional level of analysis pertains to setting the terms and conditions of government. If constitutional law is not binding on those who exercise governmental authority, then the conduct of government is no longer subject to a rule of law. The collective-choice level of analysis pertains to what a collectivity should do, as a choice of policy, within the terms and conditions specified by a constitution. This is often articulated as what "the government" should do. The policy options that should be pursued by a collectivity become the standard reference in most policy analysis. The operational level of analysis pertains to what happens in the world of action and the effects that flow from human activities. The recent emphasis on implementation indicates that the link between collective choice and collective action is problematical. An implementation gap separates collective choice from collective action. Officials may command, but subjects need not obey. Instruments of coercion can be mobilized, but activities by reluctant subordinates and subjects can neither achieve goals nor attain superior levels of performance.[1]

When policy analysts become preoccupied only with what "the government" should do, they simultaneously do two things. First, they ignore the constitutional level of analysis. Second, they presume that ultimate authority resides with "the government." Can democratic societies that are fashioned as constitutional republics tolerate such poorly conceived analyses of policy problems? Only at grave risk!

A preoccupation with management in the study of public administration neglects the whole realm of institutional analysis and how appropriate institutional arrangements might be constituted to achieve mutually productive sets of relationships among diverse elements. A self-governing society requires skill in putting together enterprises that appropriately reflect diverse interests so as to achieve shared communities of understanding that serve as the basis for informed public action. Public administration is then concerned more with public entrepreneurship than with management. Managers should never forget Rousseau's generalization: "One who believes himself the master of others is nonetheless a greater slave than they" (Rousseau, 1978: 46). Masters become slave to their instruments of control rather than searching out

ways to create mutually productive relationships among those
who serve and are being served.

Unitary structures of authority operate by systems of dominance subject to command structures characteristic of bureaucracies. By contrast, polycentric systems of governance emerge by the
way patterns of cooperation, competitive rivalry, and processes of
conflict and conflict resolution affects the intraorganizational and
intergovernmental realms. These realms are equivalent to what I
have referred to as an open public realm. The term *res publica*—the
public thing—is often viewed as the source of the word "re-pub-
lic." The public thing—the open public realm—is the basic core
of a democratic republic. Factors pertaining to "representation"
are of a somewhat lesser order of importance. A federal system
of government in a compound republic acquires its operational
characteristics from the emergent properties that accrue in the
open public realm from the patterns of interactions among the
multiplicity of organizational units operating as structural elements in interorganizational fields of effects.

In sum, our argument is not that the State will some day wither
away with the rise of global markets but rather that the conceptualization of sovereignty informing the ideal of the State reflects
ideological commitments that are out of step with the normative
and practical requirements of democratic self-government. Governments are among the many types of associations formed by
persons in a voluntaristic society. If we are talking about governments in consent-based, self-governing societies, these associations, to be sure, differ from other voluntary associations in terms
of their legitimate use of police powers. Yet no coherent claim can
be made about a monopoly of enforcement powers in a system that
holds officials who are entrusted temporarily with instruments
of force accountable for their actions. Governments in federated
polities, furthermore, offer larger and smaller arenas of enforceable actions—not higher and lower or greater and lesser "levels of
government" (Elazar, 1995–1998; V. Ostrom, 1997; Acheson, 2003;
Polski, 2003; Allen, 2005; Crawford and Ostrom, 2005). Conceptualized in this way, a "national" government—or to use Hamilton
and Madison's terminology, a "general" government—represents
a people's more universal association; as peoples unite to form

various unions, some of these "governments" may now be expected to reach across "States" to international communities of shared interests, values, and action.

The magnitude of the incommensurabilities in the two different ways of viewing systems of governance can be assessed by comparing Wilson's *Congressional Government* with Tocqueville's *Democracy in America.* Both were considering patterns of governance in American society. One looked upon Congress as the supreme authority governing American society. The other looked upon American society as self-governing. What they "saw," as a consequence, was as different as day and night. Wilson was no farther in time from Tocqueville than we are in the early years of the new millennium from the New Deal and the Roosevelt administration in the 1930s. It is not time that makes the crucial difference. Rather, it is the difference in paradigmatic perspective taken by actors and observers that creates revolutionary change. When acted upon, paradigmatic shifts in ways of thinking can transform patterns of order in human societies.

One way to reconcile the two approaches is to recognize that the theory expounded by Wilson was also used to conceptualize administrative reorganization resulting in practical experiments in government reform (Auer, 1998). Comparisons might then be made between two experimental results: when reforms addressed a particular problem by eliminating fragmentation of authority and overlapping jurisdictions and instances when reformers faced the same problem but did not undertake such reforms (McGinnis, 1999b; Parks, 1999).

We must distinguish levels of analysis: organizational, interorganizational, and multiorganizational, and levels of choice: the constitutional, collective, and operational arenas of choice. In addition, we must recognize another basic distinction pertaining to the nature of order in public economies, first developed by V. Ostrom, Tiebout, and Warren (1961), between *provision* and *production* of public goods and services (see Bish, 1971; U.S. Advisory Commission on Intergovernmental Relations, 1987a; McGinnis, 1999b). Provision pertains to the collective arrangements necessary to procure a public service. It emphasizes organizing basic aspects that have to do with *consumptive* relationships in a public economy.

Public goods are characterized by jointness of use and the failure of exclusion, as exclusion might apply to individuals. When individuals cannot be feasibly excluded, the concept *jointness of use* must be applied to some *community of people* who use a good or service in common. Several critical organizational problems arise in situations characterized by jointness of use and the inability to exclude individuals from the use of a good; the resulting features of collective organization reflect choices that bound the relevant community of users and create decision-making arrangements capable of levying taxes, articulating preferences, aggregating preferences into decisions about the desirable quantity and quality of service to provide at a desired cost to be borne by users/taxpayers, and establishing appropriate rules that apply to patterns of use. All of these aspects relate to consumption functions (Hess and Ostrom, 2007).

Like provision, the actual creation or production of a public good may be carried out in several ways. A public good can be produced by hiring employees to accomplish the task, by contracting with other producers, or by some combination of these methods. These options can give rise to quasi-market arrangements within a public economy. As long as collective-consumption functions are competently organized in relation to collective instrumentalities with powers of taxation and collective choice and powers to enforce rules and regulations, public economies can be diversely organized.

It is a mistake to focus only on production functions and to assume that units of government are primarily production units. Users of many public services are themselves essential *coproducers* (Whitaker, 1980; Davis and Ostrom, 1991; Parks et al., 1999). Teachers cannot produce education without the coproductive efforts of students; police cannot produce public order without the coproductive efforts of citizens. Public servants help to accomplish these tasks. They rarely produce the results themselves. Units of government of varying size are necessary to take account of the diverse situations and patterns of community preferences that may exist in different and overlapping communities that make joint use of various public goods and services.

Under these circumstances, presumptions about fragmentation

of authority and overlapping jurisdictions as the primary source of institutional weakness and failure in systems of governance cannot hold. Fragmentation of authority, as might apply to a constitutional separation of powers, is necessary to hold the diverse instrumentalities of government accountable to citizens as they function in an open public realm. Overlapping jurisdiction does not mean duplication of functions but allows for commensurate structuring of consumption and production functions in the absence of standard marketing arrangements. Production and consumption relationships require cooperation between producers and communities of people making joint use of what is produced. The availability of alternative production and consumption units means that alternatives are available in choosing partners with whom to cooperate in those production-consumption relationships (McGinnis, 1999b).

Alternative access to impartial and independent processes for articulating and resolving conflicts is important when competition is not maintained within proper limits and when cooperation breaks down or becomes a collusive effort to impose costs upon others. Conflicting interests, when mediated by appropriate rules of procedure and rules of evidence, generate the information so vital to informed choice in a democratic society. Conflict, as indicated in chapter 5, is also an engine that elucidates alternatives and becomes a primary source of innovation. These potentials can too easily be frustrated by the preemptive strategies that allow majorities to prevail in a political process and allow subordinates to be dominated by superiors in a system of administrative management.

As long as the appropriate structural conditions applicable to the design of the different institutional arrangements exist in similar economic, social, and cultural conditions, it should be possible to test competing hypotheses derived from different theoretical arguments, even though these arguments are derived from political theories relying on different paradigmatic approaches. Such a method is expounded in Elinor Ostrom (1999) and Parks and Oakerson (2000).

Continuing research efforts by a number of scholars have lent plausibility to arguments that were advanced when the Alabama

lectures that occasioned the first edition of the present work were
first presented during the fall semester of 1971. E. S. Savas (1977),
for example, found in an extended study of solid-waste disposal
that provision by a unit of government contracting with a private vendor for a jurisdiction, or neighborhood in a jurisdiction,
yielded better performance than relying on municipal employees
to collect and dispose of solid waste or private vendors independently servicing individual households and places of business.
Bruno Frey and Werner Pommerehne found similar results from
studies of Swiss cities (V. Ostrom and Bish, 1977: chap. 8).

Elinor Ostrom, Roger B. Parks, Gordon P. Whitaker, and other colleagues associated with the Workshop in Political Theory
and Policy Analysis have conducted a series of studies concerned
with how institutional variables relate to the delivery of police
services when measured with reference to various standards of
performance. Much of the efficiency and economy reform movement urged consolidation of local government jurisdictions into
large-scale metropolitan-wide units of government. Taking size as
a variable, small- to medium-sized police departments consistently achieve better performance than large police departments. In
metropolitan areas that have been subject to intensive study, the
largest police departments consistently respond more slowly to
calls for service, face higher crime rates, and satisfy their citizens
less effectively than small- to medium-sized departments serving
similar neighborhoods.

The most consolidated metropolitan areas require more full-
time officers on the police force to support each officer on the street
actually patrolling at any given time. The more consolidated metropolitan areas on average employ 950 full-time officers for every
100 officers on patrol, compared to 658 full-time officers for every
100 on patrol in the less consolidated metropolitan areas (Parks
and Ostrom, 1981). New York City as an extreme example employed 3,000 full-time officers for every 100 officers on patrol. It is
possible for large police forces to maintain a proportionately small
presence on city streets, but if they do, high incidences of street
crimes can be expected.

The performance of police departments was also evaluated using the dual measures of police response capabilities (the num-

ber of police cars on the street per officer employed) and police crime performance (the number of clearances of crimes by arrest per officer employed). In a study of eighty metropolitan areas, the best departments performed better in metropolitan areas with the largest number of police departments. The best departments in the more "fragmented" metropolitan areas performed better than the best departments in the more consolidated metropolitan areas.

An in-depth analysis of the effect of structure of organizational arrangements reveals complex relationships. The best police performance is achieved in metropolitan areas where there are relatively few agencies producing radio communications and homicide investigations, while direct services such as patrol are simultaneously produced by many agencies exercising independent responsibility for the operation of those direct services (Parks, 1985). There is, thus, no single optimal scale of organization for the supply of all police services in a metropolitan area. Rather, organizing metropolitan areas so that diverse scales of operation exist for different services enhances the overall performance level. Fragmentation and overlap can enhance performance when the characteristics of particular services and the needs and resources of diverse communities being served are taken into account. These same principles should be as applicable to federal systems of governance as to metropolitan areas.

It may seem intuitively obvious that fragmentation of authority and overlapping jurisdictions will yield perverse effects in any system of public administration. What appears to be intuitively obvious, however, need not be true. The principal task in the development of any science is to clarify both counterintuitive and counterintentional relationships that exist in human social relationships. It is only then that we can develop a science of administration to serve as a design science for practicing the art of administration under reasonable circumstances.

Once we begin to recognize that alternatives are possible, new frontiers for further inquiry begin to open. Finding that fragmentation of authority and overlapping jurisdiction can be associated with better performance in the delivery of police services, for example, raises new questions about why that should be the case.

In *The Organization of Local Public Economies* (1987a) and *Metropolitan Organization: The St. Louis Case* (1988), the U.S. Advisory Commission on Intergovernmental Relations is preoccupied with how fragmentation works in the public economy of metropolitan areas. Whether inequalities among jurisdictions yield inequities in service delivery needs serious investigation rather than presuming tautologies (E. Ostrom, 1985; McGinnis, 1999a; 1999b).

These studies spurred a new line of inquiry on governance in the context of various common-pool resource problems and, more broadly, the contributions of polycentricity to self-government as an alternative to plunder and the predation of States in post-colonial societies worldwide (McGinnis, 1999a; 1999b; Olowu and Wunsch, 2004). Findings from the study of irrigation systems (Tang, 1992; Lam, 1998; Shivakoti et al., 2005), fisheries (Schlager and Ostrom, 1993; Acheson, 2003), and forests (Gibson, McKean, and Ostrom, 2000; Andersson, 2004; Poteete and Ostrom, 2004; Gibson, Williams, and Ostrom, 2005) have repeatedly found that top-down policies of either centralization or full decentralization are less effective than polycentric systems with diverse local, regional, and national governance arrangements. Nor do empirical studies find that broad types of property rights (e.g., government, private, or communal ownership) are more strongly associated with successful governance of the commons (Dietz, Ostrom, and Stern, 2003; Dietz, 2005).

Intellectual crises are never resolved by wars of words. Such crises are usually indicative of alternatives that are available at one or another level of analysis. It is only as we extend the frontiers of inquiry that we clarify the dimensions of the problem and the ways human beings might cope with the alternatives that become available to them.

Even in its first edition, *The Intellectual Crisis in American Public Administration*, thus, was not confined to the paradigm problem that arose from Simon's challenge. It also addresses the paradigm problem that arose from the basic paradigmatic challenge made by Woodrow Wilson, some of his contemporaries, and those who followed in their footsteps. Still another basic paradigmatic shift occurred in the American Revolution and the diverse experiments in constitutional government that followed. Inquiry into the character of one intellectual crisis, if pressed far enough, is likely to reveal deeper issues at other levels of analysis. As we extend the frontiers of inquiry about the intellectual crises in American public administration, we are apt to press back to basic issues that stand at the foundation of our civilization. Issues pertaining more broadly to the nature and constitution of order in human societies are usually at stake. We turn to those issues next.

A Copernican Turn?

When Tocqueville referred to a "great experiment" having occurred on the North American continent to construct "society upon a new basis" using "theories hitherto unknown or deemed impracticable" and exhibiting "a spectacle for which the world had not been prepared by the history of the past" (Tocqueville, 1945: 1:25), he was suggesting that a development had occurred in political theory and in the governance of human societies that was of Copernican proportions. Following Gerard Radnitzky, we shall refer to such an occurrence as a Copernican turn (Radnitzky and Bartley, 1987: chap. 14). Tocqueville viewed this development as creating a society that had become self-governing: "there society governs itself for itself" (Tocqueville, 1945: 1:57).

In the prior history of mankind, great societies had always been organized as empires. City republics had existed in ancient Greece and Rome, and numerous free cities had existed in medieval Europe. Switzerland and the United Provinces had fashioned confederations of free cities and provinces that were vulnerable to serious problems of institutional failure. Alexander Hamilton had analyzed these problems of institutional failure characteristic of confederations in *Federalist* 15 and 16 and had conceptualized an alternative way to constitute a federal system of government. Hamilton relied upon the principle that each unit of government must be related to the persons of the citizens rather than presuming that governments could govern other governments. A system of compound, overlapping republics was used to design a federal system of government rather than a simple unitary republic.

If the American experiments in constitutional choice represented a fundamental Copernican turn in the governance of human societies, then the paradigmatic shift made by Woodrow Wilson, his contemporaries, and their followers might be viewed as a degenerative rather than a progressive development. The erosion of basic constitutional understandings, the nationalization of American government, and the inability of the national government to keep its own house in order can be viewed as the correlatives of efforts to eliminate fragmentation of authority and overlapping jurisdictions. How do we begin to consider such conjectures?

First, we need to recognize that systems of governance may be grounded in different concepts, which are given expression in different institutional arrangements. How conceptions and associated structures are put together create what might be referred to as a constitutional order. Richard Pipes's *Russia under the Old Regime* (1974) provides an interesting account of the organizing principles used in fashioning the constitutional order of imperial Russia. Edward Crankshaw's *The Shadow of the Winter Palace* (1986) supplements Pipes's account. Ray Huang's *1587: A Year of No Significance* (1981) and Tai-Shuenn Yang's "Property Rights and Constitutional Order in Imperial China" (1987) provide comparable accounts of the organizing principles and structures in traditional China. Different political systems can be constituted in different ways.

Harold Berman's *Law and Revolution* (1983) is a comparable effort at elaborating the conceptualizations and associated structures that have been important in the constitution of governance systems in Western Europe. When we carefully consider what Berman has to say, we can appreciate that the American experiments in constituting systems of governance did not spring full grown, like a mushroom, from the soil of the North American continent. Rather, Americans drew upon a thousand years of struggle, intellectual disputations, and inquiry about authority relationships in human societies.[2] In turn, those who carried forward these contestations about basic ideas applicable to the constitution and governance of human societies drew upon the intellectual resources of still earlier civilizations. The most prominent of these were the Roman, Greek, and Hebrew traditions.

Berman considers the dictate proclaimed by Pope Gregory VII in

1075 to be the critical incident setting the stage for the centuries of contestation about the proper structure of authority relationships in Western societies. This was a critical step in establishing the independence of the church from imperial and other secular authorities. From that time onward, European society has had recourse to two distinctive and independent structures of authority relationships: secular and ecclesiastical. One or the other might come to short-term dominance, but the separation of secular and ecclesiastical authority allowed for a continuing disputation about the proper order of authority relationships in Western societies that has continued to this day.

The ancient Jewish concept of law, grounded in a covenant between God and his chosen people, is the foundation upon which the Western church once judged the exercise of rulership prerogatives by secular authorities. Those same principles were in turn used within the church to judge the proper exercise of ecclesiastical authority in contestations between popes, bishops, monks, priests, and parishioners. Although the Roman Church increasingly separated itself from its covenantal roots and moved resolutely toward an apostolic confession that was more congenial to hierarchical organization, such developments were continually contested (Elazar, 1995–1998). The Protestant Reformation of the sixteenth century was but one of the recurring controversies about the proper constitution and exercise of ecclesiastical authority within Western Christendom. Dissenting Protestants, whom we today identify as puritans, dedicated themselves to the belief that each congregation is the proper governing authority in spiritual matters. They used "conventicles," a form of collective critical reflection on Anglican sermons, in their Old World associations and brought their method of discourse and disputation to New World congregationalism. In 1648 they codified their practices— separation of ecclesiastical and civil governments, the authority of each congregation to establish its governing practices, including provisions for members, the relative authority and responsibility of ministers and laity and the approach to be taken in scriptural inquiries, and the means by which neighboring congregations could be "orderly knit together" in covenanted unions.

They used the same basic principles in constituting the American system of civil governance. The concept of a covenant with God could be used to constitute political regimes in which both rulers and ruled were bound by a rule of law. The telos of a partnership with God created by mutual consent reoriented authority among moral equals who, as in the archetypal covenant, foreswore the idea of unlimited sovereignty and authority (Allen, 2005).

Another of the early products of the papal revolution of 1075 was the development of the scientific study of law and the codification of both canon law and secular law. These laws drew upon the antecedents of Roman law, interpreted and reconstructed in light of basic methods inherent in the teachings of Hebraic law. Gratian, an Italian monk, codified canon law by seeking to create "an ordered synthesis out of the tangle of apparently conflicting laws and practices that had grown up in the church over the preceding thousand years." Gratian created his *Concord of Discordant Canons* by using a general ordering principle to resolve contradictions and anomalies and yield a coherent synthesis of the whole. He did so by relying on a methodology that was grounded in the presupposition that the "principal foundation of all law [is] the timeless principle that we should do unto others as we would have them do unto us" (Tierney, 1982: 13). The golden rule can be used as a method of normative inquiry and can serve as a law of laws (V. Ostrom, 1986). An alternative method of normative inquiry was available to derive a unity of law apart from the command of a unitary sovereign.

The scientific study of law that was generated by the papal revolution created the foundation for Western systems of law. Western codes of law were more the product of university scholars and legal practitioners working with principles of Roman and Hebraic law than they were the commands of sovereigns. Systems of law have many sources and the viability of legal doctrine depends more upon rules being a mutually agreeable basis for ordering human relationships (i.e., with the consent of the governed) than commands imposed by sovereigns.

The distinctive quality of "a rational legal order," which Max Weber associated with bureaucracy, is only characteristic of Western societies that rely upon codifications of Roman law in accordance with Hebraic principles as the primary source of legal rationality. Neither Russian nor Chinese bureaucracies were associated with a "rational legal order" with general rules of law presumed to apply to all persons alike. European efforts to achieve a rule of law, or what the Germans call a *Rechtsstaat*, relied upon a differentiation of legislative, executive, and judicial functions even though those diverse structures were linked and ordered in different ways.

One of the basic characteristics to emerge in the evolution of European societies from the continuing contestation about the nature of authority relationships was the development of significant self-governing capabilities and efforts to hold rulers accountable to a rule of law. These diverse elements were never fully brought together so that one could think of Europe as a self-governing society in which "society governed itself for itself." Self-governing cities existed everywhere in Europe, but their liberties were always subject to the threat of imperial aggression and dominance. The destruction of the freedom of the city of Frankfurt, following the Battle of Koniggraetz in 1866, was, for example, an incidental consequence of Bismarck's efforts to construct the constitutional order of the second German Empire (Crankshaw, 1983: 213–214, 229–230). But that empire, established in 1871, lasted for less than fifty years. What was never effectively achieved in Europe was a way of reiterating the processes of constitutional choice that applied to free cities and provinces enabling governing networks that reached out to a larger society of continental proportions. Those efforts are now being considered in the fashioning of a European Union, though such crucial steps as the appointment of the members of the commission in charge of the administrative center are less than an open public process.

The principal modes for achieving peace through a system of government with a single center of ultimate authority are by merger, consolidation, and conquest. These yield imperial solutions. In the absence of federative arrangements using covenantal methods to achieve expanding self-governing capabilities, human societies will remain locked in struggles for dominance. And so it happens that anyone who conceives oneself to be the master of others is a greater slave than they. Those who depend upon clout to accomplish their missions in life make themselves the slaves of that force.

When we begin to explore the larger intellectual horizons that have to do with the nature and constitution of order in human societies, we see the world as abounding in efforts to design more appropriate systems of governance since the end of British, Dutch, French, German, and other empires following World War II. Independence presumed a theory of sovereignty; but nothing like a Copernican turn occurred. The principal formula for constituting independent nations was presumed to be a unitary state in command of an integrated bureaucratic apparatus. Thus the hopes for achieving a free world have given way to patterns of human predation and exploitation of almost unbelievable proportions. Until we recognize the predatory character of highly centralized states and their bureaucracies, we can make little progress in what has come to be called "development administration" (V. Ostrom, 1988; Gibson et al., 2005). Different modes of analysis are required to construct systems of order in which human beings relate to one another in mutually productive ways to improve their living conditions. Such efforts require basic skills in achieving self-organizing and self-governing capabilities (Eggertsson, 2005).

The first priority in acquiring and teaching such skills is *not* management. A prior order of skills has to do with the way that human beings constitute themselves into mutually respectful and productive working relationships. This is a basic aspect of entrepreneurship (Schneider, Teske, and Mintrom, 1995). What people do in constituting mutually respectful and productive working relationships pertains to the constitutional level of analysis and to constitutional choice. This is the process that is constitutive of human endeavors. Persons who function as public entrepreneurs in democratic societies can do so only when they think of themselves as citizens working with other citizens to build enduring patterns of association in which the community of persons involved achieves self-governing capabilities. This is how democracies can develop and remain viable over successive generations. Democratic societies cannot achieve long-term viability if democratic processes are viewed only as a struggle to win and gain dominance over others. Administrators who conceive of themselves as good shepherds exercising management prerogatives can create only recalcitrant and reticent masses. Human beings are not sheep.

As we contemplate the possibility that the American experiments in constitutional choice may have involved a Copernican turn in political theory and in the governance of human societies, we need not think of that paradigmatic turn as having accomplished a "revolution" by bringing that "revolution" to immediate fruition. We could hardly expect revolutionary potentials to be brought to fruition when the theory used to design those experiments was categorically rejected at the end of the first century in the conduct of those experiments.

Although the Americans who undertook the formulation of that experiment looked upon it as having revolutionary implications for all of humanity, they also viewed themselves as fallible creatures who could only propose and initiate the first steps on a new course in human development. Such a step is what Max Weber would have regarded as a "historical starting point." The course of human history can only have "historical starting points" that are marked by theoretical innovations of major proportions.

New ideas—theoretical innovations—never come full-blown. Instead, human beings need to be prepared to learn from experience by working with new ideas. This can never be done by rejecting the guidance that can be gained from writers of acknowledged authority, to paraphrase Woodrow Wilson. Instead, one needs to give careful attention to the conceptions and explanations offered by those who participate in formulating the designs of new experiments. Close attention would need to be given to what those experiments were intended to accomplish and to conjectures about what is likely to occur. By casting these considerations aside, Wilson rejected the use of the experimental method for assessing the American experiments in constitutional choice. Instead, he fantasized that human beings could directly see and describe social reality without a conceptual and computational apparatus for doing so.

Viewing systems of governance as experiments in constitutional choice, on the other hand, can open a new realm of inquiry about the constitution of order in different human societies. Such a method can be applied to the Russian Revolution and the Soviet experiment that followed. The theory used to conceptualize that experiment is reasonably well formulated in Lenin's

What Is to Be Done? and *State and Revolution.* Lenin anticipated a variety of developments, including the withering away of the state to follow from that revolution. Milovan Djilas, who took a leading role in the Yugoslav revolution, observes however: "Everything happened differently in the U.S.S.R. and other Communist countries from what the leaders—even such prominent ones as Lenin, Stalin, Trotsky and Bukharin—anticipated. They expected that the state would rapidly wither away, that democracy would be strengthened. *The reverse happened*" (Djilas, 1957: 37; author's emphasis).

When the reverse happens, questions arise about the warrantability of the theory being acted upon. We may have an instance when human experience had counterintuitive and counterintentional implications that departed radically from what the experimenters envisaged. This too requires an explanation. If Hobbes were alive today he would not be puzzled by what happened in the Soviet experiment. We can, if we wish, find an explanation in Hobbes's *Leviathan* for why the leadership in Lenin's vanguard party became the new sovereign in the Soviet Union. In Richard Pipes's *Russia under the Old Regime,* one sees striking similarities between the autocracy of imperial Russia and the autocracy of the Soviet Union.

At the start of a new century, we are presented with new opportunities to rethink the basis of democratic administration in a number of settings. In the 1970s, we faced an intellectual crisis in American public administration. Events of the 1980s in the United States reprised the basic problems of bureaucratic administration, while in Europe constitutional thinking took a new turn toward confederal union. In the 1990s, the end of the Cold War heralded a new age that was almost immediately eclipsed by new threats in the new millennium and the revisiting of problems left unaddressed by the passage to modernity or the post-modern turn.

Much of humanity in the twentieth century relied upon illusions in their quest for the good life (V. Ostrom, 1997; Furet, 1999). The Marxist-Leninist tradition promising a liberating Communist Party vanguard delivered autocracy and ultimately collapsed, leaving the present generation to decide whether governance can be a matter of reflection and choice rather than force. François

Furet's conjectures about the passing illusions of the twentieth
century—Marxist-Leninist revolutionaries as well as the National
Socialist and Fascist quests for grandeur—point to earlier efforts
in the passage to modernity, including the centralizing administrative tendencies that wrought terror from the noble revolutionary experiment in eighteenth-century France. Notions of the nation, often with ironically parochial views connecting citizenship
with genetic features—bloodlines—and insular ideologies of language and culture, betrayed the cosmopolitan vision of rights that
justified revolutionary writings. In the tragedies of National Socialism and Fascism especially, the parochial was elevated to the
universal, while in other homogenizing efforts, "equality" of the
most abstract character justified the occupation of territories and
the subjugation of peoples under the rubric of republican government. Today, citizens of Europe retain the challenge of revising
their national constitutions and charters for local governance in
an increasingly federated system. Will it be possible to take advantage of the distinct and shared heritage of self-determination
once enjoyed by the free cities? Will the extent of the European
Union be determined by the extent of territory once ruled by the
Holy Roman Empire? Or, will the normative covenantal basis of
federation permit a new union comprised of a diversity of cultural, social, and religious traditions? Will the temptations of empire,
so strongly felt among the nation-states of the nineteenth century,
be avoided in the twenty-first?

Empire may be justified in many ways: as an extension of Enlightenment ideals of universal right and equality as well as by
the much earlier conceptions of the rule of conquest. If philosophi-
cally more palatable, such ideals remain an abstract rationale for
domination unless self-governing conditions prevail. For that to be
the case, understandings of administration and governance must
emerge that are compatible with the realities of diverse local conditions and the cultures to which they give rise. The end of the
Cold War has not brought an end to war; citizens around the globe
must discern what the fundamental conditions beneath the generalities of a War on Terror mean and the myriad methods by which
they may be productively addressed.

How we view the world and address ourselves to the nature of social "reality" is, then, of basic importance in the social sciences and the related social professions such as law and public administration. Unfortunately, or perhaps fortunately, we too are fallible creatures. Our conceptions of social reality cannot be the *true* conception. Nevertheless, we should be able to draw upon the critical skills of others to arrive at a closer approximation of what we might respectively conceive as true and a better assessment of what it would mean to constitute a self-governing society. If each of us could participate in such a process of inquiry, we might develop alternatives by which human beings need not rely on States to rule over societies. We might learn how to constitute viable and responsible patterns of order among multinational communities. When we begin to think our way through to such possibilities, we may be prepared to understand the meaning of the American experiments in constitutional choice and begin to appreciate the immense task confronting human beings in fashioning something that might appropriately be called a free world. Unless we can attain such a level of understanding, we are likely to find ourselves trapped into fashioning new forms of cryptoimperialisms and autocratic despotisms that we falsely call democracies (V. Ostrom, Feeny, and Picht, 1988; Gellar, 2005; Sawyer, 2005).

Challenging Ways of Thinking

The adventure that we have pursued in thinking about the intellectual crises in American public administration takes us well beyond recognizing that paradigm shifts may be important to the way that scholars proceed in their intellectual endeavors and also well beyond the confines of American public administration. Ideas are always the bases for action. Human beings, and other animals, are hard-wired so that voluntary motor facilities depend upon mental processes that occur in the central nervous system. Actions depend on thoughts and habits grounded in thought. Patterns of order in human societies depend, then, on shared communities of understanding about how human beings relate to one another in ordering the ways of life that are constitutive of human societies.

People who understand how rules can be used to order conduct among human beings can draw upon their conceptions to organize human societies. Social organization appears as patterns of order that may also be institutionalized in structural arrangements. Human beings thus have potentials for fashioning their own social "realities" to some significant degree. They are never confined to only one way in formulating patterns of order. There are some ways that rely strongly upon a determinate ordering of superior-subordinate relationships characteristic of bureaucratic command structures. There are other ways that rely more upon covenantal relationships characteristic of self-governing communities. These yield quite different ways of life in human societies.

The difference can perhaps be best understood by the distinction in the terms *Herrschaft* and *Genossenschaft* in the German language. This was Max Weber's language of discourse. *Herrschaft* is translated as authority implying domination. The term has the intuitive meaning of lordship. *Genossenschaft* has the intuitive meaning of comradeship and is frequently translated as association. When Tocqueville claimed that the science and art of association must increase as people become more equal in human societies, he was indicating that they must know how to draw upon principles of comradeship of a covenantal character in achieving self-governing capabilities. Those who rely upon the power of command conceive themselves to be the masters of others and exercise lordship over others.

We still confront the puzzle of how we recognize when one or the other principle prevails. Tocqueville saw a society that relied on a science and art of association to achieve self-governing capabilities. We face some serious problems of what intellectual tools scholars and other professional analysts might use to inquire about the nature and constitution of order in human societies and how scholars and professional analysts think about and experience themselves in human societies. Do we see our world as we think about and experience ourselves? Do we think about and experience ourselves as masters and servants or as comrades and colleagues? Both patterns of order prevail to varying degrees in

different societies. How do we see the configurations of relationships being put together?

Americans cannot confine their intellectual vistas to American
society but must also be prepared to mobilize analytical capabilities for thinking about patterns of governance and ways of life in
other societies and how people might think about and experience
themselves in those societies. If we assume that all societies are
like American societies and all officials behave like American officials, we are not capable of understanding what happens in the
world (Shivakumar, 2005).

A similar problem was addressed, in part, nearly fifty years ago
by Walter Eucken in *The Foundations of Economics* (1951). Eucken
begins his inquiry by pointing to a simple event: a stove that was
heating his study. He then begins to speculate about the complex
chains of actions and transactions that had to be coordinated to
achieve that simple event. In his speculation, he draws upon some
of the analytical capabilities that economists might use to provide
a mental image of the diverse interactions of people and situations that were linked together to yield a stove heating a study.

He then raises a question about how economists address themselves to those circumstances. He finds two discrete styles of
scholarship prevailing among economists. One style involves efforts to develop general abstract models of the economy. Thus,
we might find economists talking abstractly about "the market,"
or political scientists about "the state." Bureaucracies are then
viewed as the key command apparatus that allows "states" to
govern. Reference is then made to "states," "bureaucracies," and
"markets" as the essential institutions in "capitalist" societies. In
doing so, Eucken argues that these scholars increasingly distance
themselves from economic and social reality. On the other hand,
Eucken points to economic historians who, he says, become so
immersed in the details that they simply heap facts upon facts.
An insurmountable gap is created between these two traditions
of scholarship. Eucken refers to this gap as "the great antinomy."
Eucken could as well have been discussing scholarship in public
administration: abstract models and case studies with immense
gaps between theory and practice.

Eucken continues his criticism by pointing to tendencies to

distinguish different types of economies and different stages of historical development that are discretely associated with particular times and places. He was referring to distinctions we might make today between "capitalist" societies and "socialist" societies or between "developed" societies and "less-developed" societies. Instead, Eucken would prefer to presume that there are underlying characteristics that might apply to all human beings coping with problems of scarcity that recur in all human societies. We should thus be able to apply common methods whether studying life in an "ancient" society, a "modern" society, a "less-developed" society, a "developed" society, a "capitalist" society, or a "socialist" society. Eucken was suggesting that if we view patterns of order in human societies, we should be able to base the study of social structures on the foundational elements that comprise these societies in all their diverse forms.

Eucken was arguing that we need a mode of inquiry that would enable us to "penetrate" social reality, in the sense of looking into that reality, rather than increasingly distancing ourselves from reality by highly abstract general models or painting idiosyncratic word pictures while heaping facts upon facts. We need modes of inquiry that enable us to address many different levels and foci of analysis; we must consider how studies of such variety may be related to one another, not only as matters of inquiry but also as matters of our shared social existence. Our inquiries are constitutive of societies—the relationships among scholars and our broader communal networks. This is why Eucken is closely identified with the development of a community of scholars concerned with a theory of order (*Ordnungstheorie*) (Krüsselberg, 1986; see also Boettke and Coyne, 2005; Aligica, 2005).

These issues are important to contemporary scholarship and practical efforts to constitute patterns of order in human societies. The overwhelming discourse about the nature and constitution of order in human societies still occurs by reference to such abstract universalistic concepts as "states," "societies," "bureaucracies," "markets," "capitalism," "socialism," and the like. These universalities are articulated with reference to abstract principles that are presumed to operate. Development is then viewed as a process of "modernization" that requires a centralized "state" and a "bureaucracy" to transform a "society" by means of "industrialization" and associated technological transfers. All of these factors are presumed to work as gross aggregates. Such ways of thinking manifest a simplemindedness of incredible proportions. To gain some sense of reality, we need to remind ourselves of Eucken's stove heating his study and the extraordinary configurations of relationships that were necessary to yield that simple event.

On the other hand, we have specialists in the lore of case studies who heap facts upon facts without having any consciously held intellectual tools to sort out facts and use them to assess what may be problematical in specifiable situations. These are the people who see only particular trees. The others see only sweeping forests. Unfortunately, human endeavors often require more than seeing particular trees and their idiosyncracies or sweeping vistas of forests (Gibson, McKean, and Ostrom, 2000; Moran and Ostrom, 2005). Many other perspectives are of essential analytical importance in the constitution of human societies. Each of us sustains a few important links in the configurations of relationships that make up human societies.

We cannot get along without theory to enable us to picture complex configurations of relationships, which can be neither directly observed nor definitively represented from a single perspective. In responding to Eucken's challenge, we need to sort out the basic elements that are inherent in theoretical reasoning and use these elements to develop a heuristic that will tell us what to look for. A heuristic focusing on structure, conduct, and performance, used in the study of industrial organization (e.g., Bain, 1959), is a helpful way of orienting oneself to inquiries in economic, political, and administrative theory.

A simple heuristic is implied in chapter 3 with the suggestion that the essential elements in institutional analysis are to (1) anticipate the consequences that follow when (2) individuals choosing optimizing strategies within the structure of a situation that has reference to (3) particular organizational arrangements applied to (4) particular structures of events (productive efforts and goods) in the context of (5) some shared community of understanding. The Institutional Analysis and Development (IAD) framework first presented in Kiser and Ostrom (1982) has been developed further during the past two decades (E. Ostrom, 2005) and is the foundation for multiple empirical studies (E. Ostrom, Gardner, and Walker, 1994; Koontz, 2002; Polski, 2003; Blomquist, Schlager, and Heikkila, 2004; Gibson et al., 2005).

Our reference to heuristics is analogous to what Kuhn (1964) refers to as a paradigm, Irme Lakatos (1970) refers to as a research program, or Larry Laudun (1977: chap. 3) refers to as a research tradition. We are concerned with the basic elements and assumptions upon which theories and theoretically informed modes of analysis are built. Can we assume that scholars are able to extend the frontiers of inquiry by pressing to deeper levels of analysis in reconsidering the foundations upon which inquiry is based? Rather than dealing with "values," for example, as an undefined term, can we address the problem of normative inquiry, as the first six essays of this work have done, to indicate how human beings might make interpersonal comparisons to establish the meaning of value terms (V. Ostrom, 1984)?

By clarifying the heuristic at the foundation of theoretical modes of analysis, we can be much more explicit in knowing how to take hold of a problem and proceed with an analysis. Further, we can move beyond simple universal models and recognize that the elements making up a theoretical model can be varied, giving us a much wider range of permutations in theoretical analyses. If heuristics are properly grounded, we should achieve the further capability of translating from one theoretical formulation to another.

If we were to rely on such a heuristic, we could then draw upon Karl Popper's (1964) suggestion that all human inquiry is addressed to problematical situations. From a choice perspective, analysts can confront problematical situations by first diagnosing the problem and then exploring the potential alternatives that might alter the problematical situation and achieve a resolution—if one is conceivable. From a positive perspective, an analyst can view hypothetical actors in hypothetical action situations, postulate a likely choice of strategies given incentives and constraints, and then infer what consequences will follow from actions taken, given a choice of strategy. The more fully the structure of a decision/action situation can be specified, the closer we can come to specifying the structure of constraints and incentives that will confront actors in such situations. Once these are understood, it is possible to take a game-theoretical (or an equivalent) perspective and anticipate how actors will choose strategies and act within problematical situations.

If conditions about actors in situations can be specified and applied to hypothetical situations, we have an abstract model. If those conditions are allowed to vary depending on the attributes of existing situations, we have the makings of a theoretical analysis applicable to empirical exigencies. So long as the human condition reflects exigencies that apply to all of mankind and human beings confront prototypical situations common to all societies—(1) exchange relationships; (2) teamwork; (3) the organization of teams of teams; (4) circumstances associated with communal or collective use of common-pool resources, facilities and properties, and public goods and services; (5) conflict and conflict resolution; and (6) rule-ruler-ruled relationships—we have rudimentary tools with which we can work to advance the frontiers of inquiry about the nature and constitution of order in human societies (Dietz, 2005).

Such an approach is amenable to inquiry in relation to many levels and foci of analysis. Thus, it affords opportunities to penetrate social "reality" viewed from different vantage points without having to distance ourselves from social "reality" or heap facts upon facts in painting idiosyncratic word pictures. Redundancy in pursuing different modes of analysis is necessary if we are to learn both how to generalize about and how to cope with great multitudes of facts. We would expect to find patterns of complexity, diversity, and complementarity. We need to have recourse to different levels and foci of analysis, which are commensurable with one another, in order to make comparisons and allow ourselves to be confronted by the puzzles and anomalies that arise in human experience and the critical assessments of others. Tolerating great gaps between theory and practice implies that we have so distanced ourselves from reality that we are no longer informed observers of human societies.

Eucken did not resolve his own challenge. I doubt that any one of us will succeed in doing so. Rather, Eucken's challenge reminds us that ways of thinking about social reality need as much critical attention as what is being observed. These matters are contestable among reasonable human beings and must continue to be contestable so long as human beings are fallible.

We may also draw upon Radnitzky's and Bartley's views of the task faced by fallible observers in their *Evolutionary Epistemology* (1987: 287–288, 309). Concepts and practices can be distinguished. So can concepts of truth and certainty. Choices in choice situations always involve uncertainties. Although the fallibilist does not presume to know the truth, any fallibilist stresses the possibility of error and thus "presupposes the concept of falsity and hence that of truth" (p. 287). The idea of empirical testing would be meaningless without an implicit concept of truth. We rely on the critical capabilities that can be mobilized by others to press onward to deeper levels and new frontiers of inquiry so that we reach a better approximation of what we might respectively conceive as being true. We make progress by listening to the contestable arguments advanced by others to improve our own intellectual tools and advance beyond the limits of the intellectual vision we had previously achieved. We learn, unlearn, and continue to learn as we extend the horizons of our inquiries. In doing so, we discard ideas we had used to think about ourselves and our world and develop new ideas to "transcend our old selves" and to function as human beings who continue to grow and develop intellectually, emotionally, and creatively (p. 451).

The scientific enterprise advances as we progressively adapt our way of thinking to extend what we can "see." Fallibilists will prefer the approach that successfully withstands criticism while appreciating that it is critics who offer the stimulus to "cognitive progress" (p. 288). We are more concerned with the viability of ideas than with the justification of ideas. Justification can be distinguished from criticism. The capacity to withstand criticism or to revise in the presence of criticism is important for the warrantability of ideas and their development in an evolutionary epistemology. From the perspective of the observer and the practitioner, the capacity to withstand criticism would enhance the warrantability of ideas and their usefulness to inform practice in the art of the possible. As both Hans Albert (1986) and James Buchanan (1975; 1979: chap. 5) have variously emphasized, the frontiers of human choice extend from the seemingly trivial choices in everyday life to choices of ways of life and ways of thinking.

All these levels of choice must be understood by human beings as they live their everyday lives in whatever they do if they are to achieve the autonomy of first being their own governors functioning in self-governing societies. A critical aspect turns upon the question of how observers of and participants in self-governing societies think of and experience themselves as they relate to other human beings: as individuals struggling for advancement to gain positions of dominance and become masters of others; or as fellow citizens (colleagues, comrades) pursuing courses of inquiry in addressing and resolving problematical situations in human societies.

An awareness of paradigm problems is but a step along the way toward developing a critical self-consciousness of both the opportunities and constraints inherent in the human condition and the universe in which we live. How we think about and experience ourselves is an essential component in the analytical situation of both the observer and the observed. When we use the method of normative inquiry inherent in the golden rule, we learn how methodological individualism can be used to create cognitive links among observers and the observed in studying the nature and constitution of order in human societies (V. Ostrom, 1986).

If human societies are to create good systems of governance through reflection and choice, priority must be given to the creation of opportunities for the kinds of participation that may produce an "enlightened" civic culture capable of self-government. Civic enlightenment of this sort implies not only individual learning but also a collective advance through shared inquiries and productive efforts to deal with shared problems. Public administration under such circumstances needs to be conceptualized as public entrepreneurship in the open public realms of a vibrant civic culture in which principles of equity, responsibility, a covenantally based willingness to judge and be judged as well as conceptions of obligation and right inform our actions (Kuhnert, 2001; V. Ostrom, 2006).

The primary burden of public entrepreneurship rests in mobilizing these principles of reflection and choice in a world of great ecological—and as a consequence, cultural, and linguistic—diversity. Natural resources and human communities must be governed in ways that are cognizant and respectful of the varied conditions of life on the thin crust of our volatile, significantly unexplored planet. Many ecologies, including human ecologies, are resilient, but our detours to perfect strategies of command and control have left us with too little knowledge of the public endeavors that constitute enduring communities. The intellectual crises identified in the first two editions of this book have, perhaps, global roots; certainly they have had global effects. The public entrepreneurship and enlightenment of the twenty-first century is not simply the province of professionals in policy and politics. A new science of politics demands artisanship in associations from local to global communities if we are to surpass the illusions that governed in the last millennial turn of humanity.

Notes

Chapter 1: The Crisis of Confidence

1. Several of the essays in Robert K. Merton et al.'s *Reader in Bureaucracy* (1952) reflect the experiences of social scientists with wartime bureaucracy. So do several of the case studies in Harold Stein's *Public Administration and Policy Development* (1952).

2. Dwight Waldo has responded to my comment here by indicating:

> But what I meant to say, and still do vigorously contend, is this: No paradigm of a *disciplinary* nature can solve the problem. This is because public administration is not a scientific discipline. It is a profession in a loose sense, a collection of related professions, which can do, and must use paradigms, techniques, and so forth, from *many* disciplines.
>
> Put another way, if we need a paradigm it should be that appropriate to a profession rather than that appropriate to a scientific discipline. My historic analogy has been to "the medical profession"; I would qualify that nowadays by making my analogy "the health professions." (Personal communication; Waldo's emphasis)

I am perfectly willing to accept Waldo's position on the assumption that problems of water-resource administration may require different bodies of knowledge from police administration, for example. Yet we are confronted with the question of whether such disparate fields of administration do face comparable organizational problems associated with externalities, common property resources, and public goods. If so, there may be a general logic of collective action that is applicable to both types of problems.

3. American Society for Public Administration, *News and Views* 20 (October 1970): 5.

4. Niskanen (1971) indicates some of the differences that voting rules will make on the expected output of public agencies. See generally his discussion in chapter 13 and following.

Chapter 2:   The Intellectual Mainstream in American Public Administration

1. In light of Daniel W. Martin's "The Fading Legacy of Woodrow Wilson" (1988), I want to emphasize that I am not asserting that Wilson's contemporaries looked to him for inspiration as the founding scholar in the study of public administration. He and Van Riper (1983) are correct in asserting that early scholars did not cite Wilson. Yet the underlying presuppositions associated with a theory of state, which presumes a unitary sovereign, pervade the work of Goodnow and other leading scholars in the field: Wilson does not share Bagehot's skepticism about bureaucracy. Siedentopf (1983) is critical of Wilson's treatment of the German cameralists, but as Toonen (1987) has demonstrated, many contemporary European scholars in public administration have reconstructed the historical antecedents of administrative theory to conform to doctrinal presuppositions, as their American colleagues have done, rather than conform to the historical facts about those antecedents.

2. Wilson also observes: "It is quite safe to say that were it possible to call together again the members of that wonderful Convention [of 1787] to view the work of their hand in the light of the century that has tested it, they would be the first to admit that the only fruit of dividing power has been to make it irresponsible" (Wilson, 1956: 187).

3. So far as administrative functions are concerned/Wilson asserts, "all governments have a strong structural likeness; more than that, if they are to be uniformly useful and efficient, they *must* have a strong structural likeness" (Wilson, 1956: 218; Wilson's emphasis).

4. Wilson refers to a three-stage pattern of political development, which he assumes to be applicable to the "chief nations of
the modern world." These include (1) a period of absolute rule,
(2) a period of constitutional development, and (3) a period of administrative development (Wilson, 1956: 204).

5. Weber's theory of bureaucracy did not have substantial
influence on American study of public administration until after World War II, when his translated work became available to
American scholars. The generality of the Wilsonian paradigm is
indicated, however, by the congruence between Wilson's and Weber's formulations.

6. The "monocratic principle" also implies "monopolization
of legitimate violence by the political organization which finds
its culmination in the modern concept of the state as the ultimate
source of every kind of legitimacy of the use of physical force"
(Rheinstein, 1954: 347). The persistent definition of political authority as a monopoly over the legitimate use of force indicates a
monocratic or monocentric bias in modern political theory. Can
a federal system with separation of powers be properly characterized as a "monopoly" over the legitimate use of force? I think
not.

7. Crozier (1964), in his chapter "The Bureaucratic System of
Organization," refers to Weber's place in the "paradoxical" view
of bureaucracy, which runs through much of Western political
analysis. See the frontispiece for a statement of the "paradox."

8. The disparity between Weber's conceptualization of bureaucracy as an ideal type of organization necessary for efficiency and
for development of a rational basis for modern civilization and the
consequences he anticipates as following from its perfection in a
"fully developed" form is difficult to fathom. He implies that a
system of bureaucratic rule is necessarily the fate of modern man.
He would thus affirm Rousseau's observation that "man is born to
be free but is everywhere in bondage." Such a conclusion is consistent with a "monocratic" or "monocentric" structure of political
organization based on a theory of absolute sovereignty. If all political authority resides in an absolute sovereign and if all others are
equal in their state of subjection, then Weber's conclusions follow.
His portrayal of a "fully developed bureaucracy" is surprisingly
congruent with Tocqueville's discussion of democratic despotism

in the Fourth Book of Volume 2 of *Democracy in America*.

Bendix (1960) addresses this anomaly in the concluding chapter of his biography of Weber. Bendix argues that Weber's concept of "bureaucracy under legal domination" must be distinguished from his political analysis of bureaucratization as a different intellectual exercise (p. 456). If we hold to Bendix's position, then bureaucracy as an ideal type assumes perfectly obedient functionaries. The maintenance of legal rationality does not follow except as it is postulated as a limiting condition in a logical exercise. If this is the case, Weber fails to grasp the problem of indicating the logically necessary conditions that will increase the probability that a political system will conduct its affairs in accordance with rules of law. As Bendix indicates, "Bureaucratization becomes compatible with a system of legal domination only if officials are prevented from usurping the political and legislative process" (p. 457). But what is to prevent officials from usurping the political and legislative process when a monopoly exists over the legitimate use of force? Thus it is an open question whether bureaucratization is consistent with a rational legal order or whether bureaucratization is a prelude to human bondage. We shall return to this issue in chapter 5.

9. Victor A. Thompson's *Modern Organization* (1961) is a major exception.

10. This characterization of research in the "mainstream" of American public administration is largely associated with the administrative survey movement. Currin Shields's (1952) article "The American Tradition of Empirical Collectivism" points to quite a different tradition of analysis, which Shields summarizes:

> The empirical collectivist assumes that collective action should be employed whenever necessary to solve public problems, but that the minimal action required to dispose of the problem should be undertaken. In considering a policy question, therefore, he concentrates his attention on the actual situation in an effort to fathom the all-important character of the problem and the conditions of its solution. His initial query is: is this a public problem? No a priori answer can be given to this question; the answer turns on the situation itself. If it is decided that the problem is of public concern,

then his next question is: which agent of the community is best able to deal with this problem? Is a local private agency, a county board, a national private organization (such as the American Red Cross), a state bureau, or a national agency best suited? Again he must examine the problem situation to arrive at an answer. His final query is: what sort of action is required to dispose of the problem? Each possibility he must canvass, and on the basis of past experience and future expectations he must select the form of collective action which appears most appropriate. Questions such as these the empirical collectivist can feasibly discuss with his fellows. Their discussion can center on differences of opinion about actual situations, and these differences they can resolve by appeals to experience, by examining the evidence. Thus, they can arrive at propitious decisions regarding collective action, and can settle, in a democratic manner, policy questions. (pp. 117–118)

Shields also indicates the "empirical collectivists" rely on a "'rule of economy': the minimal action to dispose of a problem — and no more — should be undertaken collectively" and "public action taken to dispose of a problem should redound to the benefit of the entire community" (p. 105).

Shields observes that "the empirical collectivist prefers voluntary to mandatory action, inducement to compulsion, restriction to prohibition. And if government action is required, he prefers public regulation of private enterprise to governmental operation of public enterprise" (p. 106).

Finally, Shields observes that the empirical collectivist's preoccupation with the welfare of the entire community leads him to take the point of view of the consumer: "The empirical collectivist is able to espouse the public interest as it is reflected in the welfare of citizens as consumers" (p. 105).

The tradition of empirical collectivism is sharply at variance with the mainstreams of American public administration. Benjamin Franklin, Alexis de Tocqueville, and Frederick Jackson Turner reflect that tradition in their writing as do a variety of practicing administrators such as John W. Powell, Elwood Mead, and William Hammond Hall and scholars such as John Dewey and Francis

W. Coker. *None* of their works has come to occupy a position of central significance in the study of American public administration.

11. The *Report* states, "In a democracy consent may be achieved readily, though not without *some* effort, as it is the cornerstone of the constitution" (p. 3; my emphasis). By contrast, "efficient management" is a matter of "peculiar significance."

Given the serious challenge to democratic government and constitutional rule being posed by the rise of totalitarian regimes during the 1930s, it is striking that the Brownlow Committee could so confidently dismiss consideration affecting "the consent of the governed" and the maintenance of constitutional rule. Such perspectives were congruent with its theory that the field of politics is outside a proper concern for administration. The commissioners apparently were not prepared to consider the possibility that a fully developed system of "efficient management" based on their "canons of efficiency" could transform constitutional rule into a problematical condition.

12. Simon (1952: 1130) clarifies his distinction of "group," "organization," and "institutions" in the following observation: "In such a nest of Chinese blocks the smallest multi-person units are the primary groups; the largest are institutions ('the economic system,' 'the state') and whole societies. We will restrict the term 'organization' to systems that are larger than primary groups, smaller than institutions."

13. Where the amount of resources and the organizational objectives are given, outside the control of the administrator, efficiency becomes the controlling determinant of administrative choice [within those constraints] (Simon, 1965a: 122).

14. See the discussion of the problems of institutional failure in chapter 3. The tragedy of the commons, for example, can occur in the absence of appropriate institutional constraints. Thus individualistic choice in the management of a common-pool resource in which demand exceeds supply would lead to "irrational" behavior when viewed in relation to other decision-making arrangements for the management of such resources.

Chapter 3: The Work of the Contemporary Political Economists

1. Discussions of professionalism and bureaucratic organization often make a direct association between the two sets of phenomena. Thus much of the discussion of professionalism among police is associated with centralization of authority and large-scale organization. Professionalization can also be treated as a separate variable from organizational structure. Both medicine and law are frequently practiced in the context of relatively small organizations in which relationships are organized through marketlike transactions. Other professions, such as the military, are organized predominantly in large-scale organizations. If professionalization and organizational structure are treated as independent variables, we would expect different structures of opportunities to prevail among superintendents of schools and city managers than in a highly bureaucratized structure such as the military service or the foreign service.

2. Most of the political economists are associated with the Public Choice Society and publish a journal, *Public Choice.*

3. In taking the perspective of an "omniscient observer," an economist confines his or her use of an individualist calculus only to market structures and relies on an assumption that general policies affecting social welfare can be determined by an omniscient and omnicompetent despot who can maximize social utility by taking account of all utility preferences. The assumption of perfect information used in formulating a model of perfect competition is essentially applied to the problem of collective choice made by a benevolent despot. Economists who use the analytical device of the omniscient observer find Hobbes's theory of sovereignty congenial for their purposes.

Most scholars in the Public Choice tradition prefer to apply an individualistic calculus to problems of collective choice in which individuals have access to less than perfect information. Decision-making arrangements such as elections, representation, and legislation are mechanisms for translating individual preferences into collective choices.

4. This and the previous paragraph have drawn more fire

from critics than any other portion of *The Intellectual Crisis*. The model of man is at the core of Robert J. Golembiewski's "A Critique of 'Democratic Administration' and Its Supporting Ideation" (1977a). This is a critical issue because much of neoclassical price theory used extreme rationality assumptions associated with perfect information. I personally reject those assumptions; and all of my own work relies on an assumption of human fallibility. There is no place for learning when assumptions of perfect information are used. These two paragraphs do *not* rely on extreme rationality assumptions. In "Some Developments in the Study of Market Choice, Public Choice, and Institutional Choice" (1989), I more fully develop the distinctions made in different traditions of economic analysis.

5. The classical theory of administration is essentially devoid of a theory appropriate to the analysis of problematical situations. In his essay on empirical collectivists, Shields (1952) emphasizes that the structure of situations provides the context for conceptualizing policy problems. John Dewey (1927) defines a public as coming into being in an effort to control indirect consequences of actions that impinge upon persons not directly involved. His concept is closely related to the concept of externalities used by political economists.

6. This position stands in contrast to Wilson's presumption that there is but one rule of "good" administration for all governments alike, or Weber's presumption regarding the technical superiority of bureaucracy over any other form of organization (see Ashby, 1962).

7. This structure of relationships applies to air pollution, water pollution, the exploitation of fishery resources, and many types of facilities. The incentive for the individual is to take advantage of any available opportunity. If one individual does not, others will. Thus the exploitation of a common-pool resource such as the whale stock in the world's oceans may proceed to a point at which the species are exterminated. Short-term advantage deviates from long-term advantage. For people to take advantage of long-term opportunities requires a modification in decision-making arrangements so that the community of individuals involved can convert a negative-sum game into a cooperative or positive-sum game.

When the relevant field of effects includes a large number of small public jurisdictions with no overlapping jurisdiction capable of regulating the conduct of the several smaller ones relative to that field of effects, the tragedy of the commons can occur in competition among the several smaller jurisdictions. In the case of whaling, nation-states may be too small to regulate the harvest of whales. Municipalities and counties may be inadequate units for dealing with problems of air pollution. Thus, Crozier (1964) is correct in indicating that the American political system is highly susceptible to institutional dysfunctions, which he characterized as the "vicious circle of decentralization" (p. 246) and which I have followed Garrett Hardin in calling the tragedy of the commons.

A solution to such pathologies can be attained by seeking recourse to a larger jurisdiction, which will bound the relevant field of effects. Such solutions, however, need not involve the creation of only one jurisdiction to the exclusion of all smaller jurisdictions. Reliance on overlapping jurisdictions is an alternative mode of organization. Still another alternative would be to rely on the decision-making capability of the next larger unit of government. Thus reliance on states to regulate interstate commerce may engender conflicts reminiscent of a negative-sum game. Federal authority to regulate interstate commerce may be necessary to avoid destructive conflict among states. As economic relations became national in scope, increasing reliance on Federal regulation was necessary for productive relationships. As economic relations become international in scope, we can contemplate a competitive rivalry among nations, which can take on the characteristics of a negative-sum game. Appropriate solutions will require capabilities to take joint action at the international level.

8. The concept of span of control, which was used to explain hierarchical structures in the traditional theory of administration, implies a substantial limit to the capability of any one supervisor to exercise control over a number of subordinates. Tullock relies on this limit to generate a theory of institutional weakness and institutional failure associated with bureaucratic organizations. The traditional theory of public administration failed to draw such inferences even though the substantial limits on control were implied by the concept of span of control.

Simon pointed out that a loss of information and control would apply to the number of tiers in a hierarchical structure as well as the number of subordinates reporting to a single superior. Thus, increasing the number of tiers in a hierarchy would lead to a loss of information and control as between the top level of command and those at the lower echelons in any organization. Narrowing the command structure at each level of organization would lead to a loss of information and control by increasing the number of levels in an organization. Simon's formulation (1965a: 24–28) suggests serious limits to the aggregate size of a bureaucratic organization.

The elements for formulating a theory of institutional weakness and institutional failure applicable to bureaucratic organizations were inherent in the traditional theory of public administration, but the logic of that theory was not developed until Tullock's work. Weber anticipated the consequences but failed to provide the logical connection between conditions and consequences. Tocqueville in his *Old Regime and the French Revolution* (1955) provides an extended description of bureaucratic pathologies associated with a highly centralized political regime.

9. The relationship of production of public goods and services to users' preferences implies that various decision-making arrangements for articulating voters' preferences and users' demands have an essential relationship to administrative performance. Voting, representation, legislation, and the availability of various remedies for aggrieved users of public goods and services to enforce demands have significance for administrative conduct. William A. Niskanen Jr. (1971) has begun to explore these relationships.

Political economists would reject the presumption that public administration should be conceptualized apart from the political process inherent in the traditional dichotomy of politics and administration. Instead, they would view various forms of voting, modes of representation, and rules for legislative action as critical processes for translating individual preferences into collective decisions to secure the provision of public goods and services. Thus different voting rules will yield different outputs of public goods and services. They would in turn be concerned with the decision rules available to individual persons for invoking and enforcing demands for the provision of public goods and services. See my discussion of the "any-one rule" in *The Political Theory of a Compound Republic* (1987).

10. It is possible for an inappropriate tax policy to exacerbate rather than relieve problems of congestion in the long run. G. S. Tolley (1969) argues that the use of Federal funds to relieve congestion may have the opposite effect. He argues that in such a situation, "the receiving entity will then have incentive to overspend. If large cities succeed in overspending relative to small cities, the tendency may be away from rather than toward desirable city size" (p. 36). In addition, he argues that the "danger of overbuilding in large cities is heightened if facilities are built in response to projection of travel demands assumed to be independent of the effect of facilities themselves on city growth." Both factors when combined lead to a *cumulative* effect, which moves in the *wrong* direction (p. 36).

11. So far as I know, no literature by political economists addresses the specific issue of authority regarding administrative reorganization. The Buchanan and Tullock (1962) analysis of decision rules implies that reliance on presidential authority to formulate reorganization plans subject only to a congressional veto is the equivalent of legislation by one-man rule subject to congressional veto.

Reference to periodic needs to "shake up" the bureaucracy presumably implies deprivation costs for those who are shaken up. How do such experiences affect the productivity of the public service? Political economists are inclined to ask such questions about the practice of administrative reorganization.

12. The possibility of diversely structured systems of ordered relationships runs through the work of many different organization theorists. Ashby (1962) distinguishes among "fully-joined systems," "iterated systems," and "multi-stable systems" and considers the relative adaptability of each. Christopher Alexander deals broadly with problems of organization and design in his article "A City Is Not a Tree" (1965) and in *Notes on the Synthesis of Form* (1964). Michael Polanyi in *The Logic of Liberty* (1951) explores the concept of polycentricity as the basis for spontaneous order as distinguished from hierarchy in a corporate order.

These different approaches to order have led to a consideration of whether an "invisible hand" operates in the public as well as the private sector. Lindblom (1959; 1965), McKean

(1965), and Bish (1968; 1969) have advanced arguments on behalf of the invisible hand in government. Duggal (1966) challenged the contention. Tocqueville speaks of an invisible hand
when he observes: "Nothing is more striking to the European traveler in the United States than the absence of what we
term the government or the administration. Written laws exist
in America, and one sees the daily execution of them; but although everything moves regularly, the mover can nowhere be
discovered. The hand that directs the social machinery is invisible" (Tocqueville, 1945: 1:70). An invisible hand can become
operable in the governance of human affairs to the extent that
bargaining, negotiation, and competitive rivalry can be used to
regulate the conduct of diverse public enterprises in relation
to one another. Thus public universities govern relationships
with one another through a variety of voluntary associations,
contractual understandings, and forms of competitive rivalry
rather than by reference to the command of superiors in an
overarching bureaucracy.

13. Daniel Elazar (1971) objects to the use of the term "decentralization" to refer to the authority exercised by smaller
units of government in a federal system. He contends that decentralization implies an allocation of authority from the center by a superior authority to a subordinate set of authorities.
Thus he argues that federalism implies "non-centralization" of
authority. His argument is sound. A federal system necessarily implies overlapping jurisdictions and concurrent exercise
of authority. Lindblom (1965) makes a similar point in con-
trasting central and noncentral coordination.

Chapter 4: A Theory of Democratic Administration: The Rejected Alternative

1. Tocqueville wrote of "decentralized" as against "centralized" administration to refer to what conforms to Weber's distinction between "democratic" and "bureaucratic" administration.
Tocqueville's references to centralization and decentralization are
apt characterizations except for one unfortunate implication. Centralization is often juxtaposed to decentralization in the sense that
we sometimes speak of centralization *versus* decentralization. The

terms need not be mutually exclusive in a federal political system in which several regimes coexist at different levels of government. The very structure of a federal political system implies overlapping jurisdictions and simultaneous reference to elements of both "centralization" *and* "decentralization." The characteristics that Weber identifies with democratic administration are precisely those that most impressed Tocqueville.

2. Tocqueville conceptualizes a democratic society to be one in which a strong equality of conditions exists among the people. He clearly recognizes that government in a democratic society requires radical conditions of inequality in decision-making capabilities. Thus, the disparity between the power of individuals living in a mass society and those vested with governmental prerogative in a highly centralized political structure is so overpowering that he despaired for the survival of liberty or free institutions in a centralized democratic society. He saw hope in the American system of overlapping jurisdictions and fragmentation of authority as permitting a sufficient dispersion of authority for freedom to exist in a democratic society. See especially Tocqueville's conclusions in the Fourth Book of Volume 2 of *Democracy in America.*

3. These essays in particular inspired Leonard White's historical studies in American national administration.

4. Thus politics cannot be viewed as *apart* from administration. Administrators as public servants or public employees are exposed to review and reconsideration of their decisions by other persons functioning in many different decision structures who occupy potential veto positions in relation to their decisions. An administrator selects a strategy in pursuing opportunities with an awareness that any act represents a move in a series of simultaneous games. If the game of administration is dominated by an exclusive calculus of pleasing superiors, the consequences will be different than if public administrators stand exposed to the scrutiny of common councils representing citizens, to inquiries by grand juries, to actions by citizens in courts of law, and to public scrutiny by a free press, as well as to the scrutiny of other executive officers and agencies.

5. It is essential that we recall Tocqueville's definition of a democratic society as being one characterized by a condition of social and economic equality. If we were to assume that great-

er social equality exists among members of Soviet society than in American society, then by Tocqueville's definition the Soviet Union would be a more democratic society than the United States. I have used Max Weber's defining characteristics for democratic administration to have the same meaning that Tocqueville used in defining "decentralized administration." Tocqueville would characterize the Soviet Union as a democratic society governed by a highly centralized administration controlled by an autocratic or self-perpetuating government.

Chapter 5: The Choice of Alternative Futures

1. Dwight Waldo in *The Administrative State* (1948: 36) observes: "Influenced by British experience and British writers, Woodrow Wilson . . . and many others had contrasted our system of separation of powers unfavorably with cabinet government, and urged the need for stronger executive leadership. Students home from the Continent were anxious to find a formula that would enable democracy to secure the manifest advantages of autocracy. The traditional separation of powers became the *bete noir* of American political science, and exaltation of the powers of the executive branch its Great White Hope."

2. John Austin in *The Province of Jurisprudence Determined* (1955) formulates the concept of positive law as that which is enforceable. He argues that constitutional law, so-called, is positive morality, not positive law. Austin's argument is consistent with that of Hobbes, but Austin does not press his analysis very far in relation to the political structure represented by what he calls a composite state. See generally his Lecture VI.

3. A strong antilegalist bias runs through the traditional study of American public administration. The problem of designing a political system that could enforce constitutional law as against those who exercise the prerogatives of government is never considered. Wilson (1887: 207) impatiently observed: "Once a nation has embarked in the business of manufacturing constitutions, it finds it exceedingly difficult to close out that business and open for the public a bureau of skilled, economical administration. There seems to be no end to the tinkering of constitutions."

The effort of other Americans to "tinker" with constitutions in the late nineteenth and early twentieth centuries could also be viewed as a critical factor in accomplishing reforms that substantially reduced the opportunities for machine politics and boss rule. Among these modifications were the introduction of the Australian ballot, direct primaries, the initiative, referendum, and recall, the popular election of U.S. senators, and other such measures.

Goodnow (1900) reflects the same bias in his reference to extralegal institutions as though any undertaking not explicitly authorized in statutory law were extralegal.

White (1948) also assumed that "the study of administration should start from the base of management rather than the foundation of law" (p. xiii). Yet paradoxically, White's writings drew heavily upon legal materials and public documents. Administration was still set on a foundation of law, but no effort was made to comprehend the relationship of administrative structures to the basic design of institutional arrangements in the American political system. Neither White, Goodnow, nor Wilson pondered the issue posed by Hamilton in the first paragraph of *The Federalist*, where he raises the question, "Are societies of men really capable or not of establishing good government from reflection and choice, or are they forever destined to depend for their constitution on accident and force?" (*Federalist* 1. I have transformed an indirect question to a direct question).

4. Quoted by Alexander Bickel in a review of Gerald T. Dunne, *Justice Story and the Rise of the Supreme Court*, in *New York Times Book Review*, May 30, 1971, p. 3.

5. The section "The Constitution of Self-Governing Public Enterprises" in chapter 3 is relevant for a consideration of constitutional decision-making perspectives as against other political perspectives. Constitutional decision making, according to Buchanan and Tullock (1962), is based on "conceptual unanimity," and the relevant criterion for Buchanan and Tullock is "Pareto optimality." Pareto optimality implies that decision rules should be chosen that will lead to advances in human welfare in the sense that no one will be left worse off.

John Rawls (1963; 1967), in a series of articles dealing with the criterion of justice as fairness, suggests that the choice of decision rules be made on an assumption that each individual has an equal probability of being subject to decisions taken by his enemies rather than his friends. If decision-making arrangements can be devised so that one's adversaries are exposed to a structural rig of the game that leads them to make reasonably good decisions, then we can expect some degree of success in devising appropriate organizational structures for human associations.

A person who invents a new game and expects that game to be successful must make certain assumptions about the capabilities of potential players and about fairness in the play of the game. Those who play the game select their strategies in order to win. The perspectives are very different. But if some set of players reaches the conclusion that a game is structurally unfair, those who bear the burdens of unfairness would rationally prefer not to play the game if they have a choice. Peasants through much of the world have long since learned that the political game in most societies is rigged against them.

The constitutional decision maker is concerned about the essential conditions of justice and fairness that apply to the rig of the game for collective decision making. The politician playing a particular election game, for example, is concerned with winning. The test of the appropriateness of a constitutional decision rule providing for popular elections is whether winning and losing over the long run without regard to particular politicians engenders the appropriate outcomes in assuring a just or fair allocation of resources in the provision of public goods and services.

Efforts to formulate legislation for the organization of water districts in California, for example, can be understood from a constitutional decision-making perspective (V. Ostrom and E. Ostrom, 1970). One reaches different conclusions about the meaning of the California efforts using a constitutional decision-making perspective than most administrative analysts would in prescribing reorganization in accordance with the traditional principles of public administration.

6. I deliberately chose to confine these lectures to the paradigm problem in *American* public administration. A problem of vastly different proportions would be raised if this discussion were extended to a comparative analysis of political systems and their

reform. The existence of common assumptions that are relevant to the design of various political institutions implies that the development of a predictive political theory applicable to the study of different administrative systems is conceivable. The evidence of institutional weakness and failure characteristic of large-scale bureaucracies is widespread. So is evidence regarding phenomena characteristic of the tragedy of the commons.

The much more difficult problem is whether reforms can be undertaken that will lead to the revolutionary transformation of one system into a different system based on a radically different design. Changes in the structure of organizational arrangements cannot occur independently of the political knowledge that is relevant to organizational practice among the persons involved. A system of bureaucratic administration cannot be transformed into a system of democratic administration except over a long period of time. Individuals in a society must acquire the knowledge, skills, and moral judgment that are necessary for undertaking joint efforts to realize common benefits. The work of Danilo Dolci is especially suggestive for students interested in this problem.

If (1) the scourge of war could be avoided on the European continent for several generations, (2) the European Community were able to negotiate a series of constitutional settlements with joint benefits (net after costs) accruing to all European peoples, and (3) appropriate European political structures were devised to permit the development of a European system of positive constitutional law, then I can imagine the gradual evolution of a system of democratic administration on the European continent.

Revolutions like the Soviet Revolution do not represent basic changes in the constitutional structure of a political system. The tzarist state was destroyed, but the Soviet state has all the attributes of Hobbes's *Leviathan* with an absolute sovereign and a new elite to function as the ruling class. The major difference is that the Soviet state has fewer symptoms of bureaucratic senility than its tzarist predecessors. Tocqueville's *Old Regime and the French Revolution* (1955) documents the continuity of bureaucracy as the central feature of the French constitution through a period of revolutionary change. Crozier's *Bureaucratic Phenomenon* (1964) substantiates its persistence to the present.

The task of fashioning political and administrative institutions for the so-called underdeveloped areas of the world is beyond the competence of American academicians. They can contribute to a political science that others may then use in devising organizational arrangements that are appropriate to an estimate of the opportunity costs inherent in different designs. Much of the literature on administrative development grossly underestimates the costs inherent in central planning and bureaucratic organization. No organizational arrangement is cost-free.

7. See, for example, the article by Albert Sigurdson in the *Toronto Globe and Mail,* December 30, 1970. Sigurdson writes: "Security guard agencies are doing a 60 million dollar business in Canada, double the level of five years ago, and new agencies continue to open across the country." Individuals are also investing heavily in private arms. A recent estimate made by the FBI is that the "private arsenal in U.S. homes now totals 90 million weapons" *(Newsweek,* August 17, 1970, p. 15).

8. *The New York Times* in an editorial on November 11, 1969, refers to a report that disclosed that two-thirds of the abandoned buildings being torn down as "unsafe" were structurally sound and probably capable of rehabilitation. If such an assertion is true, structurally sound buildings are being destroyed for failure to devise institutional arrangements with appropriate incentives for individuals to use and maintain the available housing stock. These conditions prevail amid demands for more housing.

9. A reader of an earlier draft of these lectures raised the question: "Who are the 'individual persons' who form the 'relevant public' of a public administrator? For example, is it the duty of policemen to serve the criminals?" An answer to this question requires an evaluation of the community of persons potentially affected by "criminal" activity and a sense of moral judgment regarding the consequences following from such conduct. To judge unilaterally an act to be "criminal" is contrary to basic precepts of justice. Preliminary procedures are available to take action based on a tentative judgment about the criminality of an act. Both the person who is suspected of being a criminal and the person who is convicted of being a criminal are entitled to

be treated as individual persons deserving of respect in a democratic society.

Andrei Amalrik makes the essential point when he observes in *In voluntary Journey to Siberia* (1970: 112–113):

> A court sentence ought not to be an act of vengeance but the expression of a generally accepted idea of justice. The educational value of a trial lies in convincing the defendant and everyone else that he is being judged in strict accordance with the law and with the ethical standards that man-kind has arrived at during its long history; it certainly does not lie in the Judge tediously haranguing the court or in his crudely defaming the defendant and witnesses. There is even less educational value in trials staged for avowedly propaganda purposes—as an object lesson to others. This is not a way of enlightening people but only of intimidating them, and it brings nothing but discredit upon the courts. When a man is charged with one thing but then accused of something else during the actual trial, this may help the police in achieving their limited aim, but it also results in still further deterioration of the whole system of justice.

If correctional administration is not oriented to the interest of individual persons who may have committed criminal acts, we can expect overwhelming failure in the administration of criminal justice. Correctional authorities require a substantial sense of moral judgment in counseling and working with prison populations. People are more than obedient cogs in machines. The only way to remind ourselves of this moral imperative is to relate ourselves to the individuality of different persons. When that condition becomes impossible, moral conduct is no longer possible.

10. As John Dewey once commented: "The man who wears the shoe knows best that it pinches and where it pinches, even if the expert shoemaker is the best judge of how the trouble is to be remedied" (Dewey, 1927: 207). He might have added that the man who wears the shoe is also the best judge of the appropriateness of the shoemaker's remedy.

Chapter 6: The Continuing Constitutional Crises in American Government

1. We capitalize Executive when referring to the personification of the executive establishment as an aggregate entity in relation to the President as Chief Executive. We also capitalize President when used to personify the "head" of the Executive establishment.

2. Several scholars have begun to assess the increasing use of military forces and heavy armaments in U.S. cities to augment local police forces following new tenets of military doctrine— Military Operations on Urbanized Terrain (MOUT)—developed several decades ago in anticipation of an active military presence in cities around the globe for combat and noncombat missions in "other-than-war conditions." See Warren (2004) for a discussion of the impact of MOUT doctrine on metropolitan governance.

Chapter 7: Intellectual Crises and Beyond

1. Nien Cheng in *Life and Death in Shanghai* (1987; 167) observes: "Since good intentions and sympathy for others often led people into trouble, the Chinese people have developed a new proverb that said, 'the more you do, the more trouble you have; the less you do, the less trouble you have. If you do nothing whatever, you will become a model citizen.'"

2. Steven Runciman in *Byzantine Civilization* (1956: 65) makes the following assessment of the Imperial Constitution of the Byzantine empire: "The Imperial Constitution, The Emperor, elected by the Senate, the Army and the People of Constantinople, to be the Viceroy of God but to rule according to Roman Law, was in many ways illogical and incomplete, but it had the supreme and essential merit that it worked. Its efficiency is remarkably illustrated by the fact that while in the West innumerable writers arose to discuss the difficult problem of Church and State, of Emperors and Kings and Popes and their inter-relations, for centuries Byzantium did not produce a single political theorist. The constitution

worked too well for abstract discussions to be needed." It might be conjectured instead that the emperor as viceroy of God and autocrator left no public space for disputation and contestation to occur with reference to the proper structure of authority relationships in Byzantine society. Silence is construed by Runciman as efficiency. In the absence of intellectual debates, contestations, in shaping shared communities of understanding, Byzantium failed to generate and maintain the self-governing capabilities that had earlier been achieved in the Greco-Roman city-states. When Constantinople was conquered by the Turks, the Byzantine empire collapsed without residual governing structures to maintain the continuity of the Byzantine civilization as a civilization.

References

Acheson, James. 2003. *Capturing the Commons: Devising Institutions to Manage the Maine Lobster Industry.* Hanover, NH: University Press of New England.

Agrawal, Arun. 2005. *Environmentality: Technologies of Government and the Making of Subjects.* Durham, NC: Duke University Press.

Albert, Hans. 1986. *Freiheit und Ordnung.* Tubingen: J. C. B. Mohr (Vortrage und Aufsatze/Walter Eucken Institut, no. 109).

Alexander, Christopher. 1964. *Notes on the Synthesis of Form.* Cambridge, MA: Harvard University Press.

———. 1965. "A City Is Not a Tree." *Architectural Forum* 122 (April): 58–62, and ibid. (May 1965): 58–61.

Aligica, Paul. 2005. "Institutional Analysis and Economic Policy Notes on the Applied Agenda of the Bloomington School." *Journal of Economic Behavior and Organization* 57(2): 159–166.

Allen, Barbara. 2005. *Tocqueville, Covenant, and the Democratic Revolution: Harmonizing Earth with Heaven.* Lanham, MD: Lexington Press.

Altshuler, Alan A. 1970. *Community Control: The Black Demand for Participation in Large American Cities.* New York: Pegasus.

Amalrik, Andrei. 1970. *Involuntary Journey to Siberia.* New York: Harcourt Brace Jovanovich.

Anderson, William. 1925. *American City Government.* New York: H. Holt.

———. 1942. *The Units of Government in the United States: An Enumeration and Analysis.* Chicago: Public Administration Service.

Andersson, Krister P. 2004. "Who Talks with Whom? The Role of Repeated Interactions in Decentralized Forest Governance." *World Development* 32(2): 233–249.

Arendt, Hannah. 1963. *On Revolution.* New York: Viking Press.

Arrow, Kenneth. [1951] 1963. *Social Choice and Individual Value.* New Haven, CT: Yale University Press.

Ashby, W. Ross. 1956. *An Introduction to Cybernetics.* New York: John Wiley.

———. 1960. *Design for a Brain: The Origin of Adaptive Behavior.* 2d ed. New York: John Wiley.

———. 1962. "Principles of the Self-Organizing System." In H. Von Foerster and G. W. Zopf, eds., *Principles of Self-Organization.* New York: Macmillan, pp. 255–278.

Auer, Matthew. 1998. "Agency Reform as Decision Process: The Reengineering of the Agency for International Development." *Policy Sciences* 31: 81–105.

Austin, John. 1955. *The Province of Jurisprudence Determined.* H. L. A. Hart, ed. London: Weidenfeld and Nicolson.

Ayres, Robert U., and Allen V. Kneese. 1969. "Production, Consumption and Externalities." *American Economic Review* 59 (June): 282–297.

Bagehot, Walter. 1964. *The English Constitution.* R. H. S. Crossman, ed. London: C. A. Watts.

Bain, Joe S. 1959. *Industrial Organization.* Berkeley: University of California Press.

Barnard, Chester I. 1938. *The Functions of the Executive.* Cambridge, MA: Harvard University Press.

Beck, Henry. 1970. "The Rationality of Redundancy." *Comparative Politics* 3 (January): 469–478.

Bendix, Reinhard. 1960. *Max Weber: An Intellectual Portrait.* Garden City, NY: Doubleday.

Berman, Harold. 1983. *Law and Revolution: The Formation of the Western Legal Tradition.* Cambridge, MA: Harvard University Press.

Bish, Robert L. 1968. "A Comment on V. P. Duggal's 'Is There an Unseen Hand in Government?'" *Annals of Public and Co-operative Economy* 39 (January–March): 89–94.

———. 1969. "The American Public Economy as a Single Firm:

Reply to Duggal." *Annals of Public and Co-operative Economy* 40 (July–September): 361–365.

———. 1971. *The Public Economy of Metropolitan Areas.* Chicago: Markham.

Bish, Robert L., and Vincent Ostrom. 1973. *Understanding Urban Government: Metropolitan Reform Reconsidered.* Washington, DC: American Enterprise Institute.

Blau, Peter L. 1956. *Bureaucracy in Modern Society.* New York: Random House.

Blomquist, William, and Elinor Ostrom. 1985. "Institutional Capacity and the Resolution of a Commons Dilemma." *Policy Studies Review* 5 (November): 383–393.

Blomquist, William, Edella Schlager, and Tanya Heikkila. 2004. *Common Waters, Diverging Streams: Linking Institutions and Water Management in Arizona, California, and Colorado.* Washington, DC: Resources for the Future.

Boaz, David. 2005. "Congress Should Restrain the President," *Cato Institute,* January 18, http://www.cato.org/dailys/01-18-05.html (accessed June 23, 2006).

Boettke, Peter J., and C. J. Coyne. 2005. "Methodological Individualism, Spontaneous Order and the Research Program of the Workshop in Political Theory and Policy Analysis." *Journal of Economic Behavior and Organization* 57(2): 145–158.

Buchanan, James M. 1960. *Fiscal Theory and Political Economy.* Chapel Hill: University of North Carolina Press.

———. 1966. "An Individualistic Theory of Political Process." In David Easton, ed., *Varieties of Political Theory.* Englewood Cliffs, NJ: Prentice-Hall, pp. 25–38.

———. 1967. *Public Finance in Democratic Process: Fiscal Institutions and Individual Choice.* Chapel Hill: University of North Carolina Press.

———. 1968. *The Demand and Supply of Public Goods.* Chicago: Rand McNally.

———. 1969. *Cost and Choice: An Inquiry in Economic Theory.* Chicago: Markham.

———. 1970. "Public Goods and Public Bads." In John P. Crecine, ed., *Financing the Metropolis.* Beverly Hills: Sage, pp. 51–71.

———. 1975. *The Limits of Liberty: Between Anarchy and Leviathan.*

Chicago: University of Chicago Press.

———. 1979. *What Should Economists Do?* Indianapolis, IN: Liberty Press.

Buchanan, James M., and Gordon Tullock. 1962. *The Calculus of Consent: Logical Foundations of Constitutional Democracy.* Ann Arbor: University of Michigan Press.

Caldwell, Lynton K. 1965. "Public Administration and the Universities: A Half-Century of Development." *Public Administration Review* 25 (March): 52–60.

Carey, William D. 1969. "Presidential Staffing in the Sixties and Seventies." *Public Administration Review* 29 (September–October): 450–458.

———. 1970. "Remarks on Reorganization Plan No. 2." *Public Administration Review* 30 (November–December): 631–634.

Cheng, Nien. 1987. *Life and Death in Shanghai.* New York: Grove Press.

Christy, Francis T., Jr., and Anthony Scott. 1965. *The Common Wealth of World Fisheries.* Baltimore, MD: Johns Hopkins Press.

Chubb, John E., and Terry M. Moe. 1990. *Politics, Markets, and America's Schools.* Washington, DC: Brookings Institution.

Coase, R. H. 1937. "The Nature of the Firm." *Economica* 4: 386–485.

Coker, F. W. 1922. "Dogmas of Administrative Reform." *American Political Science Review* 16 (August): 399–411.

Committee for Economic Development. 1966. *Modernizing Local Government.* New York: Committee for Economic Development.

———. 1970. *Reshaping Government in Metropolitan Areas.* New York: Committee for Economic Development.

Commons, John R. 1968. *Legal Foundations of Capitalism.* Madison: University of Wisconsin Press.

Crankshaw, Edward. 1983. *Bismarck.* New York: Penguin Books.

———. 1986. *The Shadow of the Winter Palace.* London: Papermac.

Crawford, Sue E. S., and Elinor Ostrom. 2005. "A Grammar of Institutions." In Elinor Ostrom, ed., *Understanding Institutional Diversity.* Princeton, NJ: Princeton University Press, pp. 137–174. Originally published in *American Political Science Review* 89(3) (September 1995): 582–600.

Crozier, Michel. 1964. *The Bureaucratic Phenomenon*. Phoenix Books ed. Chicago: University of Chicago Press.

Cyert, Richard M., and James G. March. 1963. *A Behavioral Theory of the Firm*. Englewood Cliffs, NJ: Prentice-Hall.

Dales, J. H. 1968. *Pollution, Property and Prices*. Toronto: University of Toronto Press.

Davis, Gina, and Elinor Ostrom. 1991. "A Public Economy Approach to Education: Choice and Co-Production." *International Political Science Review* 12(4) (October): 313–335.

Davis, Otto A., and Andrew B. Whinston. 1961. "The Economics of Urban Renewal." *Law and Contemporary Problems* 26 (Winter): 105–117.

———. 1967. "On the Distinction between Public and Private Goods." *American Economic Review* 57 (May): 360–373.

Dean, John. 2006. "The History of, and Challenges to, Presidential Lawmaking: Why the Bush Administration's Use of Executive Orders is Nothing Novel." *FindLaw Legal News and Commentary*, December 21, http://writ.news.findlaw.com/dean/20011221.html (accessed June 23, 2006).

Demsetz, Harold. 1969. "Information and Efficiency: Another Viewpoint." *Journal of Law and Economics* 12 (April): 1–22.

Dewey, John. 1927. *The Public and Its Problems*. New York: Henry Holt.

Diamant, Alfred. 1962. "The Bureaucratic Model: Max Weber Rejected, Rediscovered, Reformed." In Ferrel Heady and Sybil L. Stokes, eds., *Papers in Comparative Public Administration*. Ann Arbor: University of Michigan, Institute of Public Administration, pp. 59–96.

Dietz, Thomas. 2005. "The Darwinian Trope in the Drama of the Commons: Variations on Some Themes by the Ostroms." *Journal of Economic Behavior & Organization* 57(2): 205–226.

Dietz, Thomas, Elinor Ostrom, and Paul Stern. 2003. "The Struggle to Govern the Commons." *Science* 302(5652) (December 12): 1907–1912.

Dimock, Marshall E. 1937. "The Study of Administration." *American Political Science Review* 31 (February): 28–40.

Djilas, Milovan. 1957. *The New Class*. New York: Praeger.

Downs, Anthony. 1957. *An Economic Theory of Democracy*. New York: Harper & Row.

―――. 1967. *Inside Bureaucracy.* Boston: Little, Brown.

Duggal, V. P. 1966. "Is There an Unseen Hand in Government?" *Annals of Public and Co-operative Economy* 37 (April–June): 145–150.

Egelko, Bob. 2006. "How Bush Sidesteps Intent of Congress: Instead of Vetoing Bills, He Officially Disregards Portions with Which He Doesn't Agree." *San Francisco Chronicle,* May 7.

Eggertsson, Thráinn. 2005. *Imperfect Institutions: Possibilities and Limits of Reform.* Ann Arbor: University of Michigan Press.

Elazar, Daniel J. 1971. "Community Self-Government and the Crisis of American Politics." *Ethics* 81 (January): 91–106.

―――. 1995–1998. *The Covenant Tradition in Politics.* 4 vols. New Brunswick, NJ: Transaction Publishers.

Emmerich, Herbert. 1950. *Essays on Federal Reorganization.* University: University of Alabama Press.

Eucken, Walter. 1951. *The Foundations of Economics.* Chicago: University of Chicago Press.

Feagin, Joe R. 1970. "Home Defense and the Police: Black and White Perspectives." *American Behavioral Scientist* 13 (May–August): 797–814.

Follet, M. P. 1924. *Creative Experience.* New York: Peter Smith.

Friesema, H. Paul. 1966. "The Metropolis and the Maze of Local Government." *Urban Affairs Quarterly* 2 (December): 68–90.

Furet, François. 1999. *The Passing of an Illusion: The Idea of Communism in the Twentieth Century.* Chicago: University of Chicago Press.

Garcia v. San Antonio Metropolitan Transit Authority, 469 U.S. 528 (1985).

Gellar, Sheldon. 2005. *Democracy in Senegal: Tocquevillian Analytics in Africa.* New York: Palgrave Macmillan.

Gerth, H. H., and C. Wright Mills, eds. 1946. From *Max Weber: Essays in Sociology.* Galaxy Book ed. New York: Oxford University Press.

Gibson, Clark, Krister Andersson, Elinor Ostrom, and Sujai Shivakumar. 2005. *The Samaritan's Dilemma: The Political Economy of Development Aid.* New York: Oxford University Press.

Gibson, Clark, Margaret McKean, and Elinor Ostrom, eds. 2000. *People and Forests: Communities, Institutions, and Governance.* Cambridge, MA: MIT Press.

Gibson, Clark, John Williams, and Elinor Ostrom. 2005. "Local Enforcement and Better Forests." *World Development* 33(2) (February): 273–284.

Golembiewski, Robert J. 1977a. "A Critique of 'Democratic Administration' and Its Supporting Ideation." *American Political Science Review* 71 (December): 1488–1507.

———. 1977b. "Observations on 'Doing Political Theory': A Rejoinder." *American Political Science Review* 71 (December): 1526–1531.

Goodnow, Frank J. 1900. *Politics and Administration: A Study in Government.* New York: Macmillan.

Gordon, H. Scott. 1954. "The Economics of a Common Property Resource: The Fishery." *Journal of Political Economy* 62 (April): 124–142.

Graham, F. P. 1968. "The Cop's Right (?) to Stop and Frisk." *New York Times Magazine,* December.

Grodzins, Morton. 1966. *The American System.* Daniel J. Elazar, ed. Chicago: Rand McNally.

Gulick, Luther, and Lyndall Urwick, eds. 1937. *Papers on the Science of Administration.* New York: Columbia University, Institute of Public Administration.

Hacker, Andrew. 1970. *The End of the American Era.* New York: Atheneum.

Hamdan v. Rumsfeld, 05–184, 126 S.Ct. 2749 (decided June 29, 2006).

Hamilton, Alexander, John Jay, and James Madison. n.d. *The Federalist.* New York: Modern Library.

Hardin, Garrett. 1968. "The Tragedy of the Commons." *Science* 162 (December): 1243–1248.

Hawley, Amos H., and Basil G. Zimmer. 1970. *The Metropolitan Community: Its People and Government.* Beverly Hills, CA: Sage.

Hayek, F. A. 1960. *The Constitution of Liberty.* Chicago: University of Chicago Press.

Herzberg, Roberta. 2005. "Commentary on Richard Wagner's "Self-Governance, Polycentricity, and Federalism: Recurring Themes in Vincent Ostrom's Scholarly Oeuvre." *Journal of Economic Behavior and Organization* 57(2):189–198.

Hess, Charlotte, and Elinor Ostrom, eds. 2007. *Understanding Knowledge as a Commons: From Theory to Practice.* Cambridge, MA: MIT Press.

Hirsch, Werner. 1964. "Local versus Areawide Urban Government Services." *National Tax Journal* 17 (December): 331–339.

———. 1968. "The Supply of Urban Public Services." In Harvey S. Perloff and Lowden Wingo, Jr., eds., *Issues in Urban Economics.* Baltimore, MD: Johns Hopkins Press, pp. 435–476.

Hirshleifer, Jack, James C. DeHaven, and Jerome W. Milliman. 1960. *Water Supply Economics, Technology, and Policy.* Chicago: University of Chicago Press.

Hjern, Benny, and David O. Porter. 1981. "Implementation Structures: A New Unit of Administrative Analysis." *Organization Studies* 2(3): 211–227.

Hobbes, Thomas. 1960. *Leviathan or the Matter, Forme and Power of a Commonwealth Ecclesiastical and Civil.* Edited by Michael Oakeshott. Oxford: Basil Blackwell.

Hohfeld, Wesley N. 1964. *Fundamental Legal Conceptions.* W. W. Cook, ed. New Haven, CT: Yale University Press.

Horn, Murray J. 1995. *The Political Economy of Public Administration: Institutional Choice in the Public Sector.* Cambridge: Cambridge University Press.

Huang, Ray. 1981. *1587: A Year of No Significance.* New Haven, CT: Yale University Press.

Jacobs, Jane. 1961. *The Death and Life of Great American Cities.* New York: Vintage Books.

Kaufmann, Franz-Xaver, Giandomenico Majone, and Vincent Ostrom, eds. 1986. *Guidance, Control, and Evaluation in the Public Sector.* Berlin and New York: Walter de Gruyter.

Kaul, Minoti Chakravarty. 1996. *Common Lands and Customary Law: Institutional Change in North India over the Past Two Centuries.* New Delhi: Oxford University Press.

Kiser, Larry L., and Elinor Ostrom. 1982. "The Three Worlds of Action: A Metatheoretical Synthesis of Institutional Approaches." In Elinor Ostrom, ed., *Strategies of Political Inquiry.* Beverly Hills, CA: Sage, pp. 179–222.

Knight, Frank H. 1965. *Risk, Uncertainty and Profit.* New York: Harper & Row.

Knott, Jack H., and Gary J. Miller. 1987. *Reforming Bureaucracy: The Politics of Institutional Choice*. New York: Prentice-Hall.

Koontz, Tomas M. 2002. *Federalism in the Forest: National versus State Natural Resource Policy*. Washington, DC: Georgetown University Press.

Kotler, Milton. 1969. *Neighborhood Government: The Local Foundations of Community Life*. Indianapolis, IN: Bobbs-Merrill.

Krüsselberg, Hans-Günter. 1983. "Property Rights Theorie und Wohlfahrtsoekonomik." In Alfred Schuller, ed., *Property Rights und Oekonomische Theorie*. Munich: Verlag Franz Vahlen.

———. 1986. "Markets and Hierarchies." In Franz-Xaver Kaufmann, Giandomenico Majone, and Vincent Ostrom, eds., *Guidance, Control, and Evaluation in the Public Sector*. Berlin and New York: Walter de Gruyter, pp. 349–386.

Kuhn, Thomas S. 1964. *The Structure of Scientific Revolutions*. Phoenix Books ed. Chicago: University of Chicago Press.

Kuhnert, Stephan. 2001. "An Evolutionary Theory of Collective Action: Schumpeterian Entrepreneurship for the Common Good." *Constitutional Political Economy* 12: 13–29.

Lakatos, Irme. 1970. "Falsification and the Method of Scientific Research Programmes." In Irme Lakatos and Alan Musgrave, eds., *Criticism and the Growth of Knowledge*. Cambridge: Cambridge University Press, pp. 91–196.

Lam, Wai Fung. 1998. *Governing Irrigation Systems in Nepal: Institutions, Infrastructure, and Collective Action*. Oakland, CA: ICS Press.

Landau, Martin. 1969. "Redundance, Rationality and the Problem of Duplication and Overlap." *Public Administration Review* 29 (July–August): 346–358.

Laudun, Larry. 1977. *Progress and Its Problems: Towards a Theory of Scientific Growth*. Berkeley: University of California Press.

Leach, Richard H. 1971. "Federalism: Continuing Predicament." *Public Administration Review* 31 (March–April): 217–223.

Lenin, V. I. 1932a. *State and Revolution*. New York: International Publishers.

———. 1932b. *What Is to Be Done?* New York: International Publishers.

Lindblom, Charles E. 1955. *Bargaining: The Hidden Hand in Govern-*

ment. Research Memorandum RM-1434-RC. Santa Monica, CA: RAND Corporation.

———. 1959. "The Science of 'Muddling Through.'" *Public Administration Review* 19 (Spring): 1–17.

———. 1965. *The Intelligence of Democracy: Decision Making through Mutual Adjustment.* New York: Free Press.

Llewellyn, K. N., and E. A. Hoebel. 1941. *The Cheyenne Way: Conflict and Case Law in Primitive Jurisprudence.* Norman: University of Oklahoma Press.

Long, Norton E. 1952. "Bureaucracy and Constitutionalism." *American Political Science Review* 46 (September): 808–818.

———. 1969. "Reflections on Presidential Power." *Public Administration Review* 29 (September–October): 442–450.

———. 1970. "Rigging the Market for Public Goods." In William R. Rosengren and Mark Lefton, eds., *Organization and Clients: Essays in the Sociology of Service.* Columbus, OH: Charles E. Merrill, pp. 187–204.

Lutz, Donald. 1988. *The Origins of American Constitutionalism.* Baton Rouge: Louisiana State University Press.

———. 2006. *Principles of Constitutional Design.* Cambridge: Cambridge University Press.

Mansfield, Harvey C. 1969. "Federal Executive Reorganization: Thirty Years of Experience." *Public Administration Review* 29 (July–August): 332–345.

March, James G., and Herbert A. Simon. 1958. *Organizations.* New York: John Wiley.

Margolis, Julius. 1955. "A Comment on the Pure Theory of Public Expenditures." *Review of Economics and Statistics* 37 (November): 347–349.

Martin, Daniel W. 1988. "The Fading Legacy of Woodrow Wilson." *Public Administration Review* 48 (March–April): 631–636.

Martin, Roscoe C. 1952. "Political Science and Public Administration." *American Political Science Review* 46 (September): 660–676.

Mayo, Elton. 1933. *The Human Problems of an Industrial Civilization.* New York: Viking Press.

McConnell, Grant. 1966. *Private Power and American Democracy.* New York: Alfred A. Knopf.

McGinnis, Michael, ed. 1999a. *Polycentric Governance and Devel-*

opment: Readings from the Workshop in Political Theory and Policy Analysis. Ann Arbor: University of Michigan Press.

————. 1999b. *Polycentricity and Local Public Economies: Readings from the Workshop in Political Theory and Policy Analysis*. Ann Arbor: University of Michigan Press.

McKean, Roland N. 1958. *Efficiency in Government through Systems Analysis, with Emphasis on Water Resource Development*. New York: John Wiley.

————. 1965. "The Unseen Hand in Government." *American Economic Review* 55 (June): 496–506.

Merton, Robert K., Ailsa P. Gray, Barbara Hockey, and Hanan C. Selvin, eds. 1952. *Reader in Bureaucracy*. New York: Free Press.

Millett, John D. 1959. *Government and Public Administration*. New York: McGraw-Hill.

Mishan, E. J. 1969. "The Relationship between Joint Products, Collective Goods, and External Effects." *Journal of Political Economy* 77 (May–June): 329–348.

Moe, Terry M. 1990. "Political Institutions: The Neglected Side of the Story." *Journal of Law, Economics and Organizations* 6 (Special Issue): 213–253.

Moran, Emilio, and Elinor Ostrom, eds. 2005. *Seeing the Forest and the Trees: Human-Environment Interactions in Forest Ecosystems*. Cambridge, MA: MIT Press.

Niskanen, William A., Jr. 1971. *Bureaucracy and Representative Government*. Chicago: Aldine-Atherton.

Olowu, Dele, and James S. Wunsch. 2004. *Local Governance in Africa: The Challenges of Democratic Decentralization*. Boulder, CO: Lynne Rienner.

Olson, Mancur. 1965. *The Logic of Collective Action*. Cambridge, MA: Harvard University Press.

————. 1969. "The Principle of 'Fiscal Equivalence': The Division of Responsibility among Different Levels of Government." *American Economic Review* 59 (May): 479–487.

Ostrom, Elinor. 1968. "Some Postulated Effects of Learning on Constitutional Behavior." *Public Choice* 5 (Fall): 87–104.

————. 1971. "Institutional Arrangements and the Measurement of Policy Consequences: Applications to Evaluating Police Performance." *Urban Affairs Quarterly* 6 (June): 447–475.

————. 1972. "Metropolitan Reform: Propositions Derived from Two Traditions." *Social Science Quarterly* 53 (December): 474–493.

————. 1982. *Strategies of Political Inquiry.* Beverly Hills, CA: Sage.

————. 1985. "Racial Inequalities in Low-Income Central City and Suburban Communities: The Case of Police Services." In Kenneth Hanf and Theo A.J. Toonen, eds., *Policy Implementation in Federal and Unitary Systems.* Dordrecht, the Netherlands: Martinus Nijhoff, pp. 235–265.

————. 1999. "Metropolitan Reform: Propositions Derived from Two Traditions." In Michael McGinnis, ed., *Polycentricity and Local Public Economies: Readings from the Workshop in Political Theory and Policy Analysis.* Ann Arbor: University of Michigan Press, pp. 139–160.

————. 2005. *Understanding Institutional Diversity.* Princeton, NJ: Princeton University Press.

Ostrom, Elinor, William Baugh, Richard Guarasci, Roger B. Parks, and Gordon P. Whitaker. 1973. *Community Organization and the Provision of Police Services.* Beverly Hills, CA: Sage.

Ostrom, Elinor, Roy Gardner, and James Walker. 1994. *Rules, Games, and Common-Pool Resources.* Ann Arbor: University of Michigan Press.

Ostrom, Elinor, and Roger B. Parks. 1971. "Black Citizens and the Police: Some Effects of Community Control." Paper presented at the annual meeting of the American Political Science Association, Chicago, September 7–11.

Ostrom, Elinor, and Gordon P. Whitaker. 1973. "Does Local Community Control of Police Make a Difference? Some Preliminary Findings." *American Journal of Political Science* 17 (February): 48–76.

Ostrom, Vincent. 1968. "Water Resource Development: Some Problems in Economic and Political Analysis of Public Policy." In Austin Ranney, ed., *Political Science and Public Policy.* Chicago: Markham, pp. 123–150.

————. 1969. "Operational Federalism: Organization for the Provision of Public Services in the American Federal System." *Public Choice* 6 (Spring): 1–17.

———. 1971. *Institutional Arrangements for Water Resource Development.* Springfield, VA: National Technical Information Service.

———. 1977. "Some Problems in Doing Political Theory: A Response to Golembiewski's 'Critique.'" *American Political Science Review* 71 (December): 1508–1525.

———. 1980. "Artisanship and Artifact." *Public Administration Review* 40 (July–August): 309–317.

———. 1984. "The Meaning of Value Terms." *American Behavioral Scientist* 28 (November–December): 249–262.

———. 1986. "A Fallabilist's Approach to Norms and Criteria of Choice." In Franz-Xaver Kaufmann, Giandomenico Majone, and Vincent Ostrom, eds., *Guidance, Control, and Evaluation in the Public Sector.* Berlin and New York: Walter de Gruyter, pp. 229–249.

———. 1987. *The Political Theory of a Compound Republic: Designing the American Experiment.* Rev. ed. Lincoln: University of Nebraska Press.

———. 1988. "Cryptoimperialism, Predatory States, and Self-Governance." In Vincent Ostrom, David Feeny, and Hartmut Picht, eds., *Rethinking Institutional Analysis and Development: Issues, Alternatives, and Choices.* San Francisco: ICS Press, pp. 43–68.

———. 1989. "Some Developments in the Study of Market Choice, Public Choice, and Institutional Choice." In Jack Rabin, Gerald Miller, and Bartley Hildreth, eds., *Handbook on Public Administration.* New York: Marcel Dekker, pp. 1065–1087.

———. 1991. *The Meaning of American Federalism: Constituting a Self-Governing Society.* San Francisco: ICS Press.

———. 1997. *The Meaning of Democracy and the Vulnerabilities of Democracies: A Response to Tocqueville's Challenge.* Ann Arbor: University of Michigan Press.

———. 2006. "Citizen-Sovereigns: The Source of Contestability, the Rule of Law, and the Conduct of Public Entrepreneurship." *PS: Political Science & Politics* 39(1) (January): 13–17.

———. 2007. *The Political Theory of a Compound Republic: Designing the American Experiment.* 3rd ed. Lanham, MD: Lexington Books.

Ostrom, Vincent, and Frances P. Bish. 1977. *Comparing Urban Service Delivery Systems.* Beverly Hills, CA: Sage.

Ostrom, Vincent, David Feeny, and Hartmut Picht, eds. 1988. *Rethinking Institutional Analysis and Development: Some Issues, Alternatives, and Choices.* San Francisco, CA: ICS Press.

Ostrom, Vincent, and Elinor Ostrom. 1965. "A Behavioral Approach to the Study of Intergovernmental Relations." *Annals of the American Academy of Political and Social Science* 359 (May): 137–146.

Ostrom, Vincent, and Elinor Ostrom. 1970. "Conditions of Legal and Political Feasibility." In Garrett H. Toebes, ed., *Natural Resources Systems Models in Decision Making.* Lafayette, IN: Purdue University, Water Resources Research Center, pp. 191–208.

Ostrom, Vincent, and Elinor Ostrom. 1971. "Public Choice: A Different Approach to the Study of Public Administration." *Public Administration Review* 31 (March–April): 203–216.

Ostrom, Vincent, and Elinor Ostrom. 1977. "Public Goods and Public Choices." In E. S. Savas, ed., *Alternatives for Delivering Public Services: Toward Improved Performance.* Boulder, CO: Westview Press, pp. 7–49.

Ostrom, Vincent, Charles M. Tiebout, and Robert Warren. 1961. "The Organization of Government in Metropolitan Areas: A Theoretical Inquiry." *American Political Science Review* 55 (December): 831–842.

Parks, Roger B. 1985. "Metropolitan Structure and Systemic Performance: The Case of Police Service Delivery." In Kenneth Hanf and Theo A. J. Toonen, eds., *Policy Implementation in Federal and Unitary Systems.* Dordrecht, the Netherlands: Martinus Nijhoff, pp. 161–191.

Parks, Roger B. 1999. "Do We Really Want to Consolidate Urban Areas? [It's Like Déjà vu All Over Again]." In Michael McGinnis, ed., *Polycentricity and Local Public Economies: Readings from the Workshop in Political Theory and Policy Analysis.* Ann Arbor: University of Michigan Press, pp. 349–354.

Parks, Roger B., Paula Baker, Larry Kiser, Ronald Oakerson, Elinor Ostrom, Vincent Ostrom, Stephen Percy, Martha Vandivort, Gordon Whitaker, and Rick Wilson. 1999. "Consumers as Coproducers of Public Services: Some Economic and Institutional Considerations." In Michael McGinnis, ed., *Polycentricity and Local Public Economies: Readings from the Workshop in Political Theory and Policy*

Analysis. Ann Arbor: University of Michigan Press, pp. 381–392.

Parks, Roger B., and Ronald J. Oakerson. 2000. "Regionalism, Localism, and Metropolitan Governance: Suggestions from the Research Program on Local Public Economies." *State and Local Government Review* 32(3) (Fall): 169–179.

Parks, Roger B., and Elinor Ostrom. 1981. "Complex Models of Urban Service Systems." In Terry N. Clark, ed., *Urban Policy Analysis: Directions for Future Research. Urban Affairs Annual Reviews,* vol. 21. Beverly Hills, CA: Sage, pp. 171–199.

Parsons, Talcott, ed. 1964. *Max Weber: The Theory of Social and Economic Organization.* New York: Free Press.

Pipes, Richard. 1974. *Russia under the Old Regime.* New York: Charles Scribner's Sons.

Polanyi, Michael. 1951. *The Logic of Liberty: Reflections and Rejoinders.* Chicago: University of Chicago Press.

Polski, Margaret. 2003. *The Invisible Hands of U.S. Commercial Banking Reform: Private Action and Public Guarantees.* Boston, MA: Kluwer Academic Publishers.

Popper, Karl R. 1964. *The Poverty of Historicism.* New York: Harper Torchbooks.

Poteete, Amy, and Elinor Ostrom. 2004. "Heterogeneity, Group Size and Collective Action: The Role of Institutions in Forest Management." *Development and Change* 35(3) (June): 435–461.

Press, Charles. 1963. "The Cities within a Great City: A Decentralist Approach to Centralization." *Centennial Review* 7 (Winter): 113–130.

Radnitzky, Gerard, and W. W. Bartley III, eds. 1987. *Evolutionary Epistemology, Rationality, and the Sociology of Knowledge.* La Salle, IL: Open Court.

Rasul v. Bush, 542 U.S. 466 (2004).

Rawls, John. 1963. "Constitutional Liberty and the Concept of Justice." In Carl J. Friedrich and John W. Chapman, eds., *Nomos VI: Justice.* New York: Atherton Press, pp. 98–125.

———. 1967. "Distributive Justice." In Peter Laslett and W. G. Runciman, eds., *Philosophy, Politics and Society.* Oxford: Blackwell, pp. 58–82.

Reuss, Henry S. 1970. *Revenue-Sharing: Crutch or Catalyst for State and Local Governments?* New York: Praeger.

Revel, Jean-François. 1971. *Without Marx or Jesus, the New American Revolution Has Begun.* Garden City, NY: Doubleday.

Rheinstein, Max, ed. 1954. *Max Weber on Law in Economy and Society.* Clarion Book ed. New York: Simon and Schuster.

Ridley, Clarence E., and Herbert A. Simon. 1938. *Measuring Municipal Activities: A Survey of Suggested Criteria and Reporting Forms for Appraising Administration.* Chicago, IL: International City Managers Association.

Riggs, Fred W. 1968. "The Crisis of Legitimacy: A Challenge to Administrative Theory." *Philippine Journal of Public Administration* 12 (April): 147–164.

Rousseau, Jean-Jacques. 1978. *On the Social Contract.* Edited by Roger D. Masters. New York: St. Martin's Press.

Runciman, Steven. 1956. *Byzantine Civilization.* Meridian Book. Cleveland, OH: World Publishing Company.

Samuelson, Paul A. 1954. "The Pure Theory of Public Expenditure." *Review of Economics and Statistics* 36 (November): 387–389.

Savas, E. S. 1977. "An Empirical Study of Competition in Municipal Service Delivery." *Public Administration* Review 37 (November–December): 717–724.

———. 1987. "Privatization: The Key to Better Government." Chatham, NJ: Chatham House Publishers.

Sawyer, Amos. 1992. *The Emergence of Autocracy in Liberia: Tragedy and Challenge.* San Francisco: ICS Press.

———. 2005. *Beyond Plunder: Toward Democratic Governance in Liberia.* Boulder, CO: Lynne Rienner.

Schlager, Edella, and Elinor Ostrom. 1993. "Property-Rights Regimes and Coastal Fisheries: An Empirical Analysis." In Terry L. Anderson and Randy T. Simmons, eds., *The Political Economy of Customs and Culture: Informal Solutions to the Commons Problem.* Lanham, MD: Rowman & Littlefield, pp. 13–41.

Schlesinger, Arthur M., Jr. [1973] 2004. *The Imperial Presidency.* New York: Mariner Books.

Schneider, Mark, and Paul Teske with Michael Mintrom. 1995. *Public Entrepreneurs: Agents for Change in American Government.* Princeton, NJ: Princeton University Press.

Schumpeter, Joseph. [1942] 1950. *Capitalism, Socialism, and Democracy.* New York: Harper.

Searle, John R. 1969. *Speech Acts: An Essay in the Philosophy of Language*. London: Cambridge University Press.

Shackle, G. L. S. 1961. *Decision, Order and Time in Human Affairs*. Cambridge: Cambridge University Press.

Shields, Currin V. 1952. "The American Tradition of Empirical Collectivism." *American Political Science Review* 46 (March): 104–120.

Shivakoti, Ganesh P., Douglas L. Vermillion, Wai-Fung Lam, Elinor Ostrom, Ujjwal Pradhan, and Robert Yoder, eds. 2005. *Asian Irrigation in Transition: Responding to Challenges*. New Delhi, India: Sage Publications.

Shivakumar, Sujai. 2005. *The Constitution of Development: Crafting Capabilities for Self-Governance*. New York: Palgrave Macmillan.

Siedentopf, Heinrich. 1983. "Reflexions sur la Science Administrative Comparee." *In European Institute of Public Administration, The Development of Research and Training in European Policy Making*. Maastricht, the Netherlands: EIPA.

Simon, Herbert A. 1943. *Fiscal Aspects of Metropolitan Consolidation*. Berkeley: University of California, Bureau of Public Administration.

———. 1946. "The Proverbs of Administration." *Public Administration Review* 6 (Winter): 53–67.

———. 1952. "Comments on the Theory of Organizations." *American Political Science Review* 46 (December): 1130–1139.

———. 1957. *Models of Man: Social and Rational; Mathematical Essays on Rational Human Behavior in a Social Setting*. New York: John Wiley.

———. 1959. "Theories of Decision Making in Economics and Behavioral Science." *American Economic Review* 49 (June): 258–283.

———. 1960. *The New Science of Management Decision*. New York: Harper & Row.

———. 1965a. *Administrative Behavior: A Study of Decision-Making Processes in Administrative Organization*. New York: Free Press.

———. 1965b. *The Shape of Automation for Men and Management*. New York: Harper & Row.

———. 1969. *The Sciences of the Artificial*. Cambridge, MA: MIT Press.

Simon, Herbert A., William R. Divine, E. Myles Cooper, and Milton Chernin. 1941. *Determining Work Loads for Professional Staff in a Public Welfare Agency.* Berkeley: University of California, Bureau of Public Administration.

Sproule-Jones, Mark. 1982. "Public Choice Theory and Natural Resources: Methodological Explication and Critique." *American Political Science Review* 76 (December): 790–804.

Stein, Harold. 1952. *Public Administration and Policy Development: A Case Book.* New York: Harcourt and Brace.

———. 1963. *American Civil-Military Decisions: A Book of Case Studies.* University: University of Alabama Press.

Stigler, George J. 1962. "The Tenable Range of Functions of Local Government." In Edmund S. Phelps, ed., *Private Wants and Public Needs: Issues Surrounding the Size and Scope of Government Expenditure.* New York: W. W. Norton, pp. 137–147.

Stone, Deborah. 1988. *Policy Paradox and Political Reason.* New York: Harper Collins.

Sundquist, James L., with the collaboration of David W. Davis. 1969. *Making Federalism Work: A Study of Program Coordination at the Community Level.* Washington, DC: Brookings Institution.

———. 1970. "Organizing U.S. Social and Economic Development." *Public Administration Review* 30 (November–December): 625–630.

Tang, Shui Yan. 1992. *Institutions and Collective Action: Self-Governance in Irrigation.* San Francisco: ICS Press.

Thompson, James D. 1967. *Organizations in Action.* New York: McGraw-Hill.

Thompson, Victor A. 1961. *Modern Organization.* New York: Alfred A. Knopf.

Tiebout, Charles M. 1956. "A Pure Theory of Local Expenditure." *Journal of Political Economy* 44 (October): 416–424.

Tierney, Brian. 1982. *Religion, Law and the Growth of Constitutional Thought, 1150–1650.* Cambridge: Cambridge University Press.

Tocqueville, Alexis de. [1835–40] 1945. *Democracy in America.* 2 vols. Edited by Philip Bradley. New York: Alfred A. Knopf.

———. 1955. *The Old Regime and the French Revolution.* Doubleday Anchor Books ed. Garden City, NY: Doubleday.

Tolley, G. S. 1969. *The Welfare Economics of City Bigness.* Urban Economics Report No. 31. Chicago: University of Chicago Press.

Toonen, Theo A. J. 1987. *Denken over Binnenlands Bestuur: Theorieen van de gedecentraliseerde eenheidsstaat bestuurskundig beschouwd.* Rotterdam, the Netherlands: Erasmus University.

Toulmin, Stephen E. 1961. *Foresight and Understanding: An Enquiry into the Aims of Science.* Bloomington: Indiana University Press.

Tullock, Gordon. 1965. *The Politics of Bureaucracy.* Washington, DC: Public Affairs Press.

———. 1969. "Federalism: The Problem of Scale." *Public Choice* 6 (Spring): 19–29.

———. 1970. *Private Wants, Public Means: An Economic Analysis of the Desirable Scope of Government.* New York: Basic Books.

U.S. Advisory Commission on Intergovernmental Relations. 1987a. *The Organization of Local Public Economies.* Washington, DC: Advisory Commission on Intergovernmental Relations.

———. 1987b. *Federalism and the Constitution: A Symposium on Garcia.* Washington, DC: Advisory Commission on Intergovernmental Relations.

———. 1988. *Metropolitan Organization: The St. Louis Case.* Washington, DC: Advisory Commission on Intergovernmental Relations.

United States Codes, Congressional and Administrative Laws. 1971. Vol. 3. 91st Cong., 2d sess., 1970. St. Paul, MN: West Publishing Company.

U.S. Congress, Joint Economic Committee, Subcommittee on Economy in Government. 1969. *A Compendium of Papers on the Analysis and Evaluation of Public Expenditures: The PPB System.* 3 vols. Washington, DC: U.S. Government Printing Office.

U.S. President's Committee on Administrative Management. 1937. *Report with Special Studies.* Washington, DC: U.S. Government Printing Office.

Van Alstine, Michael P. 2006. "Executive Aggrandizement in Foreign Affairs Lawmaking." *UCLA Law Review* 54: (2) [online].

Van Riper, Paul. 1983. "The American Administrative State: Wilson and the Founders—An Unorthodox View." *Public Administration Review* 43 (November–December): 477–490.

Vile, M. J. C. 1967. *Constitutionalism and the Separation of Powers.* Oxford: Clarendon Press.

Wagner, Richard E. 1971. *The Fiscal Organization of American Federalism: Description, Analysis, Reform.* Chicago, IL: Markham.

———. 2005. "Self-Governance, Polycentrism, and Federalism: Recurring Theme in Vincent Ostrom's Scholarly Oeuvre." *Journal of Economic Behavior and Organization* 57(2):173–188.

Waldo, Dwight. 1948. *The Administrative State: A Study of the Political Theory of American Public Administration.* New York: Ronald Press.

———. 1955. *The Study of Public Administration.* New York: Random House.

———. 1968. "Scope of the Theory of Public Administration." In James C. Charlesworth, ed., *Theory and Practice of Public Administration: Scope, Objectives, and Methods.* Philadelphia: American Academy of Political and Social Science, pp. 1–26.

Wallas, Graham. 1921. *Our Social Heritage.* New Haven, CT: Yale University Press.

Walters, A. A. 1961. "The Theory in Measurement in Private and Social Cost of Highway Congestion." *Econometrica* 29 (October): 676–699.

Warren, Robert O. 1964. "A Municipal Services Market Model of Metropolitan Organization." *Journal of the American Institute of Planners* 30 (August): 193–204.

———. 1966. *Government in Metropolitan Regions: A Reappraisal of Fractionated Political Organization.* Davis: University of California, Institute of Governmental Affairs.

———. 1970. "Federal-Local Development Planning: Scale Effects in Representation and Policy Making." *Public Administration Review* 30 (November–December): 584–595.

———. 2004. "City Streets—The War Zones of Globalization: Democracy and Military Operations on Urban Terrain in the Early Twenty-First Century." In Stephan Graham, ed., *Cities, War, and Terrorism.* London: Blackwell.

Weber, Max. 1978. *Economy and Society.* Guenther Roth and Claus Wittich, eds. Berkeley: University of California Press.

Wengert, E. S. 1942. "The Study of Public Administration." *American Political Science Review* 36 (April): 313–322.

Weschler, Louis F. 1982. "Public Choice: Methodological Individualism in Politics." *Public Administration Review* 42 (May–June): 288–294.

Weschler, Louis F., and Robert Warren. 1970. "Consumption Costs and Production Costs in the Provision of Antipoverty Goods." Paper delivered at the sixty-sixth annual meeting of the American Political Science Association, Los Angeles, Calif., September 8–12.

Whitaker, Gordon P. 1980. "Coproduction: Citizen Participation in Service Delivery." *Public Administration Review* 40 (May–June): 240–246.

White, Leonard D. 1939. *Introduction to the Study of Public Administration.* Rev. ed. New York: Macmillan.

———. 1948. *Introduction to the Study of Public Administration.* 3d ed. New York: Macmillan.

Wildavsky, Aaron. 1966. "The Political Economy of Efficiency." *Public Administration Review* 26 (December): 292–310.

Williamson, Oliver E. 1975. *Markets and Hierarchies: Analysis and Anti-Trust Implications.* New York: Free Press.

Willoughby, W. F. 1923. *The Reorganization of the Administrative Branch of the National Government.* Baltimore, MD: Johns Hopkins Press.

Wilson, Woodrow. 1887. "The Study of Administration." *Political Science Quarterly* 2 (June): 197–220.

———. 1956. *Congressional Government: A Study in American Politics.* New York: Meridian Books.

Yang, Tai-Shuenn. 1987. "Property Rights and Constitutional Order in Imperial China." Ph.D. dissertation, Indiana University.

Yoo, John. 2003. "Testimony before the Permanent Select Committee on Intelligence." United States House of Representatives Hearing on "Securing Freedom and the Nation Collecting Intelligence under the Law, Constitutional and Public Policy Considerations," October 30.

Index

Adams, John, 148
Addington, David S., 139
Administrative organization, 6; principles of, 37; theory of, 8
Administrative Reorganization Acts of 1939 and 1949, 19, 118, 125
Administrative science, 6; of democratic administration, 98; of public administration, 23
Advisory Commission on Intergovernmental Relations, 129, 134, 157
Agnew, Spiro, 127
Albert, Hans, 179–80
Alexander, Christopher, 193
Allen, Barbara, 146
Altshuler, Alan A., 105
Amalrik, Andrei, 201
American Society for Public Administration, 10
Ashby, W. Ross, 190, 193
Ash Council, 118
Austin, John, 123, 196
Ayres, Robert U., 47

Bads, 46
Bagehot, Walter, 65–67, 124, 149
Bain, Joe S., 176
Barnard, Chester I., 38
Bartley, W. W., 163, 179
Behavioral scientists (Behavioralists), 9; behavioral approach, 9

Bendix, Reinhard, 186
Benefit-cost analysis, 43
Berman, Harold, 164–65
Bish, Robert L., 61, 107, 157, 160, 194
Bismarck, 167
Blackmun, Justice Harry, 133
Blau, Peter L., 9
Bounded rationality, 38, 43
Buchanan, James M., 44, 49, 55, 58, 106, 114, 179, 193, 197
Bukharin, Nikolai, 170
Bureaucracy, 7, 25–28, 102; bureaucratic administration, 18, 26, 64–65, 68–69, 80, 84, 97, 114; bureaucratic chain of command, 27; bureaucratic dysfunctions, 9, 102; bureaucratic free enterprise, 53, 57, 103; bureaucratic organization (principles of), 27, 51–56, 71; bureaucratic organizations, 26, 28, 49; bureaucratic personality, 9; bureaucratic theory of administration, 86; fully developed, 27–29, 53, 56, 84; theory of, 16
Bureau of the Budget, 33, 119
Bush, George W., 139

Caldwell, Lynton K., 20
Case studies, 8
Certainty, 44
Cheney, Dick, 139
Cheng, Nien, 202

225